"Uncomfortable, powerful, moving; few writers can give us the nitty-gritty of sex and its messiness within the grand sweep of history, and get both the big picture and the details exactly right."

— Jeffrey Escoffier, author of *American Homo*

"*What We Don't Talk About* speaks for many women who resist (sometimes quietly) the peer pressure that has no name, and for women dismayed by the politics of belief infecting our secular conversations about sex. Injustice has become a sustainable resource, and JoAnn Wypijewski eloquently documents its variations. Her reporting is solid and energetic. Wypijewski knows how to unpack a monster."

— Tracy Quan, author of *Diary of a Manhattan Call Girl*

"No other writer is telling these stories; maybe no other writer could with such generosity of spirit. 'Mercy is the scandal now,' Wypijewski writes of the ways in which too many have come to prefer the counting of sins to the dream of liberation, but this is no book of lamentations. Through a series of moments intimately observed, she summons us again to consider the possibilities for pleasure, eros as ally, in any struggle to get free. Hers is a prophetic voice."

— Jeff Sharlet, author of *The Family* and *This Brilliant Darkness*

"This book lays bare the twisted logics we employ to convince ourselves that there are easy distinctions between love, brutality, sex, and capitalism. Wypijewski's work is exemplary journalism, taking us to the hearts of neighborhoods and cities and towns from which sex panics emanate, and eliciting interviews and conversations with those affected which reveal how futile it is to search for perfect victims and villains. But her writing is also brilliant analysis, an unrelenting excavation not just of what happened and to whom, but what it means to all of us watching from the sidelines. She unflinchingly reminds us that the larger problem is not that we see and experience "bad" forms of sex, but that we don't look at sex enough to understand our complicated and uneasy relationships to it. Like few other writers, Wypijewski provides an archaeology of sex which is in turn an archaeology of power."

— Yasmin Nair, writer, activist, academic

"JoAnn Wypijewski has written steadily and courageously on topics that paralyze other reporters into silence or lukewarm compromise. She knows that our horror of crime springs from the same root as our need for scapegoats. Her essays are always perceptive, and always worth reading."

— David Bromwich, author of *American Breakdown: The Trump Years and How They Befell Us*

"JoAnn Wypijewski stimulates us to think freshly about sex and sexual politics, and she is not afraid to infuriate both those who consider themselves sexual progressives and traditional conservatives. Let's call a town meeting of the whole country to grapple with the insights, the fury, and most of all the wisdom in this essential book."

— Peter Davis, Academy Award winning filmmaker of *Hearts and Minds*, author of *Girl of My Dreams*

What We Don't Talk About When We Talk About #MeToo

*Essays on Sex, Authority
& the Mess of Life*

JoAnn Wypijewski

VERSO
London • New York

First published by Verso 2020
© JoAnn Wypijewski 2020

1 3 5 7 9 10 8 6 4 2

Verso
UK: 6 Meard Street, London W1F 0EG
US: 20 Jay Street, Suite 1010, Brooklyn, NY 11201
versobooks.com

Verso is the imprint of New Left Books

ISBN-13: 978-1-78873-805-7
ISBN-13: 978-1-78873-806-4 (UK EBK)
ISBN-13: 978-1-78873-807-1 (US EBK)

British Library Cataloguing in Publication Data
A catalogue record for this book is available from the British Library

Library of Congress Control Number
2020932062

Typeset in Sabon by MJ & N Gavan, Truro, Cornwall
Printed and bound by CPI Group (UK) Ltd, Croydon CR0 4YY

From 2015 through 2017, I had the privilege of holding the Belle Zeller Visiting Professorship in political science at Brooklyn College, an honorary post, now, sadly, eliminated under austerity. I taught various classes involving politics and language, and one class called Media Panic, Sex and the Politics of Fear.

This book is dedicated to my students, about two hundred young women and men across four semesters, who had complicated lives and abundant ideas, who didn't censor themselves or one another, who taught me a lot and who, I hope, are out in the world, smart, skeptical and brave.

Contents

Acknowledgements

John Scagliotti introduced me to Margaret Cerullo, who has been, like John, a beloved friend and marvelous intellectual spark. Margaret introduced me to Pamela Bridgewater, who, like Margaret and John, complicated my thinking in almost every conversation until she died and, with her husband, Kweku Toure, magnified the meaning of family. *The Nation*, where I worked until 2000, introduced me to Alexander Cockburn, who introduced me to Laura Flanders, who introduced me to Amber Hollibaugh, a radiant earth angel of experience and knowledge, who helped me begin to make sense of ideas about class and sex and risk for which I didn't have the words before going to Jamestown, New York, for the first essay in this collection. Jamestown introduced me to another Amber, another brave, searching soul, whose months of conversation from a jailhouse put spirit and bone to the contradictions of need and human error that tend to be lost in the blaring talk-talk about sex and danger.

Alexander, Alex now dead and gone, introduced me to many things—including the reporting of Debbie Nathan (and later to the incomparable Debbie)—but most profoundly to the riddles of love. *The Nation* re-introduced me to Lewis Lapham, the first editor who embraced me as a writer, offered money for a story and space to tell it properly. "The Secret Sharer," "A Boy's Life" and "Judgement Days" were first published in *Harper's*. Lewis commissioned "Sin, a Story of Life" at the height of the priest scandal in Boston in 2002, but hated it; Virginia Heffernan, my editor there at the time, loved it, which had not seemed to be a disagreeably contentious overall response, but Lewis was the boss, and the piece went homeless. I include it here, rather than an adaptation that appeared years later in *Legal Affairs* (thank you, Emily Bazelon and the fact-checkers there), because Lewis's frustrated but astute observation in the moment—"I think everyone is lying"—captures what I consider its strength. Many truths are embedded in scandal, but they are not to be found in the simple retelling or debunking of stories. There is pain here but there are no heroes, least of all among media SWAT teams whose aim, conscious or not, is not to encourage anyone's independence but simply to replace one deference with another, one unquestioned authority with another. "Faith-Based Justice," commissioned by Barbara Epstein for *New York Review of Books*, died with her, alas, and is included as an illustration of the travesty that occurs when the logic of scandal becomes the logic of a law court.

I met Katrina vanden Heuvel, publisher and editorial director of *The Nation*, when we were practically girls, and I appreciate having grown up with her there. The title essay was her commission, and many other pieces here appeared in "Carnal Knowledge," a feature she proposed. "Pictures from an Exhibition" and "The Wonder Years" first appeared in the Books section (thank you, Elsa Dixler and Art Winslow). "Make the Rules, Break the Rules and Prosper" was in *CounterPunch* (thank you, Jeffrey St. Clair). I have altered some titles or text, in the latter case often to restore material that was originally cut for space or split off in a sidebar. Although I have updated some bits in endnotes, overall these essays ought to be read in the context of their time.

The Nation presented more occasion for critical encounters with people across our long association than I can possibly acknowledge, but some not already named must be: Andy Kopkind (stardust now, who in bright life brought me to John), Richard Lingeman, Richard Kim, Don Guttenplan, Roane Carey, Judy Long (who also helped ready the text here), Sandy McCroskey, Peter Meyer (who also made the index possible), Zia Jaffrey, Jeff Sharlet, Susan Richardson, Carol Tavris, Leonore Tiefer, Maria Margaronis, Tracy Quan, Tia Keenan, Katha Pollitt (who doubtless disagrees with much here), Victor Navasky (who hired me as an intern), Janet Gold (who brought me on staff), Patricia Williams (a model of gracious fire, whose comments on the prologue I greatly appreciate), Judith Levine (who introduced me to *Sex Panic and the Punitive State*, by Roger Lancaster, who also commented on the prologue) and countless interns who not only checked facts but were a lively source of perspective. The same goes for everyone I worked with at *Harper's*, especially Clara Jeffery and Bill Wasik, who were my editors.

I emphasize introductions to recognize the element of luck in this business. A working-class girl from Buffalo when I arrived in New York, I have been lucky. I was lucky before that, to have had a family where, okay, the kids were spanked, but also loved mightily and taught to stand up for ourselves. The chain of relationships and influences is more like the finest chainmail, interwoven, with no clear beginning or end. I have written on many subjects besides sexual politics, and, on that, much more than is included here. I have boundless gratitude toward every source for the essays that made it into this book and those that did not, and am indebted to many more friends, loved ones, chance encounters, the voices that figure into approaching any work. Of the beloved dead, whose voices stick and who were so important to me, I remember also Ben Sonnenberg, Edward Said and Jean Stein.

Three final great strokes of kismet: a South Carolina labor struggle prompted Bill Fletcher to urge me to pay attention, which prompted me to call Kamau Marcharia, who insisted I talk to Kevin Gray, then with the ACLU, with whom I've been talking, more or less, ever since. A call from John, who said, "You should talk to this guy who's organizing gay opposition to the death penalty" after Matthew Shepard's murder, led me to Bill Dobbs, who is not only an emporium of information about sex, civil illiberty and the exercise of free speech but also the best person to shop for hardware, or ring up from detention after a protest in New York. Finally, delightfully, a surprise email arrived from "across the sea," sent by Rosie Warren, whose initiative, editorial insights and attention, together with the thoughtful work of everyone at Verso, made this book real. Thank you.

Prologue

The little girls next door are playing school. The teacher barks, and the students get detention. There are so many ways to detention: being late, being wrong, being poor in math, wanting to be popular, "with your hair all fine and your nails painted and pretty clothes—I like pretty clothes and painted nails, too, but you aren't all that." The teacher threatens them all, "good or bad," if they make her raise her voice again. She raises her voice. They are silent. She threatens to call their imaginary mothers. She threatens to take the imaginary money she's been given to get them food. It is summer, hot, late afternoon. Detention is supposed to last four hours, three months, a year. A half hour, and the teacher flags. It's not much of a game with one player. Okay, she announces, everyone can go to gymnastics. "Get in a line, class! No talking! Straight line!" The others obey. She arranges rolling garbage carts for them to jump off of onto the black-tar driveway. Happy shrieks conjure heaven for the first time, as a breeze comes up and an ice cream truck plays its wistful tune and a rat, which none of them sees, scuttles from one yard to the next. "Do it again," the teacher shouts. "You. Are. In. Training!"

◆

Let's leave the little girls alone for now with their game, the meanings of which and the elaborate circuits of example, accommodation and rebellion it reflects are, in a sense, the pursuit of this book. I will return to them.

Let's think, at the outset, on the meanings of more widely circulated reflections of reality in early twenty-first-century America. Three stories bumped up against one another as spring slid into summer of 2019, their coincidences unremarked upon, for all the words that each elicited in isolation. These stories are in no way equivalents. Their facts are necessary, but the stories coincide not at the level of fact; instead, together they represent a mood, a relationship—longstanding but specially adapted for delirious repetition and shapeshifting in the era of Trump and #MeToo—between the crowd and punishment.

On May 31, 2019, Ava DuVernay's *When They See Us* premiered on television. A drama in four episodes, it tells the story of five man-children, aged fourteen to sixteen, at the center of a media storm in New York City in 1989 that was so powerful, so laden with the debris of assumption, prejudice, official and unofficial trickery, that it blocked the light for decades. In real time it was a story of tropes: a young investment banker, part of the city's rising new class, went for a jog at night in Central Park; the same night, in Harlem, a large group of teenagers, part of the city's stuck old class, went into the park to play, to let off steam, to cause trouble, just because … Off one path, the jogger, Trisha Meili, white, was raped and beaten so gruesomely that words fail. On other paths, some of the teenagers, black and brown, raised havoc, assaulting people, variously hued, until police arrived and the kids scattered. Amid the chaos, no one in authority acted to follow a lead from a rape that was disrupted in the same general part of the park two days earlier.

Five boys (let's call them boys, an interpretive term but more accurate than "wolf pack," which they were called at the time) were eventually interrogated, coerced into confessing, tried and formally convicted for the attack on Meili. The sixteen-year-old,

xiv

Korey Wise, had not been arrested but simply accompanied his friend to the police station. He was interrogated anyway, and said blandly to police and prosecutors on videotape, "This was my first rape. This … I never did this before. This will be the last time doing it." The words are startling, at once horrific and so remote from the most elementary understanding of the world of crime and consequences that they ought to have provoked skepticism among at least some substantial segment of the professional journalists who were focused on these dreadful events. *Who is this kid, and what causes him to speak this way?* As a class, journalists were not skeptical. Even when it was known that Wise was developmentally disabled, that he had made the statement after spending many hours in the station alone under pressure by authorities, they were not skeptical. They had effectively tried and convicted Korey Wise and the others before they knew their names. Pete Hamill of the *New York Post*, a dean of big-city column writing, wrote the prosecution's opening statement promptly after the attack:

> They were coming downtown from a world of crack, welfare, guns, knives, indifference and ignorance. They were coming from a land with no fathers. … They were coming from the anarchic province of the poor. And driven by a collective fury, brimming with the rippling energies of youth, their minds teeming with the violent images of the streets and the movies, they had only one goal: to smash, hurt, rob, stomp, rape. The enemies were rich. The enemies were white.

The Central Park Five, as they came to be known, were vindicated in 2002, after a man doing time for rape and murder called Matias Reyes confessed to being the sole perpetrator and matched the DNA found at the scene. (None of the five had.) It would be ten years, following a book by Sarah Burns in 2011 and a TV documentary in 2012, before the mass public met the record of trampled justice. In 2014 the city settled a civil rights lawsuit with the five for $41 million. Not until

DuVernay's dramatic series, though, did the public really see the boys who became men in captivity, their families before the storm, their fathers and mothers, and the human dimensions of what happened to them—especially to Korey Wise, who alone was charged as an adult, tried as an adult and punished in multiple terrible ways in adult jails and prisons for almost fourteen years. The same institutional media that formerly had aped the police and prosecution, scornful of defense, now, thirty years later, embraced the emotional power of DuVernay's theatrical recreation.

They could not, however, sit with the weight of damaged life left by the storm and take its full measure. Editorialists evaded their own profession's responsibility and turned their fire on a former assistant district attorney, the police and Donald Trump, deserving but easy targets. What had been a moral panic—"the ultimate shriek of alarm," as then-governor Mario Cuomo put it, by institutions, individuals and social forces (overwhelmingly white) over crime (typed as black)—was being resolved in the stock manner of moral panics: with enemies and a pointing of fingers by the righteous pure. Former ADA-turned-novelist Linda Fairstein, whose zealotry as head of the sex crimes unit had fueled her to abandon prosecutorial ethics in persecuting the boys, and who maintains that she, her office and the police did nothing wrong, has been denounced, shunned and marked for silencing, primitive forms of social discipline now deemed progressive. Although DuVernay has stated that her objective was to reveal the many impacts of structures of injustice, the review site *Roger Ebert* conveyed the tenor of much of the crowd's political response: "eliciting empathy and a desire for justice, [the drama] demonizes the right people and demands your fury." The storm, the scandal, has yet to be fully comprehended.

The next two stories lie outside the borders of critical historical assessment. Unfolding in the present, they exist in the region of raw emotion, the region of danger and fury. Here be demons.

Between January and the end of June 2019, a defense attorney was the subject of a public row over not only the presumed guilt of a notorious defendant but, in particular, his own guilt by association. In January, Ronald Sullivan, a Harvard Law School professor and celebrated attorney in both high-profile and obscure cases, joined the legal team representing Harvey Weinstein in a pending trial on charges of sexual assault and rape in New York City. Soon after, a group of Harvard students, along with their newspaper, the *Crimson*, erupted in protest—among other things, spray-painting "Down w Sullivan!" on Winthrop House, where Sullivan and his wife, Stephanie Robinson, lived with their family and served as faculty deans since 2009. More than 300 students signed a petition calling for their removal; supporters gathered 1,000 signatures for them to stay, which was rarely mentioned. In March, the dean of Harvard College announced a "climate review," an investigation typically initiated in Title IX sexual harassment cases, to determine if Sullivan and Robinson's continued presence at Winthrop endangered or otherwise harmed students. Anyone providing information was guaranteed anonymity. Fifty-two members of the Law School faculty wrote an open letter supporting their colleagues. The Black Law Students Association stated that Harvard should be capable of addressing sexual violence and supporting victims without "scapegoat[ing] Professor Sullivan." The Association of Black Harvard Women denounced him. In May, protests escalated, as did the language of alarm. An article in the *Crimson* alleged that a "culture of fear" had pervaded the house over much of Sullivan and Robinson's tenure as deans. Seven former and current Winthrop staff spoke of a "climate of hostility and suspicion," a "threatening environment," a "toxic culture." "We're all obviously terrified," said Madeleine Woods.

No complaint had ever been lodged against the deans for failure to care for students, or inattention to sexual violence, or condoning threats or violence. Such a complaint is not required under Title IX, which governs relations on US campuses today, and upon which federal funding may depend. The case was complicated by the traditional role of house master (the old name for faculty dean) and the roles of professor and lawyer—the expectation of nurturance versus the expectation of intellectual challenge versus the expectation of vigorous defense, and the question of whether those expectations must conflict. It was complicated by old complaints against Sullivan and Robinson by former staff at the house—that they acted like bosses, and not very nice ones. Some Harvard faculty insist the specter of Weinstein was mainly a coincidence. In the white heat of the moment, though, the specter predominated, and complaints took on the coloration of horror. On May 10, Sullivan withdrew from Weinstein's defense, citing scheduling conflicts; the next day, he and Robinson were sacked as faculty deans effective June 30. The *Crimson* described student activists as "shocked and excited" over what one characterized as a victory "against rape culture."

Weinstein had not faced criminal prosecution for the accusations by Hollywood actresses that sparked the #MeToo phenomenon in 2017, so the New York case invariably symbolized a reckoning for all his alleged bad acts. It became a symbolic substitute as well for all the actions never taken against all the accused whose names have tumbled through public space since #MeToo emerged, including and maybe especially Donald Trump. This substitution effect typifies cases involving public demons. Since Weinstein is a public demon, his case raises a challenge that is central to the case of every hated defendant, a challenge that should have been decisively met in 1989 in New York but was not, and to which Sullivan adverted when he told students, "It is particularly important for this category of unpopular defendant"—one who is seen as "guilty, … vile or undesirable"—"to receive the same process as everyone else, perhaps even more important."

Sullivan was being a teacher in that moment. His statement was an attorney's affirmation of the principle of equality under the law, but as a former public defender and a longtime advocate winning freedom for the wrongfully convicted, he knows that in practice "everyone else" is not an undifferentiated category, and the accused don't all "receive the same process." Moreover, he knows that his audience knows this too. So, the statement implicitly provoked questions, ones that inhere in the application of the law, particularly criminal law. Those questions presume a continual public wrestling. One can picture an open-ended dialogue for many voices.

How can you talk about a "category" of defendant, as if that category transcends race, sex, class and histories of oppression? … The law is embedded in those histories, of course, because it is embedded in history, and the world is full of oppression; pushing toward equality is a political project. Equality has to be the principle … *I'm sorry, there is no equality; the system is rigged, and talking about Weinstein as just another defendant evades his real power in the world* … Does rigging our concept of justice against the despised person and attacking his lawyer advance equality? I don't see the evidence; there's been a lot of despising going on … *There's been a lot of rape going on, too; there is no justice for women* … There's no justice when you're accused of a sex crime. Bam! you're guilty … *We have to respect the suffering victim of any crime, and we have to protect the rights of the criminally accused. There's a tension there, and we can't ignore it. As a society, we tend to ignore it in high-profile cases with defendants who are extremely unpopular —which is why what happens in those cases, when guilt is presumed and everyone is watching, is so important* … It's a measure of any society, how it treats the "damned and despised" … *And it's not a measure how it treats women's suffering? Women haven't been believed, and have been essentially tried for coming forward. That's not a problem?* … That is a problem, and the legal system must be accountable. People's fates can't be based on belief, though. Women are defendants too. Women are the mothers of defendants. Everyone wants to be believed;

how do you resolve that? ... *Shit, there are people every day who go before a court, and every day face the prospect of suffering because no one's going to believe them; most of them never get a trial, they fill the prisons. They're not all nice people, but we should care that they are effectively denied their rights* ... You're talking about people who are poor and powerless. That's structural injustice, but so is letting a criminal buy his way out because he can afford a fancy legal team. No crime victim wants to see that ... *You shouldn't say "criminal"; that's for the state to prove* ... The state can be wrong. Popular opinion can be wrong ... *Not about Weinstein* ... Let's not talk about Weinstein, but we should talk about power. No criminal defendant has power in the criminal justice system, and no defendant, however wealthy, can match the resources of the state. This is crucial. If we can't see the defendant, irrespective of person, we can't properly see the state—its awesome power to police, prosecute and punish, a power that by its nature, also irrespective of persons, establishes a fundamental conflict between the state and every individual ... *Yeah, if you're in the dock, you better believe you want a strong advocate, because if the state is going to exercise its ultimate power over your life, it better have to prove its case* ... That's the problem: power over your life. Most exercises of male power aren't in the courts and never will be. That's patriarchy. That's the issue ... *Struggles for justice aren't discrete things. Due process, presumption of innocence, burden of proof—as terms they sound analgesic, like aspirin, or cruelly absurd because of all the times people, especially poor people and minorities, don't get them. But they exist in contested history, where rights are not conferred; they, too, are the product of human struggle against oppression and unchecked power. That struggle is continuous and exists simultaneously on many fronts. So, we should be asking, What responsibilities does it demand of the citizen?* ...

Some version of that dialogue was not organized following Sullivan's statement. Protesters said discussion was beside the point. They weren't denying Weinstein's right to the representation of his choice; he could choose many lawyers, they said, but Sullivan shouldn't be one of them, because his participation could be "trauma-inducing" for Winthrop residents (the term from a student on the *Crimson*, not a Winthrop resident). Rather than an invitation to intellectual work, Harvard's administrators sent students questionnaires: is Winthrop House "sexist," "non-sexist," "hostile," etc.? Those are standard to the Title IX process, as is confidentiality, and it is argued that Harvard was legally bound to begin the process. What emerged as a result, though, were two principal forums for speech: one, the investigation, conducted in secrecy (unavoidably, and for reasons that are understandable regarding allegations of impropriety but at odds with a dispute over the compatibility of professional roles); the other, a noise machine that, though prompted by politics (the pariah status of a criminal defendant) and fueled by politics (the energy of #MeToo), then proclaimed that the demand to remove the deans had nothing to do with politics.

None of Sullivan's antagonists spoke of guilt by association; these are liberals, and that term is too bonded to the anticommunist witch hunts of the 1950s. They spoke of fear and security. They said Sullivan and Robinson must go. They did not speak of disloyalty, but their words bore its whiff: protection is the first duty of deans, and by putting defense of a dangerous man ahead of the chance that some students might thereby feel endangered, Sullivan was shirking his duty. However much that may comport with a conception of Harvard house masters *in loco parentis*, one might reasonably ask how criminal defense attorneys can ever be good parents to actual children if the rational basis for feelings of fear cannot be challenged.

Students picketed Winthrop House with tape across their mouths; meanwhile, Sullivan said he'd received notes of support from other students, some saying they feared reprisals if they spoke publicly. After Sullivan and Robinson were ousted, one of the protesters' allies in the press, Lucy Caldwell writing in *The*

New Republic, described Sullivan's statement about unpopular defendants as "intellectually dishonest, if not downright nefarious" and "condescending." Students know all about how the criminal justice system works, she argued; they also know that Weinstein is a wealthy, powerful man. Earlier, one of Sullivan's Law School colleagues, Jeannie Suk Gersen, had written in *The New Yorker*:

> In the thirteen years that I have been a law professor, teaching and writing on criminal law and sexual assault, I have regularly provided legal counsel: both to alleged victims and to people facing allegations of wrongdoing at school, in the workplace, or in the legal system. In the past year, the climate for such work has changed. There is now such a stigma attached to people accused of sexual misconduct that anyone who defends legal principles on their behalf risks being mistaken, in the public mind, for a defender of sexual violence.

Caldwell wrote that Sullivan's supporters were deluded to think they were defending academic and professional freedom: "instead, they're defending a status quo that has caused so many women to suffer for so long."

Sullivan and Robinson are black. It has been regularly mentioned in passing that their appointment in 2009 as house masters was a first for Harvard. The college was founded in 1636. The house system was established in the 1930s. That Harvard took more than seventy years to confer the honor of master upon black faculty members but in the blink of an eye, relative to its history, endorsed suspicion of the pair's continued presence in the house; that it made Robinson invisible and effectively forced Sullivan to profess his worthiness, to cite his bona fides as an advocate for victims, the downtrodden, the family of Michael Brown, killed by police in Ferguson; that it terminated their contract immediately after named and unnamed sources in a newspaper accused them of long being high-handed, incompetent and scary; that, in rebuffing reasoned argument and indulging feelings, vandalism and innuendo, Harvard chose to "police certain ideas and [not] police others," to borrow Sullivan's words—these elements of the story were subject to little analysis taken together. After Sullivan told an interviewer that he thought race was a factor in the administration's decision to order a climate review over a clash of ideas, his opponents said that claim was ridiculous: ideas were not at issue; his ability to make a home for students was. Maybe Sullivan had a feeling. Maybe it related to unspoken knowledge of white professors whose hands-on relations with students haven't precipitated investigations. And maybe the dean of Harvard College was correct in saying by May 11 that the situation at Winthrop House had become "untenable." But gripped by emotion for months, the school became a rough court, and Sullivan and Robinson defendants, guilty as charged.

The anthropologist Roger Lancaster has a term for communal feeling forged from the negative energies of fear, suspicion, vigilance, mutual identification against the demon—and all his works and associations—and for shunning and punishment as empowering, unifying goals. He calls it a "poisoned solidarity." Anti-black racism at the crude level of group expression qualifies, as does the vast public's post-9/11 accommodation to guilt by association, torture, Guantánamo, endless war, assassination by drone, and other masquerades of protection, excepting "torture for fun" (the government's argument against "deviant" low-level soldiers at Abu Ghraib, examined in this book). Trump's scare campaign against immigrants as invaders, rapists and thieves is a latter-day iteration of his contribution to the chorus howling for revenge against the five boys in 1989. "It's more than anger," he said then, "it's hatred … I want society to hate them." It is important to recognize that Trump had a minor solo in that chorus, if a memorable and loathsome one. As an entrepreneur of enjoyment in the dehumanization of others, he understands that unity through vengeance sells—and has sold since before he took the main stage with his signature bombastic exploitation of real and imagined fears. He did not, however, create the conditions that would be ripe for that exploitation. For the average person living in New York in 1989 Trump's intervention in the jogger case didn't particularly stand out, maybe because he and those who despise him now—great swathes of white feminist New York, white liberal media New York, white political New York—were all on the same side then. It was the power side, and its instant dehumanization of the accused, accented by a fervent belief in confessions, ignited a reaction, sometimes ugly in its insensitivity to the jogger, among the boys' backers, called "the black side" by some reporters in court.

As so often, the power side won, but society was diminished in that victory, and women were no safer: five were raped and bloodied by Matias Reyes after the jogger; one of them, Lourdes Gonzalez, was murdered, while her children listened behind a locked door. Reason—pursuing Reyes from the unnamed woman's April 17 lead—might have saved them; rage could not. Lancaster describes this poisoned solidarity as a feature in America's long-running moral panic over sex as a source of unparalleled danger from monsters among us—panic that sometimes explodes in the public square but by now has been normalized in the social conscience, habitual, ready to burst out in tweetstorms that may gather like hurricanes or disperse like a passing rain, but either way hit their mark. The inciting events vary. The instigators may be on the political right, but often they are liberals or professed progressives. The demon may be guilty or not; the crime, grievous, nonexistent or anywhere on a scale of harm. Rage unites them. Bombast is the conventional linguistic mood. Falling in line is the objective. And instead of a positive spirit of organic social solidarity to take concerted action for the common good, there is the perverse thrill of simultaneously quaking together in fear and sticking it to the devil.

So comes the third story. On July 3, 2019, a *New York Times* front-page headline read, "He Is Accused of Rape but Has 'a Good Family'." The report that follows does not explore the cluttered pathways of wrongdoing and redress. It, too, is a story of tropes. She is sixteen, "visibly intoxicated, her speech slurred." He is sixteen, also drunk, how badly we aren't told. They are at an "alcohol-fueled pajama party." They are in New Jersey. "The boy filmed himself penetrating her from behind, her torso exposed, her head hanging down, prosecutors said." It is important that we are voyeurs from the start. She is sixteen and drunk. He is sixteen and drunk. He later shares the video by text, according to investigators, with the message "When your first time having sex was rape." Prosecutors move to try the boy as an adult. The judge in family court says, No, this is a juvenile case. He says a lot of other things. He says what happened wasn't rape. His definition requires strangers with weapons in a dark alley. Such a case, he suggests, would fit the profile for adult prosecution. This does not: the youngsters staggered to a dark place holding hands; the boy comes from a good family, is an Eagle Scout, at a terrific school, with terrific grades. "He is clearly a candidate for not just college but probably for a good college." Is the girl aware that prosecuting him as an adult would destroy the boy's life? All of this happened in 2017 and 2018. The story is news because an appeals court rebuked the judge. It is front-page news, two weeks after the fact, because the *Times* wished to celebrate the rebuke. "A judge's rationale for leniency is rejected," a subtitle crowed. It is easy, with the disturbing details firmly in mind, to overlook what was being celebrated: the go-ahead to prosecute a sixteen-year-old as an adult.

The judge was arguably not the best equipped to decide this case, but we cannot know what would have happened if the prosecutor had entered family court in 2017 seeking swift accountability, correction and restitution. GMC, as the boy is called in court papers, was sixteen and drunk, but also, if the facts set out so far be true, or even mostly true, sixteen and mean, sixteen and selfish, sixteen and stupid, sixteen and dishonest, sixteen and in need of a lesson. Mary, as the girl is called, told her mother the next day that she worried that "sexual things had happened at the party," according to the appellate court summary of the case. Also according to court papers, before the video was made several boys sprayed Febreze on her butt and slapped it. Later, as Mary vomited on the floor, GMC had already left the room. The next day he texted friends, "I fucked her, not raped her. Calm down. If you have the video, get rid of it." When Mary asked him whether he'd made a video, he denied it. When she discovered he had lied, she asked him to stop sharing the video and destroy it, and he did not. Her mother called the police. An officer told GMC and his friends to delete the video, which they did.

Two years after that alcohol-fueled desert of the senses, there had been no lesson that might have mattered to a high-schooler. No consequences to make GMC take responsibility. No restorative justice in response to actions that, legal determinations aside, were wrong. No attention to the concerns of Mary. For her, the case goes on with only vituperative action, because the state was not interested in harm reduction or amends or correction in the realm of sixteen-year-olds. It was not interested in ensuring that GMC grow mindful of the ways that boys are acculturated to carelessness and violence, that he understand the harmful, capturing effect of technology. It said GMC's behavior was beyond his years, adult behavior, really, "sophisticated and predatory." The judge called that nonsense. Separate from everything else he had to say, this was the determinative rationale for rejecting the motion to treat the boy as an adult. The law in New Jersey is silent on good grades and test scores and Eagle Scoutery, but it does stipulate that a charged action must be sophisticated and predatory to meet the criteria for waiving a juvenile case out of family court. What the *Times* called leniency was affirmation of adjudication in the juvenile system. That is what the newspaper has advocated as appropriate treatment in general—and for years, ever since mass incarceration became a strain on the liberal conscience that once enabled it—for accused teenagers and children, who are presumed immature and impulsive, more so when addled by drugs or drink. In the particular case, though, the nightmare image of the predator, the animal, is irresistible. The appellate court said the prosecutor's assessment was valid, and the judge should have deferred. The crowd jerked in unison, *Get him!* If knowing of a dark place qualifies as predatory, and drunkenly making a cell phone video of drunken penetration of an impaired individual and texting an admission of rape fits any definition of *sophistication*; if language, that is, can be so unmoored from reason, we're all in trouble—or dishonest.

Both, actually. The *Times* story quickly metastasized. On Twitter a woman identified GMC by his full name as a student at Syracuse University. SU's *Daily Orange* did a lengthy report on July 7, by which time the student had either withdrawn or been expelled. Tweets flew fast and giddy. His name, his face, a photograph of his family home, the family address, a GIF from the TV series *Empire* with André repeating, "I said I'm gonna kill him" and other cries from the crowd:

Know his name, know his face
Ruin his life let the world see this don't employ him
Say his name! Say his name!
I don't feel save [sic] returning to a school that has a
  KNOWN sexual predator
Damn, he even looks like a rapist too
He should go to prison for the rest of his life
Jail time
Let's hope the inmates take video of his first time as well
It's so scary to think … like how many other trash people are
  among me/us and we don't know?
Boy need some years in prison and the judge need to lose his
  seat in the judicial system ASAP
There is no way this guy shouldent [sic] get 20 years
I believe castration should be on the table for punishments
That judge sounds like a rapist himself.

By mid-July the judge was out, forced to resign. GMC's case was expected to move to a criminal grand jury. Under New Jersey's juvenile waiver law, teenagers as young as fifteen may be tried as adults. Their identities are not protected, their court records are not sealed; if convicted they have a permanent criminal record, are subject to adult sentences and may eventually be locked up in adult prisons. If convicted of a sex offense, after serving their sentence they may spend the rest of their life on the public sex offender registry, which Laura Cohen, director of the Criminal and Youth Justice Clinic at Rutgers Law School, calls "a dangerous public policy" whose harms are "profound and numerous." Unless acquainted with the registry's strictures, most people in the US approve of this form of social death.

GMC is eighteen now, and hated. He is in that category of unpopular defendants whom Professor Sullivan calls "guilty, … vile or undesirable." Neither the *Times* nor court papers identified him as white (he is), yet almost immediately blogs and tweets asserted he had "gotten off" because of his race and privilege. *Good family* is apparently code for *white* among some vocal segment of the righteous. This is disturbing on so many levels, most obviously its subtext that non-white families must be bad, imagined once again, tacitly this time, as inhabiting a world of "indifference and ignorance … a land with no fathers"—or Eagle Scouts, good test scores or college dreams. Once his name, face and address were plastered on the internet (the address supplied by a Democratic aspirant to Congress for 2020, Carol Hafner), the furies were unleashed over the benefits of his color and wealth, with the inversion that anger was directed not at the unconscionable number of black youths tried as adults but at the absence of equal injustice for all.

Youth advocates and criminal justice reformers have long opposed trying juveniles as adults, and argue for further reducing punitive measures, including confinement, in favor of rehabilitative ones. Juveniles treated as juveniles, research shows, are less likely to commit crime again. (Also less likely to be physically, sexually and emotionally brutalized, less likely to commit suicide.) In 2015, when sixteen- and seventeen-year-olds in New York were still automatically treated as adults, as in 1989 (the law would not change until 2017), Jonathan Lippman, chief judge of the New York State Court of Appeals, made the cogent point to CBS News: "Here is the problem, they're not adults!"

Thirty years after a different set of good-family men and women of the media and other good-family liberals abetted the bad-family biases of police and prosecutors, the crowd's essential reflex is the same. The facts are different, the degree of panic is different, the cases are distinctly different. Certainty about a teenager's irredeemable life is unchanged. The criteria are different. White people can declare, *The enemy is rich. The enemy is white* in a new timbre, confident that no one will call them racist. For all its pretenses to social justice, this is poisoned solidarity. The enemy may be poor and black tomorrow, desperate and immigrant the next day—in fact both groups are, today. The validating enjoyment from demonizing "the right people" is as dangerous as ever, and unchanged. The situational view of rape is unchanged too: rape is a heinous crime, except when wished upon those accused of it.

All of which makes the crowd's tearful praise, just a few weeks earlier, of DuVernay's intimate portraits of the Central Park Five—their good or pretty-good families, their childhood hopes and silly banter, their humanity—appear to have been more a matter of sentiment than principle. If it be principle, the episode devoted to Korey Wise's agony behind bars should have inspired a public revolt against ever trying teenagers as adults, and amplified the moral fight against Prison America. As it is, the tears seem to have been shed only because Wise was the wrong guy. Yet for years he and the others (who suffered in juvie lockup) were presumed to be the right guys, convicted and declared the right guys, guilty, vile, undesirable. Does our pity depend on something so wispy as innocence? Wise and the others were not angels, they were boys, who were hystericized into wolves; in welcoming them back into the human family as victims, we have missed a step. Complex humanity, the mess of life, demands principled humanity. The victim is one of us. The suspect is one of us, whether ultimately found guilty or not.

I didn't start writing about sex to write about crime. Not all the pieces in this collection concern it, though many do. The first time I wrote on sex and culture, in an essay included here about Madonna, I was drawn to pleasure in the midst of danger, danger manifest physically in the AIDS epidemic and politically in persistent attacks on sexual freedom, sexual expression, homo- and other sexuality in the rule-breaking category. Desire is the subject there. The attacks (from Jesse Helms' denunciations of gays on the Senate floor, to collaboration by anti-pornography feminists with the Reagan right, to official silence as tens of thousands of gay men died of AIDS) were part of the historical context, then understood, as was the ongoing fightback from ACT UP (whose rowdy affirmations of life over fear somehow disappeared in critics' recent revisionism of New York in the late 1980s as a city in terror, paralyzed). Pleasure—the possibilities for it, the absolute necessity of attention to it as part of any radical politics, the meaning of and conditions for it, the substance of intimate life—continues to be my interest.

But sexual danger is at the fore in public discourse. Not since the height of the AIDS crisis has sex been so prominently welded to menace, except this period's version of safe sex, rather than emerging from a community's erotic sensibility, is a checklist of yes-or-no questions drafted to standardize consent and, primarily, to avoid legal action. (As the book's first entry shows, the erotic linkage of sex and safety was perverted by the criminalization machine, which continues to distort the rational impulse for precaution into an irrational license to punish.)

Scandal, the context for many of the pieces here, has become the background noise of life, a thrum that's stripped the word of its original meaning. Anticipating retribution enlivens people regardless of ideology, and has accelerated into ordinary, terrible fun. Mercy is the scandal now. Reason almost is. Eros is a suspect, and satisfaction in the humiliation of enemy-others is so everyday that as a culture we seem incapable of recognizing it as an extension of the violence we deplore. *What we don't talk about* is the red thread running through this book. What are the reasons, what are the causes and complications beneath the roar of the crowd, the stories we think we all know? What are the consequences of joining in? I don't pretend to have exhausted such questions, and I still hold out for a future where we are not handmaids of punitive authority but authorities over our own bodies, pleasures and risks.

This brings me back to the little girls at the start, playing school. The games of children are typically symbolic tests of the limits of their authority and autonomy. Often, the games involve fear, indulging it as a way of displacing it, gaining mastery, discovering *Ah, this is life* despite real or imagined danger. That is why the games of children are frequently risky (and sometimes go terribly wrong) or are simply heart-racing, involving fantasies of witches and monsters. When I was a little girl, playing in the yard across the fence from where these new little girls were playing, my brother and I made a game with neighborhood kids which we called Come, Little Children. It was basically a game of tag, but we ratcheted up the thrill factor by making whoever was It a witch. The witch sang a weird little song, creepy and enticing—*Come, little children, come, come, come ...*—accompanied by luring hand gestures and gyrations, trying to tempt the other children, lined up along a safe zone against the front of the garage, to step off and run for their lives, imaginatively speaking, either outwitting the witch to get to the next post of safety or coming under Its thrall. This was in the 1960s, but it could have been centuries earlier, so traditional is the extraction of joy from the sensation of fear (because the witch, who had earlier been just another child, a sibling even, was scary).

The little girls' leaps from wheeled garbage bins onto the blacktop, and their peals of laughter, reflect this age-old practice of pleasure-seeking through defiance of fear. Their wild risk-taking, though, exploded in a context of repression. Training games are customary, the child's *Let's pretend* enacting grown-up behavior—preparing them for the world they will inherit while also rehearsing, in rough form, their relationship to authority. As Marina Warner shows in her fantastic book *No Go the Bogeyman*, the mimicry of such games is often madcap, comically exaggerated in the anarchic spirit of play, metaphorically robbing the authority figure of some of its power. The teacher in this game, the oldest of the bunch at maybe ten or eleven, did not seem to be poking fun at her model, and except for a few groans, the littler ones in detention did not challenge her —the whole exercise less an imaginative enactment than a reproduction of reality, as numerous schools have determined that what best suits working-class children are the regimens of prison. On first impression, then, this was a game of obedience, not autonomy. Yet the rigors of improvised gymnastics gave loft to the leader's own dreams of performance even while intensifying her responsibilities. Instructing the smaller ones on discipline and technique as they prepared to leap, and leap again, protected them from injury and brought them joy in the afternoon. It could have gone otherwise, of course. There is nothing simple about play.

Long before any of us learn about sex, we learn about authority: our parents' over us, the wider world's over our parents, their response to that wider world's power, and the costs of any yes or no. The game of school was one game by one group of little girls on one leafy afternoon on the hard side of a hardish town, what used to be the black and Polish East Side of Buffalo, New York, and is now the mostly black, latinx and

Bangladeshi East Side. The girls appear to be loved, well cared for, polite, curious. I know almost nothing about their family's relationship to the landlord, the tax man, the bill collector, the policeman, the boss or social service agent. I know that at a nearby health clinic, adults drop in to talk sometimes about the stigma of being from the East Side, which, as everyone plainly sees, the city's leadership doesn't know what to do with. In this particular neighborhood about half the people are officially poor, reports of violent crime are among the highest in the city, and at least a third of the boys and girls in middle school and high school have seen someone shot, stabbed or assaulted—meaning almost every child knows a child who has witnessed violence, and the victim might be a parent, a sibling, a neighbor or friend. The kids learn to hit the ground when they're told to, and in school what they don't talk about is often what they can't talk about. Over the past couple of years, the city's grown-ups have sought ways to unburden children of the things they carry. One little boy has found a way, sort of, through playing the violin. It is necessary that the community come together to talk about violence. Violence is what nobody wants, not even, perhaps, the stick-up boys who, once upon a time, not long ago, may have been labeled "emotionally disturbed" in school because of the things they carried, and were then put on the short bus or in detention or suspended. Violence is a subject that doesn't wear out, but its most insidious forms don't require a weapon.

That little-boy violin player especially likes the "Ode to Joy." It has been called a balm for things he doesn't want: anxiety and nightmares, disabling grief over his father's murder. As for what he wants … How much unarticulated desire is bundled in that choice? How long will he, will any children but especially boys, be allowed to be sensitive? How do they talk about wanting when they want so much? When they might be afraid of their wanting, or the paths to it are obscured?

Listening to the little girls across the fence, I wondered what would be their blossoming pear tree, the emblem that stirs them in their bodies and their souls, as it did Zora Neale Hurston's Janie,

> like a flute song forgotten in another existence and remembered again. What? How? Why? This singing she heard that had nothing to do with her ears. The rose of the world was breathing out smell. It followed her through all her waking moments and caressed her in her sleep. It connected itself with other vaguely felt matters that had struck her outside observation and buried themselves in her flesh. Now they emerged and quested about her consciousness.

I wonder at all that must quest about the consciousness of these children, and all that will, and the distance between lived experience on an ordinary day and the rote political language of essences and -isms that is too straitened to contain it. By way of analogy, it is maybe not incorrect to say, as one high school teacher's guide to *Their Eyes Were Watching God* does, that the book "explores sexism, race and class discrimination, and the disappointment of loveless marriages," but then it wouldn't be incorrect to say that the book explores a black town, the Everglades, a hurricane and what to do when your man has rabies. Either way, Hurston is spinning in her grave, because the language is insufficient and the optic narrow. Janie's story is about getting free, about a woman coming to know her own body and mind, and daring, along the stony road and against the common sense of the time, to live and love authentically. Sexual politics cannot ignore the many forms that danger and domination take, else how could it be called politics— hence the explorations of this book—but it is nothing without freedom as its star, and the effort to change the common sense of the time, for the sake of every mother's daughter and son. I try to remember that.

Summer 2019

1

The Secret Sharer

They say a stranger brought sex and danger to Jamestown, New York. Not just sex, and not just danger—though no one admits to much of that being here even now—but sex-anddanger as an unhyphenated reality, a threat so great that government health officials flouted precedent and papered the county with posters of his face, red-bordered warnings, Most Wanted-style, that Nushawn Williams (*aka* Face Williams, "F," Shyteek Johnson, Jo Jo Williams, Lashawn Fields, Headteck Williams, Shoe Williams, Face Johnson), the twenty-year-old with the dark skin and short braids and occasional display of a "pleasing personality," was carrying the AIDS virus, and anyone who'd had sex with him, or with someone who'd had sex with him, ought to come down to a clinic for testing. His confidentiality might not have been honored, but yours surely would be.

This happened in the fall of 1997, before the subject of sex with multiple partners had made its swift transit from public menace to political crisis to national presidential joke. Williams was a small-time drug dealer who'd come to upstate Chautauqua County from Brooklyn in 1995. He was not a pioneer in any sense of the word. His occupation and migratory route were as commonplace as his discovery, in September of 1996, that he'd tested positive for HIV; as commonplace as the county jail cell he was in when he learned of that test result; as common-place as denial.

He'd been intimate with a number of young women both in western New York and in New York City before and after being told he had HIV. He is not known to have used intravenous drugs or to have had sex with men, though Chautauqua County health officials are not interested in determining the source of his infection. He's been X-ed out of all the usual categories of *patient*. Back before this was so—when Williams was like anyone else who'd tested positive and was first told the terrible news—he gave those officials the names of twenty-two area women for notification. Then, in January of 1997, he left town. Over the course of a year, four young women who were traced from the names Williams had provided tested positive; then one of their male partners did; then six more women whom Williams had never named but who had listed him among their partners. It was at that point—after the one person who tracks every HIV case in the county had sorted out Williams' aliases—that health officials decided his private life was a public emergency.

In the close-elbow manner of small-county politics, the sheriff and his father, the judge who gave the legal go-ahead to breach Williams' confidentiality, agreed. State authorities agreed as well. So the posters went up, and the press came flocking. Williams' face and his HIV status were flashed on network television, on CNN and throughout the print press even as he was again confined to jail—this time at Rikers Island in New York City, for selling $20 worth of crack to an undercover agent in the Bronx. In Chautauqua County, some 1,400 people, most of them high school students, were tested for HIV in October and November. Parents who once lived next door to Williams brought their children, even infants, for tests. In the end, thirteen young women, aged thirteen to twenty-four, had tested positive and claimed Williams—more precisely, unprotected sex with Williams—as the source. Through them, one other (a baby, not Williams' child) also tested positive. The press moved on to riper scandals, leaving Jamestown bleached and raw, its kids sullen from too many questions and too many answers half-heard. The posters, which Williams' friends began to rip down almost as soon as they went up, disappeared. Williams was history and, for a while at least, someone else's problem.

But suspicions of strangers die harder, especially in an area where some people, high-placed people, pride themselves on provincialism; where police are known to harass and judges known to issue one-way bus tickets to kids who come from out of town; where more adults than anyone cares to admit reckon uneasily that the presence of sharp young black men from Rochester and Buffalo and Brooklyn—mostly Brooklyn—is as alluring to some local girls as the sight of a deer to a hungry hunter, and for the same reason.

Jamestown's cupboard is bare. Its children, the ones who'd been invisible until association with Williams gave a few of them a moment of dubious fame, are walking bored and lonely and desperate for something that reason tells them they're never going to find here. It's less Jamestown's fault than its condition. And less its condition—less some malady that grew up in isolation in Chautauqua County, sixty miles from Buffalo, amid the dairy farms and fruit orchards, creeping suburbanization and crumbling urbanization—than it is America's. Jamestown just called attention to it by putting Nushawn Williams' face on a poster and telling itself, like a girl who believes with all her heart that she can't be pregnant until the contractions have her crying for deliverance, that everything was okay until he came to town.

"I don't understand it. Why would all these girls sleep with this guy without using a condom? What is it they figure— forty-eight girls he slept with? It's not like they'd never heard of AIDS." The UPS driver moonlighting as a bartender at The

College Inn, a neighborhood bar near Jamestown Community College, took a quick drag from his cigarette and went about setting up the next round of drinks. "It's stupidity, that's all. Just plain stupidity. They know what can happen, and they do it anyway."

"Do you always use a condom?"

"If I'm in a relationship, no. But if I'm just having fun, absolutely—every time. Sometimes two and three."

Through puffs of smoke, everyone at the bar, working men from their late twenties on up, distracted temporarily from their betting games of dice and darts, agreed, and agreed too that only stupidity or youth's faith in its own invincibility—"you know, *It can't happen to me*"—could explain why the girls took such a risk.

It was a familiar rationale, though reason rarely played a part in it (as it doesn't in the fiction that two condoms are safer than one). Kathleen Lombardo Whitmore, of AIDS Community Services in Jamestown, allowed that one day of AIDS education a year in the local public schools wasn't enough, that free protection wasn't readily enough available, that many of the girls seemed to have low self-esteem (a term that has become the catch-all explanation for any teenage sexual activity); but in the end even she declared in exasperation: "I don't think they think! I don't think a lot of them care."

In the white heat of the crisis, Whitmore had appeared on *The Montel Williams Show*, where she said, with admirable self-reflection, "I'm wondering where my message is going. Our agency's been there for five years—is anybody listening?" Indeed, none of the young women who are HIV positive and attribute their condition to Williams had ever been seen at AIDS Community Services, had ever dropped by to pick up free condoms or dental dams. It wasn't the easiest place to find. Until HIV and AIDS asserted themselves as necessary, even acceptable, subjects of conversation here, the agency's name was not listed along with Catholic Charities, United Way and other social service groups on the sign outside the old mansion on Fifth and Main whose basement it occupies. Even inside, one must ask a worker at another agency to point out the unmarked door that opens to the darkened stairway leading down to the offices. It barely advertised on radio, not at all on billboards, and Jamestown has no buses on which to place ads or even to transport people who don't live within walking distance.

That said, the question about *message* veered toward the heart of the matter at a time when, after a decade of awareness, half of all new HIV cases involve people under twenty-five; when the number of women diagnosed with AIDS rose 63 percent between 1991 and 1995, faster than any group in the US; and when the single biggest group of women are infected through sex with men they love, or say they love, or ally with in pursuit of love. Whitmore did not speculate about love or need or the often impossible choices women face when making decisions about safety. Instead, she used her one shot at a national audience to ask the friends and former lovers of Nushawn Williams whether they had thought about abstinence.

Abstinence? I had come to Jamestown because although there had been some 300 media reports on the story, everything seemed too simple. It was the inverse of Monicagate, where everything's gone rococo. In the Nushawn Williams scandal, the girls were presented as stupid or slutty or victims. The *Geraldo* show went live to film a young woman in New York as she got the results of an HIV test she had undergone after learning about the health alert upstate and realizing that she too had been with Williams. When she found out she was negative, she said, "It's like I'm a virgin all over again," a sentiment eagerly seconded by the unctuous Geraldo. By inference, it was also like a problem in logic: if negative equals virgin, then positive equals ____? Out of deference to the Jamestown girls' age, or perhaps their color (almost all are white), the press mostly shunned the traditional iconic complement, whore, and called them victims instead—victims who were "looking for love," a pursuit described as if it were a pathetic novelty rather than a hazardous preoccupation of humankind throughout history.

Jamestown was deemed "depressed" and "dreary" but also somehow "safe" and "mostly bucolic"—"Middle America" with "a solid, conservative social fabric," the kind of place where, as Mayor Richard Kimball put it, "it [is] hard to believe that something like this could happen." Mostly, though, whether in dreariness or small-town naiveté, it was exceptional—the setting for a local tragedy, not the emblem of a national truth.

Williams was the simplest of all, a "lethal lothario," a "sexual predator," a "one-man plague," a "monster." Dr. Robert Berke, the Chautauqua County health commissioner, said, "He's not a monster. ... We have the devil here," and Montel Williams told millions of television viewers that the death penalty would be the right punishment for what Williams had done. What he'd done, according to health and law-enforcement officials, was intentionally infect or try to infect young women with the AIDS virus—intent here resting solely on the fact that he'd been told he was HIV positive and didn't tell them. He's been charged with statutory rape for having sex with the thirteen-year-old, and further charges have been bruited: first-degree assault for every woman he had sex with who is now HIV positive, and reckless endangerment for every woman he had sex with who is HIV negative. Each assault rap could get him up to twenty-five years in prison; each endangerment rap, seven.

Chautauqua County district attorney James Subjack and New York State attorney general Dennis Vacco initially outdid each other in telling the media of their desire to prosecute Williams on such charges. Six months later, with no formal action taken, the two were being evasive, low-key, as if the legal machinery they'd endorsed with such confidence was flawed and they weren't at all sure they wanted to try it out, once again, with all eyes watching.

A preview of the kind of justice Williams might expect upstate has already been played out in New York City. Like legions of young black and latin men caught in the criminal justice system for petty drug sales, Williams had been awaiting formal sentencing on the crack charge in the Bronx when the posters proclaiming him a public sex enemy went up. He had already sealed a plea bargain with the DA to serve one year in jail. Normally, a judge just approves such deals, but on February 20, 1998, Judge John Byrne of the Bronx Supreme Court threw Williams' deal out—largely on account of the potent mix of rumor and allegation in Chautauqua County. Due process? Presumption of innocence? Integrity of a solemn promise? The same questions can be brought to bear on the decision by upstate officials to breach Williams' confidentiality and convict him as a "cold-blooded murderer" in the court of public opinion. On the straightforward matter of the drug charge, Williams was given a Hobson's choice: more jail time because of unproven and unrelated claims in a different jurisdiction; or the risk of a trial on a charge to which he had already, famously, pled guilty once. On April 20, Williams decided to abandon his plea and take his chances at trial.

In the state capital, meanwhile, New York legislators used the crisis to plump for a range of legislation that even Dr. Berke acknowledges would have done nothing to prevent it:

§ laws making it a felony for anyone who is HIV positive to have sex without first telling a partner;

§ laws forcing doctors to report the names of all positive cases to the state;

§ laws requiring persons who test positive to reveal the names of all their partners or face criminal charges;

§ laws establishing a state registry of everyone who tests positive;

§ laws allowing the use of this registry to divulge the names of positive individuals while notifying anyone who has ever had sex with them;

§ laws compelling the testing of prisoners, criminal defendants and arrested persons under a variety of circumstances.

None of those laws would have made any difference in the case of Nushawn Williams, who had an HIV test while at a county clinic for treatment of another sexually transmitted disease; who identified almost two dozen sex partners and agreed to let health officials contact them under the current system, which Berke says "worked perfectly in this case"; who went by so many aliases as to make name reporting irrelevant, was identified publicly under the "clear and imminent danger" provision of existing law, and may well be prosecuted even without a special statute criminalizing HIV status.

More important, they would have made no difference in protecting him from the virus in the first place, and they will make no difference in the lives of the young women of Jamestown—or in the lives of their mothers or sisters or kids. They will not make HIV-positive individuals more responsible to tell, partners more responsible to ask, or any of us more responsible to hold out for our own safety in time before, as one Jamestown woman put it, "the question *Why am I doing this?* gracefully turns into *Why did I do that?*" [1]

"What makes you vulnerable is what's complicated," said Amber Hollibaugh, national field director of women's education services at Gay Men's Health Crisis in New York. "It's the secrets that people can't talk about that put them at risk— always, always. It's not a question of whether people do 'risky things'; that doesn't deal with the real issues in the lives of real women and real men."

No one knows what goes on behind the doors in any town, just as no one knows what goes on between two people. But from what's in plain sight, it's hard to understand how anyone could consider Jamestown safe in the fullest sense of the word.

Nothing here rivals the devastation of parts of Buffalo—the ruined avenues empty at night but for a single driver and a guy powering his wheelchair through the mist. But neither is there the energy that animates other parts, even poor parts, of that wounded city. Jamestown's inner city, mostly white and black neighborhoods where Williams and many of the young women lived, consists of solid blocks of two-story frame or brick houses on hilly streets that rise up sharply from a stretch of factories on one side of the Chadakoin River—the old Swede Hill—and lead more gently out of downtown and into what's called the Valley on the other side. Rounding out the inner city, away from the center along Second Street, is the latin section. Only rarely do you find a house boarded up, and there are fine, even beautiful, structures here. But most are worn rough, and too many have doors lost, steps broken, hallways naked to the street. People make an effort or they don't, but the effort is often too small and probably too hard-won as well—a garden but not the steps, a gate but not the door, a curtain but not the window, some Christmas lights but not a coat of paint. On these streets, most likely they don't own the place anyway.

A lawyer named John Goodell told me he and others were angry that some reporters had said Jamestown was depressed. Indeed, the *Jamestown Post-Journal* printed a front-page story on November 7, 1997, lashing out at the national media and reminding readers of the city's virtues. Goodell took this a bit further. "Have you seen our ghetto?" he asked. "I bet you'd be happy to have our ghetto in New York." It seemed a slim choice, trading one zone of poverty for another, and all I could think of was Billy Preston's words: "Nothing from nothing leaves nothing ..."

I found myself raiding the icebox of pop culture a lot while in Jamestown, and not only because so many white, black and brown teenagers here testify to the universality of hip-hop style. There are also the city's own contributions to the culture: Lucille Ball and 10,000 Maniacs. Lucy grew up here. The Lucy–Desi Museum, around the corner from the high school, is a monument to mirth and marriage, though if you find the right button to press and wait long enough you can hear how, just before the divorce, Lucy clenched her teeth, dug her long red nails into Desi's shoulders and growled, "I could kill you." The Maniacs have far less claim on the local consciousness, except that they practiced in a warehouse that became the focus of a satanic-cult hysteria here in the late 1980s. Parents kept children home from school in record numbers one Friday the 13th when word spread that blue-eyed blonde virgins would be sacrificed. Countercultural kids were considered the dangerous element in that panic; one of them wore a jacket to school with the slogan FUCK AUTHORITY and eventually had to leave town because he was so beset with threats.

There was no blood sacrifice, nor any satanic cult (though one blue-eyed blonde who'd later be with Nushawn Williams did get a black rose from some kids making sport of the scare), just as there was no perfect happiness for the screwball come- dienne whom some old-timers still denigrate as a teenage slut, running wild with a bootlegger's son before leaving town. But the culture has a way of conjuring up a good fright when that's what's needed as distraction.

Jamestown had its start in 1811, when James Prendergast, a doctor from Tennessee, set up saw and grist mills by the Chadakoin rapids. From 1823 to 1873 it was the largest furniture-manufacturing city in the country, and up until the late 1920s was second only to Grand Rapids, Michigan. The lush forests that in 1800 blanketed the land, broken only by Indian footpaths, were gone a century later. The Indians were gone too. By then Jamestown was known as The Pearl City, owing to its production of pearl ash, used in making soap and glass. In the early days, while those with some capital set them- selves to lumbering or artisanry—or, later, to establishing textile mills, small metalworks and photographic-paper businesses —the poorest settlers survived by hacking at the forests, burning the wood to ash and bartering this for staple goods from store- keepers, who sold it to asheries. As the forests passed from memory so did the asheries, along with the reason for the city's moniker.

These days there are many "good parts" of Jamestown and, beyond the city limits, rambling houses and gracious country in the resort areas near Chautauqua Lake. (There are also year-round cottages off dirt roads hard by the water that recall places I've seen in Mississippi.) Jamestown High School's Red Raiders play football on a million-dollar field covered with AstroTurf, and on special occasions they have been known to step out in identical gray slacks and blue blazers, courtesy of local donors. Some old fortunes remain here, concentrated in five foundations worth $160 million combined, and the entertainment pages note high culture events befitting that part of the past memorialized in standard histories.

But downtown presents only mute mementos of the "air of constant activity and bustle" that guidebook writers of the New Deal found in 1940. The population, 45,500 then, is now 34,500 and falling. The rumble of public transport is gone, the Art Deco station for the Erie Railroad sooty and abandoned, its clock frozen like a prop out of *Great Expectations* at 9:25. The elegant Hotel Jamestown is an old folks' home, as are several erstwhile commercial buildings, reflecting the only segment of the population that is growing. At the other end of Second Street from the high school, the cavernous Furniture Mart, to which buyers and dealers once flocked from all points, now houses Kelly Services, one of five temp agencies.

A slight, wise-eyed Puerto Rican girl named Tania, who left home at fifteen and later became a roommate of Nushawn Williams, went through one of those agencies for a job at Bush Industries, a furniture maker and the city's biggest employer. She worked graveyard shift on the packing line when she was seventeen, along with nine other teenagers with whom she shared a two-bedroom flat. "They showed us a video when we first came in there saying how much better it is 'cause they have no union," she said. "You know, 'If you have a problem we can work it out.' But if you complain, they fire you. They was paying us $5.15 an hour, and fifteen cents goes to the agency. I didn't mind, 'cause when I got my check, you know, I was just glad to have the money. But then we all—all ten of us—got hurt at the same time: our backs. Not all the same minute, you know, but around the same time. They give you carfare to the hospital, but you got to pay your own way home. You got to pay for the hospital too. The doctor told me to stay home three days; I stayed four and they fired me. But it don't matter, 'cause you can just go to the agency and they'll hire you right back."

Manufacturing started to bleed from Jamestown in the 1950s; from the 1960s to the early 1980s it was in full hemorrhage, and it's still in slow decline. But unlike in Buffalo, where one shutdown at Bethlehem Steel alone cut loose 7,300 workers, here people left the plant gates quietly, a few hundred at a time, until 5,000 to 8,000 industrial jobs and perhaps the same number in support industries and services had disappeared. To consider the numbers now is staggering: job loss in the magnitude of anywhere from a tenth to a third of the population. Of course, it happened over time. There was other work—service work, part-time work, work out of town. Not all the manufacturers closed. And there were malls that went up in the suburbs, chain restaurants that moved in, a new civic arena downtown, the nursing homes, Walmart, Kmart and all the other marts that duplicate strip malls on the edge of every unlucky town in the country. People soldiered on, and, in the same way that a lifetime of days looking in a mirror makes aging tolerable, they barely noticed as the town fell apart around them. Perhaps for the same reason, they barely noticed the young subcontractors from Brooklyn who started coming to town in the early 1990s to work in the drug trade then expanding along Route 17 from New York to Jamestown and from there on to Buffalo and Canada. Their children took note, though, well before Williams came on the job.

Today in the legal economy, unemployment is 5.2 percent, but as Sam Teresi, who heads development at city hall, put it: "We're following the national trend. While the figures are looking pretty good, it takes two and three members of the family now to equal the old wage of one. And every big company is using temp agencies. If that's frustrating for a teenager, it's also frustrating for a forty-year-old head of household who has no health insurance and a family to take care of. At this point we've weathered the storm—essentially we've bottomed out. Now we're looking at how to sustain real, incremental growth. Manufacturing has to be a major leg in the economic stool, but we're realistic. Jamestown is not going to become the oasis in the industrial desert that is America."

Teresi conceptualizes the integrated pieces of a new economy as vividly as he juggles metaphors. But he also knows that if "good jobs at good wages" ever were enough to ensure the good life, they aren't anymore. A generation of deindustrialization did more than remake the landscape and reduce the living standards of places like Jamestown, where the median family income is about $26,000 and almost a quarter of families with children under eighteen are poor. It made insecurity—always a feature of working-class life—the central experience. After twenty-six years of a citywide experiment in "labor-management cooperation," there is no sign that the working class has any more power or any more pride. For too many of those without enough, there's not enough of anything: not enough time, not enough confidence, not enough culture, not enough choices, not enough love.

On the last weekend before Christmas it seemed I had the downtown to myself. Two fine-jewelry stores, a camera shop, a florist doubling as a confectioner and one or two other merchants displayed holiday lights and brimming determination. But all the action was at the D&K Store, where people clothed in weariness waited to pick through bins—89¢, 99¢, $1.99, $14.99 tops—of sequins and wood blocks, pipe cleaners, tube socks, flannel shirts, pocket screwdriver sets, ceramic figurines: the flotsam and jetsam of the retail trade for the working poor.

"We gotta get your daddy something now," a wan young woman said, pulling along two pasty tykes and searching the aisles for anything that might say, *I'm special*.

> *Do you love me, baby?*
> *Can you feel me, baby? I been away a long time.*
> *Is it still me, baby—the one on your mind?*

I drove away from downtown with Puff Daddy's *No Way Out* playing in the car at full volume. On Tania's suggestion, the album had become my soundtrack for seeing Jamestown.

> *Can I touch you, baby? Is that all right with you?*
> *Can I love you, baby? What we're about to do*
> *could make the whole earth move, I'll tell you my first move.*
> *Climb up in it slow. I ain't tryin' to hurt you.*
> *Can you feel me, baby? Should I keep it right there?*
> *Is it still me, baby? Take off your nightwear ...*

At the health department they say nothing links the girls who tested positive besides Williams—no common social or medical profile. Dr. Neal Rzepkowski, a family physician who treats a lot of them, told me most of his patients had a prior history of sexually transmitted disease or had engaged in anal sex; otherwise, there is no "type."

In the first flush of the crisis officials said there was a very definite type: girls who traded sex for drugs. This persisted in the public mind even after the sheriff asserted that "in no way" was that the case; too many girls had started turning up talking about love. I was meeting mostly girls who had moved in the same circles as Williams: some, like Tania, who'd never had sex with him but knew those who had; others who had; one who was positive. Although I've been told there were girls from "well-off, solid families" who'd had sex with Williams as a tryst with danger, the young women I was meeting were all working-class and precarious. I drove along imagining the rapper's lyrics as a kind of baseline unifying the fragments of life history I'd heard:

You're seventeen and you left home years ago. Your mother bugged you or was tougher than you thought your father would be, or she just threw you out. And you love her but she never had time—or maybe she had time but not as much as you wanted. You "wanted it all." But she couldn't help it really 'cause there were other kids and she had to work all the time; or she could help it, but she spent all her time with her boyfriend and then got on you about yours! Or she paid too much attention, or there was too much fighting, or she was always sick, or you got pregnant, or you couldn't take another day of your father harping on everything you'd done wrong, or ... or ... too many reasons you'd rather not talk about. So, you're living with relatives, friends' families or kids alone and in the same boat as you. You're working midnight to eight to pay the rent and utilities, to pay for food and clothes. You're trying to go to school, but it's hard to stay awake and it's a drag to be hassled as if you're a child. You're sick and you need an excuse. The excuse is supposed to come from your mother, but you don't live at home. The teacher says, "Well, get one from whoever you live with." So you get it from your girlfriend; she's who you live with! But the teacher thinks you're being smart, so you get in-school suspension. You don't mind that so much 'cause at least they leave you alone to do your work or think. And you're with all the other kids who are always in detention, the "bad kids," the ones "who are just looking for a place to fit in—they'll accept anyone." You actually tried to be a prep once, 'cause it's not like you're poor or nothing, but you had to dress a certain way, walk a certain way, talk a certain way—it was too much. And you dreamed of being a cheerleader but you were too fat, or you were a cheerleader but with everything else you were trying to keep together it was too much. And you have average grades or below-average grades, but it's been clear for a while that no one expects much from you, and anyway school's a bore so you drop out. You hear little kids counting the days till they can drop out too, asking, "Can I drop out as soon as I turn sixteen, or do I have to wait until the end of the year?" Anyway, you hang out with your friends. There's not much to do unless you swim or play basketball, but you won't go to the Boys and Girls Club 'cause "that's for really grubby poor kids, these little kids who just piss in the pool and turn it yellow," and you don't like the Y 'cause that's where the preps go and "they have this attitude they give to anyone who don't have as much as they do." Sometimes you go to JCC to play basketball and that's fun, and there are girls who run track with this club Striders and they go off to meets out of town, which is okay if you like to run but if you don't, well, you don't. And there's just nothing to do in this town but get high and fuck—well, and hang out and play cards and watch BET on cable, but really nothing else. There used to be a teen club and that was good 'cause you could go dance all night, but that closed up. You can't get into the bars unless you're twenty-one—well, you can sneak in—but the only really good DJ is at the Rusty Nail. They got a good one sometimes at Rascal's. No?! Rascal's is a gay bar?! Well, anyway, it's not like you drink that much or get high that much—maybe a beer or some weed—though you know some kids who are in AA now because, you know, life is hard sometimes, and "in this town if you fall you don't just miss a stair or two; you fall down the whole damn staircase." And it's not like you just sleep with anyone, either. You're not like "those little girls who are just whores, you know, real pigs, who go with anyone." Those little girls are disgusting, and some of them are real shystee bitches—"you know, not what you'd call real women"—the kind who talk behind your back and steal your man as soon as you go to jail. Oh, yeah, you can go to jail so easy in this town. Your boyfriend—he's black and from Buffalo—he was in jail for a month and a half for throwing a stick at a car. He was mad—"he has problems with anger"—so he threw this stick and these white kids jumped out and started a fight, and one of them had an outstanding warrant but your boyfriend's the only one got locked up. And you know this other boy—he's black and from Brooklyn, he knew Face there—he went to jail for two months for driving without a license. Two months! You've been to jail a bunch of times, "always for the little things, never for the big things," but those little things add up. Or maybe they're not little things. You were at a boot camp once—eighteen months. And later you were in for four months—breaking probation—'cause you cursed out your landlord, said you'd blow up his house when he wouldn't do what you needed. You have problems with anger too, but it's not like you have a history with explosives. Now you're through with "the business"—the pharmaceutical business, what do you think? selling drugs—'cause you just don't want to be in jail again. You're eighteen, nineteen, and you're not talking about a little time now. But in the business, on a good night, you could make three, four thousand dollars in a few hours— "Jamestown is full of crackheads"—and that sure beat packing boards or sorting screws for five or six dollars. Yeah, you got to get out now. Maybe go to Atlanta, "where there's some culture"; you and your boyfriend might have a chance in a black city. Nothing's easy, though. Your little sisters think it's glamorous 'cause you been out on your own since you were thirteen, fourteen. "But they don't know how hard it is, how real hard." It's not so bad, though; it's not like your friend in Rochester who has a three-year-old kid by her mother's boyfriend who still lives in the house and visits her room every other night—and her room is right next to her mom's! Or like your girl in Buffalo who had HIV—maybe from Face, nobody knows—and who was killed last year. It was an accident, a gun went off that wasn't supposed to, but you never had a friend who died before. She was eighteen. That was in Buffalo, and Buffalo's dangerous. "Jamestown isn't dangerous, it's just boring."

I wish this pain would go away
I wish this pain would go away

Marx was wrong. Sex, not religion, is the heart in a heartless world. It may not turn out well; in fact, it almost certainly will not. Most every girl I met trailed a broken heart somewhere in her short past; if she didn't, it was because she was still with her first boyfriend, or because she had never let anyone get too close, or because at eighteen, having determined that "we're both clean," she was planning for her wedding right after graduation and heartbreak would catch up with her soon enough. Whatever the case, sex brought the promise of something good, something intimate, something sweet and fleshy and maybe pleasurable; it brought that promise as surely as it carried the darker risk of pain and sorrow. But everything carried that—and more than the risk, the plain, lonesome reality. To be held in someone's arms, to be kissed, to be entered and, in the act, forgiven for not being the most beautiful or the most responsible or the most stable; to be forgiven for the reckless dream of wanting, a baby, a partner, a life; to exert that power of forgiveness over someone else: only sex carried the slim hope of something better.

It is difficult now, when his mugshot has appeared across the country and young women have appeared on television weeping over their predicament and his betrayal, speaking of his violence and irascibility, to imagine that there was also a time when Williams delighted them and they delighted him. It is as if these young women, cast as victims of sex, must be denied every pleasure of their past and every power of decision—good and bad—so as to prepare for some future prosecution in which it can be shown that he was just a criminal and not a man, a young man, negotiating his fears and needs through sex as surely as they were.

Andrea is nineteen, white and HIV positive. She told me she was with Williams for a month or so at the end of 1996 and that she always "despised" him.

"Always?"

"The whole time."

"But you say you were with him for a month, so there must have been an upside. Was it really just that he bought you presents and took you to restaurants?"

"He made me feel like I was somebody, like I was special. He was always there, and my other boyfriends were never there."

"Anything else?"

"Well, the sex was great. And he held me in his arms when we slept, and that was important to me. And he kissed me real softly ... I thought I loved him, but it was only infatuation. I wanted him because he was something I was told I couldn't have."

Andrea claims she used a condom with every man she was with until Williams. She claims he wouldn't hear of using one, though she also insists, "He told me when we first had sex that he put on a condom." To accept that requires believing that she never touched him, never paid attention, that she simply lay back, closed her eyes and took it.

"Oh, I never touched men. I never played with them or nothing; I think that's disgusting. I never did oral sex either. I try not to look at them too often—their penis, I mean, it's ugly."

Great sex? "They can go down on me. And I make sure I always get mine."

Andrea has been in and out of psych wards, group homes and jails since childhood. When she was four her mother's fiancé took her to a park and abused her in some way involving oral sex. Her mother, Wendy, traces Andrea's problems to that event. "At that age," she says, "there's part of them that understands it's violating and part of them that enjoys it." She says Andrea became obsessed with sex from that moment. At six she was on Ritalin. At twelve she ran away from a group home in Florida and met up with a man who was twenty. She told him she was seventeen, though seven years later, without makeup, she still has a baby-doll face. She remembers sitting on the edge of the bed in a motel, her knees shaking, before he took her virginity. "I thought I was going to be with him for a while," she said. "A week later he was charged with armed robbery, and I felt like such an idiot." In the years that followed she'd come home to her mother's comfortable house, stay awhile, wind up in another institution, run away again and again—selling drugs, being pimped on the street, taking up with men for a ride or a place to stay. "I thought the end point would come when I got caught or when I was dead," she said. "On the street you always have to watch your back. HIV was the least of it."

It still is, in a way. Maybe not for Andrea—who dyed her blond hair black to avoid being recognized, lives at home again and strives to maintain the disciplines of safe sex and a medication schedule—but for many young women in America. "It's the life that is lethal," Amber Hollibaugh had said. But the life can't be prosecuted; Nushawn Williams will have to do. He can stand in for every man who ever violated Andrea and every man who violated the others—and there are probably more fathers and brothers and boyfriends in that company than anyone wants or dares to take account of. He can pay for every rotten thing that ever happened to them that nobody knows how to deal with. If in the end he is convicted, none of the Andreas or Andreas-to-be will be stronger or safer, but somebody will call it justice.

Andrea said, "He was the only man who ever scared me." And although that is hard to believe set beside the frightful details of her life (just as it is hard to believe that she didn't know he sold drugs, that she always used condoms until she met him, that she had intercourse with only nine or ten men in her life, that she never before had a sexually transmitted disease and therefore knows her infection traces back to him), by all reports their time together was brutal. Yet the knives are drawn for him not for beating her but for holding her in his arms, kissing her softly, fucking her often and well—for the only things in a world of pain and binds from which she exacted a little pleasure and commanded a little power.

The frenzy over just how many teenagers are having sex in Chautauqua County, protected or unprotected, obscured a series of more unpleasant truths about the county's families. "It's still a great place to raise a family" was not only on the lips of politicians and the head of the PTA; even Andrea's mother had said it, allowing that things had gone awry in her own case. In their descent upon Jamestown, journalists had sought out various family folk who had lived upstairs, next door or otherwise in proximity to Nushawn Williams. These people were offered in stable counterpoint to his volatile world—much as the *Post-Journal* runs engagement notices of recent high school graduates on one day and mugshots of area men for whom there are outstanding warrants on the next.

Right before Christmas, I was at the Chautauqua County Jail visiting a former girlfriend of Williams named Amber when I learned that a woman who had appeared in the media as the mother-next-door was also being held there. It seems the woman had written a bunch of bad checks—possibly in hopes of accomplishing something before the holidays that would calm her husband's temper—but the details are sketchy, and her arrest was never reported. Amber, on the other hand, was a minor celebrity. She had spent considerable time with Williams and, in a manner that revealed as much bravery as vulnerability, had shaken up Jamestown by telling reporters that although she was angry at Face, her eighteen-year-old heart wouldn't let her join in reflexive condemnation. "He's not a monster," she'd simply said. "I did once love him." Afterward, she says, some plainclothes cops pulled up alongside where she was walking and promised to laugh at her funeral. Her father said, "I hope she dies." Amber was arrested outside a county clinic after receiving her HIV test results (negative, which she says she reveals only because a rumor mill insists she's positive). She was sentenced to serve a year for running up $600 on a stolen Sears credit card and for a drug sale she got busted on because a cousin agreed to wear a wire and set her up. Shortly after the press bus left in November, Amber said, the father-next-door was also in jail.

"He's what I call a good friend but a bad man," she said. It was a distinction she'd made before about men who love their neighbors and hurt their lovers. This man is in his twenties, with many children. But he did it right. He's married, he doesn't cheat, doesn't sell drugs, and although the family doesn't have much—he doesn't work often—on the outside it puts up a fair face. On the inside it's hell. In the days of high panic, his wife told the media that she'd counseled Williams to get away from his girlfriends if he couldn't restrain his anger. Now people tell me they wonder if she'll live to see her own children grown.

The Division of Criminal Justice Services states that domestic violence in Chautauqua County is increasing, from 232 reported cases in 1993 to 566 in 1996. The suicide rate is not comforting either. On the Tuesday before New Year's, a twenty-nine-year-old woman had been dead on the couch for twelve hours when she was found by a caseworker. Her children, three and four years old, circled in confusion close by. Crime is low by state standards, but it's the tenuousness of things more than the upward curve of any statistic that unsettles: the notices around town about a young woman who vanished, the drinkers at the precipice of rage, the unprompted warnings from people on the streets that perhaps you should be frightened when nothing seems frightening. On the social charts, teen pregnancy and car accidents involving twenty-five- to thirty-nine-year-olds under the influence are also up, after having dropped a few years back. The rate of child abuse more than doubled, from twenty per 1,000 to fifty-one per 1,000, between 1991 and 1993. This rate is about twice as high as in the rest of the state outside of

New York City, and it represents only reported cases. Around the corner from one of the houses where Williams lived bumper stickers announce, WHAT THIS COUNTRY NEEDS IS A BREATH OF FRESH PRAYER, and after posters of his face went up, Lucy Zulick of Good Shepherd Mission Outreach, an evangelical church in the nearby village of Clymer, declared: "This problem began when we took God out of the schools and put condoms in. When they took heaven out, hell came in, and one word can sum it up: Sin with a capital S." Chautauqua County schools aren't required to talk about condoms, much less give them out, but on Super Bowl Sunday five children from a family of religious zealots were in a county emergency room with bruises and both old and new fractures. The five-year-old with the broken nose said she got hit for not sweeping the floor right.

"The family? I think it's like a balloon that you keep blowing air into, and it's holding more and more, but at a certain point it can't hold any more and it just explodes." Nancy Glatz, a practical nurse and a caseworker for Early Head Start in Jamestown, was talking about how everything has changed—the role of the city, the economic base, expectations of work and generational progress, the responsibilities of government. And everyone acknowledges there's no going back. When it comes to the family, though, there's only going back—to a Lucy–Desi ideal that was never true in the first place.

It's common these days to hear talk of the Golden Age of the working class, when the household was strong, the factory secure and upward mobility seemed certain. This is the happy-family working class I came up in back in the 1960s and 1970s in Buffalo. I was hardly alone. But beside all of our happy families there were always unhappy ones, in which work was unsteady, violence came easily, and mothers and daughters and their daughters too lost their youth in vows of love that never turned out as they'd hoped. No one likes to remember those families, not even the children who come from them. They are the people who lost at a time when the country's story admits only of winners. But someone always did the low-wage jobs, always got on the slow track in school. "I never wanted to be like my mother," a young Jamestown woman told me, speaking of one of my contemporaries. "She had me when she was fifteen. I got pregnant at sixteen and ended up doing exactly what I never wanted to do."

About seventy-five families—most with two adults—participate in Nancy Glatz's Head Start program. She describes the general scheme of their lives as chaotic, constantly on the edge of want, dangerous in so many ways beyond the physical. Often there is no phone; there is no car, or one car and it's the man's car. Having control of so little else in life, he carries the Medicaid cards and every other family document, and he decides who is welcome in the house. Sometimes when he goes out, he takes the rest of the family's boots and coats with him. But every time the caseworkers first visited these families, the women said that except for a few small problems everything was fine. It was only later—sometimes years later, when they began to trust that any revelation would not automatically call down Child Protective Services to haul away their kids—that they opened up. Still, there's the shame, the fear that in a small town to say you need help because of alcohol or violence or mental illness or just the awful narrow limits of your life is to risk being branded sick or something worse.

When Wendy went on national television and stated that Andrea had been abused, all kinds of people in Jamestown responded bitterly, *And where were you?* No one seemed to know or care what this crime must have cost her, a woman who'd left her good-for-nothing husband, who'd hoped she could "save" the man who hurt Andrea and broke with him right after it happened, who says she was molested herself as a child, whose hit-and-miss strategy for dealing with this multiple horror was to shut away her own past, cart her daughter to a series of (as it turns out, dubious) therapists, throw herself into such Good Mother roles as scout leader, and never, ever allow herself to be touched by a man again. Nothing she did saved Andrea from HIV, and the nasty truth is that there are harder cases than Andrea's. They're the married women with HIV, the women in committed relationships, the ones who wouldn't have dreamed of asking their men to use a condom, and whose very existence upsets all standard notions about HIV.

"I see people come in here, and it kills me," Rose Torres said one afternoon in her office at AIDS Community Services. "I'm twenty-five, and I think, 'Okay, it can happen to me, but not to my mother,' and then these ladies my mother's age walk in. People don't want to talk about that." Indeed, Rose's colleague, Kathleen Whitmore, didn't.

"What about women in relationships?" I asked Whitmore. "If you're a 'bad girl' maybe people think you have no right to safety, but if you're a 'good girl' you have no need for safety. How do you deal with that, since statistically the majority of women with HIV got it from a partner, not from a one-night stand?"

"What do you mean when you use the word *relationship*?"

"Married women, people who live together—a month, a year, twelve years. How do you ask a guy to use a condom when asking suggests he's cheating, and cheating suggests you're failing?"

"Well, I kind of think you can tell when someone's cheating, don't you?"

"Do you ever use a condom?"

"I'm married."

There have been fifty-two cases of full-blown AIDS in Chautauqua County since the epidemic began being tracked in the US in the 1980s, but most of those, Dr. Berke said, "have been secret." The county women with HIV whom nurse Margaret Geer has been visiting to help with insurance claims, social services and the like all thought marriage or commitment was a prophylactic until someone in the family got sick. Only one of their men was an IV drug user, and only one had clandestine homosexual encounters from what Geer has been able to determine, though the men might not tell everything. (Did they ever share a needle? Did they ever have sex in prison?) What they do admit to is sex with other women. One called it "my sport." And what strikes Geer about the women she visits, all working-class, is their isolation, their lack of confidence, the huge degree of control they ceded to their men, and the silence that, until HIV was added to the mix, covered it all. Lately she's begun visiting one of Williams' partners.

Nationally, two of the top known concentrations of women with HIV are in Newark, New Jersey, and Macon, Georgia. In Newark the profile of "women at risk" fits those most at risk of any torment of poverty in a hard city. In Macon it's different. Women there learned they were HIV positive when they went to give blood for Desert Storm at Robins Air Force Base. Many of their husbands are vets who years earlier had had trouble with drugs, cleaned up and came home to set their lives right. They didn't talk much about the past, not at all about HIV. The CDC estimates that anywhere from 200,000 to 300,000 people don't know they're positive, and the majority of the public that thinks HIV is someone else's problem grows bigger with every poll. Almost every straight person I talked to before leaving for Jamestown, most of them well-educated grown-ups in New York, said there must be some secret I'd have to unearth about these girls. "It's almost impossible to get it just from sex between men and women," they said, even though sex between men and women is the fastest-growing mode of HIV transmission.[2] Amber Hollibaugh says that when she started the Lesbian AIDS Project some gay women said she'd never find more than a dozen cases—*Everyone knows we don't get it!*—but now the project involves 400 women in New York City alone. In Jamestown some of Williams' friends said they believe him when he says he thought the authorities who told him he was positive while in jail were just trying to scare him into leaving town. But his friend Amber, who was with him on and off for nine months, now thinks that he was mostly in denial: "When I went to visit him, he said, 'Do I look sick? I don't feel sick.' I think he convinced himself that it wasn't true—and, you know, you can convince yourself of anything."

Watching Williams escorted out of a Bronx courtroom, giving a half-smile and two-fingered salute to someone in the gallery, I thought of Ohio. "That was his big dream," Amber said, "to move to Ohio and make a life. He went there when he was younger; his dad used to live there—now, I don't know if that's true but it's what he said—and he loved it." By now the rough sketch of Williams' biography has been drawn often enough, and it contains precious little of the stuff of dreams: born in the Crown Heights section of Brooklyn, his mother addicted to crack, his father jailed when he was four; a sweet kid attractive to females from an early age, an angry teenager who was in special ed for reasons unclear and who robbed one of the few people who tried to help him; a Blood, a dealer, a "wild cat" who survived a shooting in a housing project and a string of charges, including one for murder (he was acquitted); a guy with more sexual partners than Bill Clinton and, yes, a "pleasing personality."

But what did they see in him? The question, overt or indirect, has riveted reporters and TV presenters. It's funny how the opposite question—what did he see in them?—is never asked, only implicitly answered in the assumption that he was "looking for victims" and they were easy "prey." There's more than a touch of racism behind the media prurience, since, except that so many of them are white, the young women in this case mostly swam in the same stream of trouble as Williams. It would have been stranger if they hadn't found each other. But America could have a lifetime of "conversations on race" and the white press would still twitch at the idea of a black man in bed with white women. This time the history of white perceptions of savage blackness was compressed in an economy of symbols—the reproduced poster, the headline language of beastliness, a young woman's photograph, all of which worked together like a logo. The symbols made it unnecessary for most reporters even to remark on the interracial nature of the liaisons; allowed them, actually, to write or speak as if such pair-ups among young people in Jamestown were as common as they are, in upstate New York or anywhere, judging from the 57 percent of US teenagers who pollsters say have been in interracial relationships. *Common*, though, is not part of the vocabulary of the media in scandal mode. The scandal, the news, was therefore best conveyed by images, which effectively told the story, superseding all other language. In the story of Williams, pop culture's trinity of sex, race and danger was perfectly realized.

Still, it's too neat, and too disregarding of the women who are HIV positive, to say, as some have, that the panic is reducible to white, straight male America's historic fear of black male sexuality. Racism poisons the brew in Chautauqua County as it does everywhere, but the fact is it wouldn't have much mattered if Williams had infected one white girl (unless she was the mayor's daughter), just as it wouldn't have much mattered if the only person traced to him was the black thirteen-year-old, who I was told could pass for the seventeen years she claimed to be when everyone was partying.

In the catalogue of victimology, working-class women count only in bulk. Before Williams became an issue, no one with power got excited that Ernest Lockett, another black man in the county, had infected his white partner, Nan Nowak, and through her their daughter, Nadia. They were just another throwaway family. Nor is the state any more concerned with the health of such families now. Legal action has gained currency as a reasonable response to infectious disease, so Lockett is being prosecuted for assault, an action that Nowak had advocated but the state had resisted for years. If convicted, he will be one more black prisoner. Ernest, Nan, little Nadia: nobody knows their names. In the Williams case, numbers assumed such fetishistic value that Dr. Berke declared Williams had "damaged hundreds and hundreds of lives," even when at the time the positive individuals associated with him numbered nine, and perhaps half of those had the virus before he was told he was positive. The state announced he'd named fifty to seventy-five partners in New York City, who in turn were placing untold others at risk. Those numbers were totally manufactured. According to sources at the New York City Health Department, Williams named about fifteen city women, of whom fewer than half have been found and none have been linked to him by HIV with any confidence. But the larger number was excitedly reported, implying an ugly chain of equivalence: one mayor's daughter is worth twenty small-town "risk takers" is worth seventy-five big-city sluts is worth …

When numbers are so thrown about, the individual recedes, which is exactly the purpose of such panics. In propagating the extraordinary, they distract from the crushing ordinariness of life and death in the age of AIDS: from the 380,000 deaths and the 900,000 HIV-altered lives; from the man or woman infected every hour without notice or care; from the catastrophic failure of public health and the common, terrible but no less human realities of one man—one youth, really, for Williams was not more than eighteen when he came to Jamestown—for whom the best of all possible futures, a regular life in Ohio, might as well have been the biggest, most impossible fantasy anyone had ever had.

What did they see in each other? Maybe a hope of family. And if they only replicated its distortions, who deserves the blame? At a kitchen table one night in Jamestown, a fellow who calls himself Killer explained that the crew he leads, a gang that seems a long way from the Crips of his dreams, is "like family and religion rolled into one." Listening to him describe his responsibility to instruct and discipline his "children," to dominate his "Queen"—and hearing his acolytes vow obedience—was like an hour spent captive with Christian radio. Yet what is spoken and what is true may differ. Earlier, when I talked with Killer's girlfriend alone, she had characterized their relationship as one of tender honesty, in which they faced their weaknesses and pooled their strengths, in which they had decided to abandon the underground as too risky but were still trying to find a way out of their low-end factory jobs. Equality was assumed. She said that with every man she insisted on using a condom, that she insisted with this one until they'd committed to each other and both had been tested. Surrounded by his friends and subordinates, Killer put aside his jokey charm and imagined firearms and "fucking with the police" and "big-time fraud." He said he had never used a condom; he never would, not even now, not even to protect his Queen. He'd rather die.

So who is right? Probably both and neither. People burdened by fears have always sought to make something of a romance or swagger-dance of their life, and others have sought to deny them their contradictions and protective deceptions. I met Killer and Queen in a flat occupied by a group of teenagers and young-twenties, a driftway of bare rooms with almost bare mattresses on the floor for which they paid rent in cash or product or IOUs (this was kept vague) to an older woman with whom they sometimes sat around watching TV in the afternoon. They were poor and young and groping for home.

I have not spoken with Nushawn Williams. His court-appointed lawyer in New York, William Cember, turns away journalists' requests for interviews and has warned Williams that anything he says will be used against him, by somebody. Cember is not wrong, but the protective effort is another form of capture, leaving Williams visibly invisible. There's no reason to suppose, though, that Williams alone among men must be one-dimensional. It's regularly assumed, for instance, that every present he gave, every gentle thing he did, was a ploy to exploit a young woman. Now, he might not be a "good man"; he might be a little crazy (psychiatrists report he is competent to stand trial, but that doesn't mean he has no problems); and he certainly was wrong not to tell his partners about HIV. But at least sometimes might not a gift have been just a gift, a gesture of feeling and a bid for notice? How many ways are there for a street dealer with scars all over his body and a heavy rap sheet to express eligibility, even if some girls say they "go for thugs"? Isn't it possible that he too might have been "looking for love," that in the exchange of tokens and physical desire the trade in "self-esteem" might have gone both ways?[3]

It was the way he "carried himself," Amber said, that first attracted her to Williams. "Like a millionaire." I grasped something of that allure one Saturday after 2 a.m. at an all-night downtown diner called Mattia's. Jamestown's fifty-odd bars had just closed, and the restaurant welcomed the broken figures of what's left of white working-class culture. I'd seen such faces earlier at the Ranch and the Bull Frog, faces joyless and worn and just a little menacing, just enough to shame you for the freedom of your life and the outsider's curiosity that made you assume the right to impose on their dignity. At Mattia's they were joined by a few soft drunks, a few frisky matrons, a few creamy prep-types and the drug dealers or drug-dealer hangers-on, who alone laughed and walked proud and with every flirtation or quick remark to a table of young women proclaimed, *Life!*

Girls who spent time with Williams say he was funny. He improvised songs and told silly jokes and put on accents. He could also be cruel and demand that they take off their clothes and get fucked when that's not exactly what they had in mind. Amber describes a life of alternating sweetness and brutality, in which she would hit him and let him cry in her lap for his childhood; in which he would choke her and put his arm around her in the dark and let her cry for hers—for her girlhood rape and all the pain behind her toughness. He cooked her spaghetti dinners, putting "his own spices" in sauce from a jar and lighting candles on the table, and in the afternoon he had quick sex with others whom she tried not to think about or not to believe. About the violence, which she remembered casually, almost as one would the events of a summer vacation, she said, "Obviously I believe in second chances ... I guess the reason I didn't leave is that I'm a violent person too. He just had to say something smart and I'd hit him. I don't know, my dad used to hit me, my mom used to hit me, I fought with my brothers. I thought it was normal." She bargained for what safety she could—denying him sex, leaving town for a while, taking a blow, giving one back, demanding respect, not getting it, then getting it, provoking him, evading him, insisting on a condom, not insisting, not even wanting to insist, trusting, not trusting, and never once assuming that protection might rest with persons who were as much her oppressors as his. Finally she'd had enough.

When I first met Amber I asked her about danger, and she said that before all the posters and the panic, HIV wasn't anywhere on a scale of one to ten for her. She hasn't been sheltered from AIDS. A cousin and her boyfriend died of it; Amber's stepsister's uncle died of it; his boyfriend was either positive or had AIDS when he moved away after the uncle died. She just didn't worry about it for herself, not in Jamestown. Her biggest fears, she said, were being in jail and being alone. Now she was both, not having heard from her latest man, the one whose name is tattooed on her stomach, the one to whom she could tell anything, the one who would not hit her. They had a fight, he doesn't write easily, has no phone—couldn't afford to accept the charges, wildly inflated, if he did—and no ID. No one visits at the jail without ID. Somehow it seemed too small to be talking about risk, but we talked about it anyway.

"What would life be without putting yourself out there sometimes?" she said. "I tell this to my mother. My mother's life is this: she goes to work, goes to the bar—she's not a drinker or anything, she just goes there—goes home. Every day: go to work, go to the bar, go home. I asked her, 'What's the point, Mom? What is the point of your life?' What could she say?

There's nothing she could say. That's why I have to get out of Jamestown. It's not anything about the town; it's me. It makes me unhappy to be here. And I don't want to be unhappy."

"But do you think there are things you could do to protect yourself more from hurt?"

"There's no way. No way. Because whatever you do, as long as you're alive, there's a scale of hurt. There's the kind of hurt you get from loving someone, and the kind of hurt you get from keeping just to yourself and not letting yourself love nobody. So either you're gonna get hurt because of someone you love, or you're gonna be lonely. Either way, you're hurting yourself. The point is, you're doing it to yourself. You're making the decision."

In a time of epidemic, every woman has to decide for her own safety, and every man for his. Out of New England recently came a report that four out of ten persons who are HIV positive don't tell their sex partner, and two-thirds of those don't always use protection. Somebody didn't tell Nushawn Williams—some woman, he says—and maybe somebody else didn't tell her. The cascade of recrimination for all the anguish in Jamestown, as in America, is endless if you want to go that route; and many do. Almost thirty states have laws criminalizing the behavior of people who are HIV positive. Without disclosure, consent is no defense, and in most places neither is the use of a condom. More than 300 persons have been prosecuted for reckless endangerment, or assault with a deadly weapon, or attempted murder. Many of these are prisoners who spit at or bit corrections officers (often in the course of being beaten), even though there's no known case of HIV transmission by those means. And many are people who didn't tell the truth.[4]

The truth? Suppose Nushawn Williams is prosecuted for sex as proposed. Imagine two "victims." Both of them consented, neither insisted on protection, both engaged in the same act of vaginal intercourse. Suppose, just to complicate matters, that they both enjoyed it. But one of them is positive and one is negative. The same "crime," the same "weapon," but one conviction could bring almost 250 percent more jail time. Proponents of this scenario say it's no different from murder and attempted murder, except in this case the "bullet" hit in exactly the same spot and the victims were willing participants. Suppose further that the woman who is positive had another sexually transmitted disease—herpes, chlamydia, gonorrhea—that made her more vulnerable to contracting HIV. Suppose that the person who gave that to her, and thus compromised her health in a way that the negative woman's health was not compromised, never told her he had it. Suppose, moreover, that she didn't tell Williams, though exposure to something like herpes could be quite dangerous for someone with HIV. And suppose, beyond all those suppositions, that when it comes to sex people lie about a whole host of things, or they forget, or they have vendettas, or they need to protect someone, maybe themselves. How can it even be known, finally, whether the weapon is indeed Williams' body and not someone else's?

DNA! But DNA matching in HIV cases, according to Dr. Marcia Kalish at the CDC, "doesn't prove anything. It simply supports the fact that there could have been recent transmission. It's not like matching blood; you don't have that definite answer. It's just a very small piece of the puzzle."[5]

The terrain gets slipperier when you think for a moment about the real way people have sex—the way risk arouses and arousal subordinates thoughts of risk, the way shame influences almost any discussion of desire, the way denial is always, always at work. If a woman begged for it up the ass because she wanted to avoid pregnancy or maybe because she actually likes it (yes, even nice girls do), would she admit it, or would she worry that such an admission would put her in a different category of victim, the one occupied by drug users and homosexuals? If a person was told he is HIV positive but also "knows," the way so many straight Americans "know," that "it's almost impossible to get it just from sex between men and women," might he have assumed—still in considerable disbelief about his condition—that the risk was rather low and he was just unlucky? And then how might this assumption—on which hangs the balance of guilt or innocence—have played out in the sex act? As the calm preface to judicious decision-making, or as one of a hundred flighty things in a highly fractured process of thought? So how does a court of law have the means or the right to decide any of this?

Intent is a necessary requirement for criminal prosecution. In California recently, an appellate court ruled that assault charges could not be brought against an HIV-positive straight man who failed to disclose his status, because some studies show that the annual rate of heterosexual transmission from man to woman is quite low—5.7 percent—and, applying the reasoning of the betting parlor, it could no more be said that he intended to cause harm than that somebody who put money on a horse favored seventeen-to-one intended to lose. It was a victory against criminalization, but by this logic it might be argued that groups whose odds of transmission are higher, or who, unlike the avowed heterosexual, have been branded with the scarlet A, ought to be criminalized. Criminal intent is extremely difficult to prove in consensual sex cases, gay or straight, which is why laws proscribing the behavior of HIV-positive individuals simply say that knowledge equals intent to harm.

Which brings us back to the fuzzy matter of truth. In the Bronx courtroom in late February, a defense attorney was telling a colleague that he would favor new criminal law to prosecute people like Nushawn Williams, "people who know and don't tell." People who don't know—that's another matter. So, suppose a man, maybe a man like this lawyer, has unprotected sex. And suppose he doesn't think HIV can touch him, so it never occurs to him to be tested. Then suppose he doesn't tell his wife he's had sex with others, and one day she discovers she is HIV positive. With the same outcome, the lie of Nushawn Williams is a crime while the lie of the hypothetical lawyer is an unfortunate mistake. To be consistent, every lie would be a potential crime and every one of us a potential criminal.

In the sex panic around Nushawn Williams—as in the scandal around President Clinton, for different reasons—scarcely anyone pauses to consider the big lies that make the smaller ones inevitable. In Chautauqua County, Kathleen Whitmore travels to public schools for the allowed one day of AIDS education and is regularly told by administrators, to her frustration, just please say nothing about anal sex or oral sex or condoms (unless they ask), nothing about homosexuality ("there are no gay kids here," one teenager told me); of course, nothing about pleasure. Dr. Rzepkowski, who is gay, out and HIV positive, has spoken at some schools about all those things and has never been asked back. After the news about Williams hit, a high school teacher in the county, Marcia Lindquist, was suspended after talking to her students about abstinence, because it was not appropriately abstracted from sex.

This is not provincial ignorance. In the entire history of the AIDS epidemic, the federal government has done exactly one national mailing on the health issues involved. There is no serious education on the relationship between other sexually transmitted diseases and HIV, and no effective prevention effort, even though people with one of those diseases are three to five times more likely to contract HIV, and people who are HIV positive and have another sexually transmitted disease are more likely to pass on the virus. These other diseases can, of course, be cured or suppressed, but it is as if public knowledge on the subject were frozen in 1981, and along with it the shame-brand that compels people to hold tight to their secrets and risk the very thing they hope to avoid: dying of embarrassment.

One in five Americans over the age of twelve has genital herpes, and up to eight in ten have oral herpes, which can also be transmitted to the genitals, but no one talks about that anymore. Over 50,000 Americans contract syphilis every year, but at current spending rates the disease will never be eliminated.[6] There's not a public school in the country that has a curriculum on human sexuality—its complications and wonders and varieties, "the emotional part," as Tania put it, and the physical part without evasion or disdain. Too many young women I met still spoke of "feeling dirty" because they'd had sex, or were eager to label someone else dirty. Mainstream feminism is nowhere on this issue, and nowhere in the lives of these girls, who often don't use birth control and don't approve of abortion because, like sex, a baby is a little piece of goodness.

Now government officials grandstand on the need to "protect our kids," but a comparison of rates of HIV infection for young people, particularly young women, at the beginning of the epidemic and today ought to nullify the state's claims to legitimacy as an ally in safety. Former surgeon general Joycelyn Elders said, "I'd have a bag [of condoms] on every corner, so all you'd have to do is reach in and pick them up," but we know where such ideas got her. A runaway shelter in Jamestown offers a refuge so that kids don't have to choose between sleeping with their father, sleeping with another man or sleeping on the street, but it can't keep them longer than thirty days, and funding for homeless assistance nationally is down 14 percent since 1996. The government conducts research on the spread of HIV among young people, and wants to keep statistics on everybody, but plans for universal surveillance are not being accompanied by plans for universal education or universal treatment, and there are no broad support networks for kids who learn they are positive and have no family, no insurance, no solid income and no emotional preparation for hearing that their life is in jeopardy. By providing the names of his partners for tracing, Nushawn Williams did exactly what public health officials advocate and was then vilified by those same officials as "some kind of scorekeeper." It would have been better for him if he had lied. And with the specter of name reporting and national registries and more energetic prosecution, increasing numbers of people will decide that it is better for them never to get tested. But most grotesque in a rich field of hypocrisy is that anyone in authority should ask, *Why didn't he tell?* when from its beginning HIV infection has been treated more as a social condition than a disease, when the files of the Lambda Legal Defense Fund bulge with cases of discrimination, and when you don't have to know any of those details to know that being a carrier of the AIDS virus on top of being a black out-of-town drug-dealing ex-con is very bad news. Just how bad is symbolized by the spit mask Williams had to wear while being transported to courtrooms and even to meet visitors in New York—a gauzy bubble over his head with a black opaque strip over the area of his mouth, the whole contraption attached to a wooden collar with a stick jutting out, "like a dogcatcher uses to catch dogs," Amber said.

The mask, the jail cell, they were just waiting for him—much as jail awaits the "bad kids" of Chautauqua County who are not already inside. Either that or marriage or death, and sometimes all three. Again and again in Jamestown I met well-meaning adults who said they only hoped girls in trouble would "meet a guy with a good head on his shoulders," their one chance for safety. Classrooms at Jamestown High bear handmade signs urging students to JUST SAY NO to all the familiar vices, and the school system has a strategy group to keep kids on the straight and narrow that is affectionately called the Pizza and Flashlight Committee. The concept, according to assistant school superintendent James Coffman, is "if you attract them with pizza they will come, and if you shine a light on the cockroaches they will go away." The cockroaches are the Nushawn Williamses of the world, "The Outsiders" depicted in a student's drawing reprinted last fall in the *Post-Journal*—archetypal white toughs hanging out, drinking and smoking—and the girls who, by daring to go with such boys, deserve whatever they get and whatever name anyone chooses to call them.

For kids who are one step away from that category, just on the cusp of expulsion, the county runs an alternative education program. They go to school in the evening, when the regular students are home, and the emphasis is on behavior modification. A policeman escorts them in, watches them remove engagement rings and other jewelry, and stands guard the whole time. Sometimes the chief of police comes to teach English or Behavior.

The idea is "to make everyone part of the team," Coffman told me. It's an experiment borrowed from Erie, Pennsylvania, forty-five miles away, and Coffman urged me to remember that the program is in its infancy. I believe he was sincere when he said that the county wants to help these kids succeed. Over the years it has put a tremendous amount of energy into various schemes advanced by one or another national expert. But often the experts haven't a clue. Observing one evening's session—the teachers exhausted from working all day, the kids surly though full of secret knowledge, the cop on the beat, the lessons stripped of anything that might provoke surprise or curiosity or love—I took it as preparation for prison.

Jamestown is the kind of place that can make a person's hate pure, and not for anyone in it, or anything particular to the town. I left it as I've left countless places in America where people labor for so little and the spirit has been so robbed—praying that every kid I met could get out, and moved by the strength of the people who fight for the future: Ron Graham, who coaches girls' track and consults on youth programs; Matt Milovich, who runs the shelter; Sam Teresi; Nancy Glatz; Rose Torres. There are others. And there are more still who refuse to pass judgement on the young people caught up in the crisis. "Unless you walk in their shoes, how can you know what life is like for these girls, or even for that fella?" an older woman who works as a cook and waitress said to me. For months people have been meeting to decide what to do next. "Low self-esteem" has been identified as the basic problem of "kids at risk," but some aren't so sure.

"I think it's too easy," Rose Torres said. Rose worked at the runaway shelter and was on welfare with her three-year-old daughter before coming to AIDS Community Services. "I can have a lot of self-esteem and still make bad choices—based on need, based on want. I'm still going to do what I have to do. It may go against reason. Am I going to stay in an unhappy relationship with someone who abuses me, with someone who cheats on me, because it will let me take care of my child? If I go to a hospital and they say they can't do something for my sick child because Medicaid won't cover it, do you think I won't do anything to get that child what it needs? If I just want to be loved and I don't make someone wear a condom for all the reasons any of us might not do it, is he a monster? Am I a victim? I'm not a victim; I'm a volunteer. We need a little honesty. Why do any of us make the choices we make? A lot of women don't have a lot of options."

None of the young women with Nushawn Williams had enough options. Neither did he. Neither does Jamestown.

(1998)

2

What We Don't Talk About When We Talk About #MeToo

Amid the chorus of stories that define the #MeToo phenomenon, there remain other, unattended stories. These others do not displace the chorus. They do not say, *You are wrong, shut up.* They do not exist in the world of *Keep quiet* or *Be good.* They do not deny the reality of power, of men's long dominance over women or of conformity as a silencing force. They say power is cunning, power is a hydra; it has more heads than any story or group of stories can describe. They say history does too. They invite us to inspect the hydra.

What follows is my invitation.

We both were young, twenties, but I was older. We worked for the same outfit, but I was paid. We kissed while walking home from a party, and then at the back of a bus, and then in his stairwell. He had made the first move, but only I could say, in the midst of our distraction, "Of course this means I can't hire you." He was an intern, I a department chief. The declaration astonished him—whether because he sensed I underestimated him I cannot say. Ultimately, he so surpassed the qualifying test's requirements that not hiring him would have been absurd. Years later a catty friend would say ambition alone drove the boy's kisses: "After all, he was gorgeous, and you ..." I was his boss and lover, he my assistant and lover, each of us on the seesaw of power and weakness that those dual roles implied until, over time, the temperature changed.

That is a true story, true to me, and the telling, I suppose, encourages you to believe it. But what do you know? Say I were a man and the intern a woman. Say I called her a girl and someone said that her desire for a job figured in the encounter. Say you knew nothing of her side of the story, as you know nothing of his—as, actually, you know only the barest details of mine. Say, finally, that she knew the value of her kind of beauty in seduction and social competition—how could she not?—but also its curse. Does that imaginative exercise open what for me is a sweet, if complicated, memory to sinister interpretation? Is the intern now a victim? Am I a predator? And yet the information is unchanged, as revealing and partial as it was at first telling.

The story, like any told from a single point of view, raises an unnerving question about certainty: how can we determine the truth from what we cannot know? In his *Histories*, Herodotus tells readers that *x* is what he heard but could not confirm, that *y* is what his informants say they believe, that *z* is something he highly doubts but is, in all events, a cultural consensus. Readers might not have verifiable truth, but they are invited to interpret what those views might say about the people who hold them (or the writer who chose to record them). At the detective's desk, a story of crime is pieced together from multiple sources; even then a charging document is not the truth, it is subject to challenge. In literature, truth is an investigation not an endpoint, so the story is an instrument for revealing the complexity of being alive, and wisdom, rather than certainty, is the hope.

In politics, truth tends to be whatever those holding the bullhorn say it is. During the spectacle of the Golden Globes ceremony, television viewers would have seen this graphic commercial:

He said. She said.

He said. She said.

He said. She said.

He said. She said.

The truth has power.

The truth will not be threatened.

The truth has a voice.

The New York Times.

Afterward the ad flickered from New York subway platforms. As cultural messaging, it resolves the problem of uncertainty by saying, first, that truth lies in the teller and, second, that social truth—the reality of sexual violence—may obliterate the particulars of any individual life by the sheer number of tellers saying "Me too."

Given the timing of its debut at the start of Hollywood's award season, the "She said" cascade could be read narrowly to represent producer Harvey Weinstein's accusers and the *Times*' role in his fall. It is now accepted as fact that Weinstein is a violent criminal. He may be, but in actual fact we don't know. Saying that should not be controversial: review enough cases brought on the basis of multiplying accusations in periods of high emotion, and you resist trial-by-media. That it is controversial indicates just how much people are willing to trade for certainty—also, how sheltered some are from the idea that they could ever find themselves on the wrong side of a police investigation. Weinstein basked in the bully role, but his descent would be more satisfying if it did not rely simultaneously on conviction by say-so and a generalized agreement that he disempowered every man and woman who wasn't on his security detail, from assistants to actors to journalists.

Affirmations of powerlessness are more telling than sordid details. Not because the latter might be untrue but because the former reduce a many-layered story of sexism, violation and human weakness to a bleached tale of monstrosity and cowering. If some of the most privileged people on the planet were paralyzed by fear, this story implies, what defense do the rest of us have against the Bad Man?

As Natalie Portman explained, we are helpless: "It's only some men who do the harassing, but it's all women who fear the violence and aggression. It has an effect like terror ... everyone is afraid to walk down the street alone at night."[1]

Desperate situations demand desperate measures. After the terror of 9/11: war, torture, mass surveillance, the gulag. After the terror of Weinstein, to what ends must we go to feel safe?

That is not a glib question, nor is the terror reference insignificant. It points to a broader politics of fear structuring our time. Rage, revenge, the *frisson* of command as the list of accused men grew—these emotions reigned as #MeToo burst into the air-conditioning system of the culture.

Rose McGowan joined the cry for jettisoning laws and legal distinctions ("These rape and child molestation statutes of limitations—what the *fuck*? That's murder. That's *killing* somebody"). Jenna Wortham imagined "the possibility of a new world order," perhaps unaware of the term's association with boasts of US leadership in global violence. After the appearance of the Shitty Men in Media List, the pell-mell anonymous *J'accuse* on the internet, Wortham expressed initial unease in *The New York Times Magazine*, only to conclude:

> A friend compared the feeling [after seeing the list] to the final scenes of "V for Vendetta." She liked seeing women as digital vigilantes, knowing that men were scared. I did, too. I wanted every single man put on notice, to know that they, too, were vulnerable because we were talking.

Teen Vogue columnist Emily Lindin tweeted of the list: "Sorry. If some innocent men's reputations have to take a hit in undoing the patriarchy, that is a price I am absolutely willing to pay"— a curious way of putting it, since Lindin would absolutely not be the one to pay. Dylan Farrow, whose stated memories of molestation by Woody Allen are anything but simple—one brother (Ronan) launched a career off them while another brother (Moses) says they are false memories, implanted— blasts "our collective choice to see simple situations as complicated and obvious conclusions as a matter of 'who can say?'"

Notwithstanding some thoughtful commentaries, fury has led. And, as after 9/11, why wouldn't it? Who is not moved by suffering, or does not want to be resolute in opposing violence?

There is a rub, though. Strip the veneer of liberation, and an enthusiasm for punishment is palpable. Look beyond declarations of revolution, and there is an under-analyzed conception of patriarchy. Take seriously the argument that any social conflict will have winners and losers, and there remain cavernous, unplumbed realities of loss. Look squarely at the presumption of guilt in light of experience, at the bundling of diverse behaviors under the rubric of sexual abuse, at emboldened efforts to dispense with legal protections for the accused, and the *Zeitgeist* feels like sex panic.

Exponents of #MeToo bridle at the term. After Daphne Merkin worried in the *Times* over waves of accusation, and Mimi Kramer called her "a beard for covert anti-feminism" probably put up to it by a man ("That's Dean Baquet [*Times* executive editor] trying to muddy the waters, no?"), other voices rose to pre-empt talk of sex panic, which they promptly mischaracterized. So, a definition: a sex panic, or moral panic, is a social eruption fanned by the media and characterized by alarm over innocence (stereotypically, white women and children) imperiled. The predator is a lurking, mutable social presence, a menace against which the populace must be mobilized—and has been since at least the "white slavery" panic of 1880s–1910s, but almost continuously since the mid-twentieth century.

That politics of fear has not been trivial. Examples range from the fever over (homo)"sexual psychopaths" (1950s) to serial rages since the late 1960s against: sex education; gay "sex rings," gay teachers, gay threats to family; "stranger danger"; Crime!; Porn!; satanic ritual abuse in day care; sexual abuse dug up from "repressed memory"; AIDS predators; "superpredators"; internet predators; Sex Offenders as a separate category of human being; "pedophile priests"; epidemic campus rape.

Whether formulated for political organizing (the right's "Save Our Children"), or inflated/concocted from genuine claims (the priest scandal), or entirely concocted (the day care frenzy), or fueled by exaggerated statistics and unstable classifications (the college "hunting ground"), these panics—whose practical and ideological work continues past their peak—have shared features. Sex figures as a preternatural danger, emotion swamps reason, monsters abound, and protection demands any sacrifice, including the suppression of opposing views.

In the cauldron of panic, definitions collapse. Abuse might be a comment, a caress, a violent act. Suspicion of deeds rouses the same alarm as deeds. Sex, misunderstandings and mistakes about sex may be labeled deviance depending on the speaker, depending on the subject; there is no time, no air for distinctions. Rape, a terrible and serious crime, is conflated with behavior that may not be criminal at all—with the perverse effect that efforts to ensure fair criminal investigations and eliminate bias against people who report rape are undermined. Insisting on distinctions, on skepticism as a fundamental element of journalistic inquiry and, most of all, on the rights of any accused is called denial.

Sex panic reverses the order that governs law, where, formally at least, innocence is presumed. In panic all the stories are true, and the accused are guilty by default. Law having been declared a flawed tool for achieving justice—as, indeed, it is—

"naming and shaming" takes its place. That shame likely re-inforced the foundation from which the panic grew in the first place need not be examined. Garbed as justice, accusations become moral lessons of Good's triumph over Evil; they thus become increasingly difficult to question. Their proliferation becomes proof of legitimacy. Victims are encouraged, "Speak your truth." Everyone else is commanded, "Believe."

Typically, panic generates another story, written in the language of law, now resuscitated as a sturdy instrument of justice, reinforcing repressive power but protecting the rest of us from monsters ... until the next panic.

In *Sex Panic and the Punitive State*, Roger Lancaster examines these mass convulsions alongside the expansion of state violence. That hydra's head is unpleasant to behold, more so when cries of the oppressed have been used to feed it. Liberals and feminists stirred many of these panics and have deployed an inflammatory language that they would mock were it coming from the right. Here, Oprah's brief emergence as a presidential dream prospect was overdetermined. There is "a dark evil pervading our country," she railed in 2008 over strangers lurking on the internet to destroy children. "What you are going to see will shock you to the core." Earlier she had launched Oprah's Child Predator Watch List. During the satanic panic her show entertained hair-raising fictions about day care, and in 1991 she pushed "the Oprah Bill" while, based on such fictions, blameless souls languished in prison or clung to the wreckage of their lives. President Clinton signed the bill, which created a national database of convicted child abusers for checking up on day care providers.

The language, the lists, the insouciance toward false accusations ... As a nation we have been shocked to the core, only to be shocked repeatedly, and to feel as fearful and powerless as ever.

The repetition should disturb us. As citizens of the biggest prison state, the leading exporter of violence, we should consider how even arguments against violence may be colonized by it.

When Wendy Kaminer, Zephyr Teachout, Masha Gessen and others warned about the indifference to due process, women from *Socialist Worker* to *The Washington Post* scoffed. Ana Marie Cox in the *Post*: "The courts aren't where our national conversation is taking place so let's not dither about the dangers of proclaiming guilt or innocence."

That ignores the way culture and social attitudes bleed into the law, shape policy, define guilt and innocence, and determine punishment beyond the borders of any particular discussion. It ignores the crippling of due process and the ratcheting up of criminalization in all contexts across decades of serial media-fueled panic. Due process, as should be glaringly obvious—sit on any grand jury where police officers' specious grounds for suspicion win indictments against poor, dark-skinned people all day—may be constitutionally guaranteed, but securing it in practice, even defining what makes the law and its processes just or unjust, are fundamentally social and political matters. Most Americans, in fact, have dithered or worse as campaigns of alarm worked to label vast cohorts of people suspect and turned the screws of punishment. Bill Clinton's grotesque 1994 crime bill did not occur in a vacuum. Folding the Violence Against Women Act into it was calculated co-optation, and liberals cheered VAWA even as it enabled longer sentences, more prisons, more death.[2] Michelle Alexander is right; no claim to conscience can ignore the realities of carceral politics. Sex panic ignores them all the time.

Some 70 million people, nearly one-third of US adults, have a criminal record, according to FBI statistics. Since the 1980s, the rate has spiked. Some 50 percent of black men and 40 percent of white men are arrested by age twenty-three. Women and girls are hardly immune. As the Brennan Center for Justice puts it, "if all arrested Americans were a nation, they would be the world's 18th largest. ... Holding hands, [they] could circle the earth three times."

The War on Drugs accounted for much of this. The War on Sex has been waged concurrently and—as noted in an excellent anthology by that name, edited by David Halperin and Trevor Hoppe—now drives the fastest-growing imprisoned population. That war has standardized irredeemable existence. In sex cases, any sentence is often, effectively, a life sentence. Some 860,000 people are Registered Sex Offenders, social exiles for whom daily life is absorbed by punishment and shame. Many were put on the list as juveniles. Many have nowhere to live, nowhere to work, no access to college. If they are parents, they may be barred from taking their children to a playground, or school, or using the internet to help with homework. If they live with parents, the parents may be forced to give up alcohol, to hide baby pictures, to make formal disclosure of the danger within to any workman or visitor. Privacy is abolished. Surveillance reigns. For many, until they die.[3]

Progressives used to distrust zero tolerance, a term that just got a facelift. Some snapshots of its real face are in order. In 2008, Virginia police were called because Randy Castro, six, had swatted a female classmate's butt; sexual harassment was written into his school record. In 2011 in Gastonia, North Carolina, nine-year-old Emanyea Lockett was suspended for three days as a sexual harasser after calling a teacher "cute" (his version) or saying "'she is fine' in a suggestive tone" (the school's version). In 2015, a Tampa school threatened to press sexual harassment charges against a nine-year-old boy for writing notes to a classmate; one said, "I like you" in a scrawled heart. In 2010, Palm Beach County police arrested a five-year-old boy for sexual battery because he kissed the buttocks and penis of another five-year-old.

Nothing says patriarchy like the police state.

We had adjoining rooms at a hostel and didn't lock the doors. We had talked for years about politics, race, earthly pleasures too. We had never spoken about our mutual attraction, but when I went to his bed one night unbidden I felt certain he would not object, and he did not. In a thousand ways we had signaled desire, and I would not have thought him presumptuous if he'd come to my bed. But only I could feel so unthinkingly insulated from the risk of miscalculation, being young and female and white, whiter then than now.

Young activists raising the banner of #MeToo are not to blame for this world of punishment and fear. They did not make it. But every human alive is responsible to history. We inherit it, and will bequeath whatever it is we do with it.

It should be impossible to think of sex and accusation and not think about race. History grabs back. White America lynched some 4,000 black people, mostly men, from 1877 to 1968. Ida B. Wells documented the worst years. The rape of a white woman rationalized all vigilantism, but, Wells reported, two-thirds of those killed were not accused of this "outrage upon the community." Murder was a more frequent accusation, but lynching's apologists did not shout, *They're killing our men!* One might consider how unstable the white man's sense of his worth must have been; also how anti-miscegenation law emboldened this weak but vicious whiteness to become its enforcer. Any affectional alliance between a white woman and a black man was an outrage. A white man's rape of a white woman was not, and black women had no rights that anyone need respect.

Wells determined that black power, not sex, was the real outrage: growing prosperity after Reconstruction, and the suspicion that a black man's control of his own property and family and destiny might impinge on the white man's destiny, power and property, including his woman. The woman was hemmed in but not entirely powerless. She had only to say she'd been touched, as with Emmett Till. For the man or boy condemned, the accusation was the ultimate power; for the woman, in terms of what she could make of her own life, it was largely an illusion of power.

I expect that progressives today presume that all those white women were lying. Carolyn Bryant was, in the Till case; she admitted it, as we learned in 2017. At her husband's trial, Bryant testified that the boy had grabbed her. "I was just scared to death," she said then. Young Emmett didn't scare her, but her husband may have.

It is understandable that today we should not only disbelieve every accuser from that time but recoil at the suggestion of individual complexity. Discernment vanishes in a context where every accusation led to death.

So, here's a problem: what if even one white woman was telling the truth?

It is a terrible question, not because it would justify the punishment—nothing could do that—but because it wouldn't matter. Where every white accuser was believed and every black man, woman or child guilty, truth was irrelevant, falsehood was irrelevant; justice was impossible, whether delivered by a court or a mob. Actual victimization, like actual responsibility, was irrelevant. It is reckless to forget that logic now, even if the stakes for the accused bear no resemblance, even if the headline predator is white and high on the hog.

Hollywood cemented the predator in mass culture; the movie business thus ought to be recognized for its role in shaping attitudes about who does and does not deserve a hearing. *Birth of a Nation* did not invent the black sex fiend in 1915, but by making the Southern anti-Reconstruction view of history the American view, transforming the Confederate traitor into the savior of white womanhood and projecting it on a phenomenal scale, the film nationalized white panic, sex panic and the idea that an aggrieved white populace has a right to commandeer justice. The ecstatic white response to the film inspired more anti-miscegenation laws and the KKK's recrudescence. Amid crime spikes in the 1970s, Hollywood revived the revenge fantasy but washed the predator white in *Death Wish*, whose latest iteration is hitting theaters just in time. In each case the predator is depraved, beyond rights; a hearing is out of the question. More important, the predator ensures that his hunter, the hero, need never require a hearing. As the Bad Man, the predator exists to authorize the bad that the Good Man does, to convert it into good, and thus to affirm that justice is whatever the white avenger says it is: undebatably, the only process due.

Justice is being tossed around like a ten-cent word. What was justice for the black woman whom nobody believed? The answer there is simple, for she had no right to a hearing, whether as accused or accuser. If by some breach in the rules of race she had been believed while her brother and lover and son were still guilty by accusation, would any call that justice? What is justice now wherever the hydra head of violence is interpersonal, is racial, is economic, is state policy? One in four women, one in two black women, loves someone in prison. One in eight women, one in five black women, lives in poverty—economic violence that makes every other kind more likely. It is not an accident that experiments in restorative justice have emerged from black communities. It is not an accident that Tarana Burke invented the idiom *Me Too* while working in the thick of life with women and girls of color. Burke's *Me Too* was not a bullhorn slogan; it was a signal for another kind of hearing, a tool for helping young women speak about experience and begin to engage the compound realities of life with clarity and confidence. Its hijacking as a hashtag is said to symbolize a resurgent feminism. But what does that mean?

Feminism has taken many shapes. In 1977 black radical and lesbian feminists issued the Combahee River Collective Statement. One of its authors, Barbara Smith, reiterated the collective's ethos on its fortieth anniversary: "You can't work on one vector of oppression and think you're going to solve whatever problem you're addressing. You have to be able to understand how systems of oppression connect." What conversations might we be having now if Combahee's analysis of power—rooted in the black woman's interrelated experiences of production, reproduction and violence—had become standard feminist analysis all those years ago? If this black radical vision of sexuality, solidarity and human liberation had centered radical analysis?

The *might have been* is unanswerable. So much got in the way. Sexism, racism, homophobia, backlash. Among history's legacies there is another, related: the path that some white feminists and liberals took in the 1970s, and where their best intentions for supporting crime victims led. The roadbed they laid would be paved and posted VICTIMS' RIGHTS by enraged citizen groups, law-and-order advocates and policy makers bent not only on the privatization of public interests but on dressing up racist projects in the guise of safe streets, safe families, safe women and children.

The sympathetic aspect of the victim obscured the movement's essential function: to assert vengeance as a social good. Consider now how far along that path we've traveled: how normal it is to speak of victims (rather than accusers or complainants); how expected are victim testimony, victim impact statements, victim involvement in prosecutions; how widespread is the view that a criminal trial is not about determining facts and repairing the breach crime creates in the social fabric but about enlisting state power for the satisfaction of the aggrieved individual. Consider, finally, how placidly we are meant to nod our heads at sentencing as a victim or victim's family wishes violence and suffering upon a person who is convicted; how righteous a sentence of 60, no, 100, no, 235, no, 360 years is made to seem.

Responsibility to history requires that we attend to its surprises. South Carolina's modern-day anti-lynching law was supposed to target racist violence; in 2003, 69 percent of its targets were black men. The Obama administration's rules for

Title IX investigations into campus sexual assault were supposed to address gender discrimination; they emboldened tribunals that discriminated against the accused. This pantomime of justice has likely been racially biased as well, though we are rarely asked to inquire into that.[4]

When I saw *Three Billboards Outside Ebbing, Missouri*, people in the theater voiced approval as Mildred Hayes, the antihero seeking the resolution of her daughter's rape and murder, tells the police chief:

> If it was me, I'd start up a database, every male baby was born, stick 'em on it, and as soon as he done something wrong, cross-reference it, make 100 percent certain it was a correct match, then kill him.

Mildred's speech captures the wild agony of a parent whose child has been annihilated. The audience reaction was a souvenir of how much society has abdicated its responsibility in bowing to revenge.

I was a temp, sharing the office with the secretary of my boss's second in command. She had been there for years. Her boss screamed from across the hall, "Get in here, you old cow" or "fat sow." Farm animal slurs. I told him his language was vile, and complained to my boss, who must have stifled him, at least while I was there. My office mate told me to ease off. "He's a good man," she said. "When my mother died, he gave me three days off; he didn't have to do that."

Humiliation was the secretary's daily work experience. Her boss was a sexist, but his assaults were not sexual. They were part of a terribly ordinary structure. In that structure, a hand on the butt or a lewd joke or even the boss flashing his dick is the least of it. That is an indictment, not a justification. In that structure, three days to grieve is a blessing. What do we see when we inspect the hydra head of the working day? When we look unblinking at the embodied experience of men, women, trans, wherever they belong to a workforce under control?

For the boss who does the controlling—who need not be a man—sexual harassment is one tool. Humiliation, inventively variegated, is another. Physical danger, overwork, layoffs, are others. Their aim: discipline, profit. Their form: assaults on body, mind, spirit.

An insurance adjustor is assigned to train the low-wage worker who will displace him. An electrician who smokes reefer picks up a flask of urine from his brother each morning and straps it to his body to keep warm in case he's picked for a random drug test. A farmworker prunes citrus in the heat with no water, no shade, no toilets or washing facilities. An industrial-laundry worker sorts sheets stained with semen, blood and shit, then must suffer captive-audience harangues because she wants a union. An office cleaner must work so fast "you can't work any more." A nanny is raped, then fired by the rapist's wife. (The Bureau of Justice Statistics estimates 43,380 workplace rapes and sexual assaults a year.) A mechanic is ordered to crawl into a toxic chemical tank to make a repair for which he's not trained; he dies. (The Bureau of Labor Statistics reports 5,190 fatal workplace injuries in 2016, up 7 percent from 2015.) An exotic dancer walks barefoot down a stairway strewn with glass. A fourteen-year-old ballet dancer works in pain. (The BLS reports 2.9 million nonfatal injuries and illnesses for 2016.) A food co-op manager is murdered by an enraged worker. A beautician is murdered on the job by her husband. (The BLS reports 500 workplace homicides, up 19.9 percent.) A medical-supply worker grows faint from the glue used to make artificial-kidney hoses and is exposed to a carcinogen. (At least 53,000 workers die each year from occupation-related illnesses, a UC Davis study estimates.) A waitress develops blood clots. A recycler loses his leg. (The BLS reports 892,276 severe injuries or illnesses requiring days off.) An autoworker does mandatory twelve-hour shifts; her younger part-time, precarious co-worker loses his mind. (The BLS reports suicides up 27 percent.) A female manager is shut out of all-boys planning meetings. A university tradesman says the professoriate makes him feel subhuman. A day laborer is never sure he'll be paid if he's picked for a job. A chicken processor stands in cold water all day. A prisoner works for nothing. A deputy warden sits in the parking lot wondering, "How can I do this another day?" Salma Hayek asks on behalf of Hollywood women, "Why do we have to fight tooth and nail to maintain our dignity?"

Hayek's exquisite insulation notwithstanding, the real work experiences noted above are not intended to draw tearful sentiment. Workers in any struggle inevitably say, "It's about dignity." It's about being used, and used up; it's about life versus the depletion of the working day.

"I Am a Man," striking sanitation workers asserted in Memphis in 1968, welding a rejection of racism and economic and physical exploitation. Insurgent women in labor, law and the liberal arts have long added gender and sexual oppression to that mix. #MeToo discourse borrows the anti-harassment piece but separates it from work's full reality, which is to say capitalism. The result is a pinched, again privileged, conception of power. If sex in the workplace were the sole measure of dignity, strawberry pickers who haven't been sexually harassed should be happy agents of their destiny, sex workers who control the terms of their trade should be basket cases, and 26,400 Hewlett-Packard workers discarded by Carly Fiorina should have had no problem.

He was my professor. He kissed like a dream. I met him at a bar. I agreed to go to his house. I recall aquavit, "Sun Goddess" on the stereo. I was too drunk to walk home, and he too drunk to drive. I was surprised to wake up beside him because I had

gone to bed alone. He offered to make breakfast and then to make love. It was tempting, but I was a hung-over virgin and the room was ringed with photos of his estranged wife. Maybe she was not so estranged. Breakfast sounded nice. I learned recently that he still teaches, and wondered, dismally, Were I to tell this story differently, might I ruin him?

I don't think I was lucky my professor was not a rapist, and I was not alarmed. College women were not naive about the risk of violence in those days, the mid-1970s. We walked together at night, and either signed up for self-defense training or shared tips on kicking, gouging or otherwise disabling assailants. We'd come up watching Westerns—also rebellions that exposed a nation hooked on violence and inequity. We were living at the cusp of the liberationist '60s and the fear-jacked backlash. We understood that independence brought risk. I gravitated to classes taught by women and men for whom freedom and its guises were weighty questions. Sexuality was part of the political territory everyone was negotiating. So much of that terrain was new. It encouraged women to explore desire, not to say yes. I was stupid to get drunk that night, as was the professor—as are people generally when drinking to excess—but we weren't playing a game of blind man's buff.

#MeToo has put ambiguous sexual interactions and harassment or assault in the same box. This is not a #MeToo story (my history of assault involves stick-ups with weapons for small change). It's an awkward story about pleasure and hoped-for pleasure, and ultimately about honesty and eggs.

Like all stories, it exists in a social context. There, reality has many dimensions. People are worked by orders but also make decisions, and sex (not just for heterosexuals, who have dominated the public discussion) is complicated: by personality and socialization, by class, by race and gender and historical memory, by concepts of what is "normal," what is "dirty" or "hot," and by anyone's experience of repression and desire.

What doesn't alarm one person might alarm another, but before asserting "This isn't about sex, it's about power," let's confront that cliché's central evasion. Because, clearly, while a boss imposing sex is about power, and rape is about power, what keeps tumbling out of the closets is also some pretty bad sex. And because bad sex often involves unsorted anxieties and lacunae about who we are and how we engage with others, to say that it's beside the point is to say that we, storm-tossed persons, are too.

Why, in these ambiguous stories, are the men so insecure and inept? Why are the women so pliable and prone to freezing in place? Sex therapists say temporarily freezing is a common human response, so women who've always imagined ourselves only either walking away or slapping a guy who "got fresh" need to update our manuals. Going limp, though, is no more desirable than being a self-centered clod. Speaking up *can be* arduous. That isn't the answer, it's the question. How do people practice sexual consciousness, confidence?

The monster/victim script forecloses that conversation. The personal story as public fodder does too. Cornered in a false debate between belief and blame, it leaves room for nothing but silence or rage.

Being fiction, Kristen Roupenian's wildly popular, if superficial, story "Cat Person" at least allows interpretation. The male character is a cardboard monster by the end. Before that, he is mainly awkward, fat, hairy—an ugly man like Weinstein, like so many men in the initial line-up of monsters—traits the reader is enlisted not to ponder but to rebel against. Why? One could scarcely imagine that fat and furry "ugliness" is beauty for a vast gay subculture, or that the beauty trap might also stunt men. The female character is lithe, aware of her perfect body if nothing else. Neither one sees the other. Sexually aggressive, she is also terrified. Sexually obtuse, he is a boor. Post-coitus she wants to slither away; he wants to watch TV. The story should have ended at their first awful kiss. Simply asserting that women are conditioned to say yes—a response to similar, nonfiction accounts of bad kisses, bad dates, bad sex—skirts the problem that neither person seems equipped with sensual intelligence. Why? Is virtual communication anaesthetizing? Has the long night of sex panic—shadowing generations, along with 9/11 and war—begotten a kind of sexual nihilism?

Sex exists in personal and political time. Perhaps the hydra head of fear looms larger, and more insidiously, than public discussion so far has allowed.

My stories here, vestiges from a time before sex panic became permanent, are messy, not simple. At a party last winter, amidst the blizzard of accusations, a woman who'd come of age in the 1990s mentioned "the unfinished business" of the sexual revolution: "What went wrong?" Even without a backlash, what went wrong is what always does: capitalism bit down, absorbed the liberationist impulse, mass-produced the sex but everywhere devalued knowledge, meaningful education, manifold reality; and liberationist forces were too besieged or internally at odds to withstand it. What remains is a menu of sexual acts to perform and a simulacrum of freedom: at one end, Hollywood stars, the ultimate symbols of marketable feminine sexuality, protesting objectification; at the other, legions of ordinary joes opening emails urging, "Get bigger, last longer, become the beast she always wanted." In between is only more dissonance, including TV sex as no-foreplay gladiatorial combat initiated by powerful female characters created by a powerful female producer.

As a dream-path to a world of peace and equality, the sexual revolution would always be constrained by the contradictions of the society that birthed it. The great diversity of human personality could be forgotten in assumptions about how "freedom" should feel. Yet getting free was a serious project. Gay liberation seized on it. Women's liberation did too, until anti-sex feminists marched into a cul-de-sac, and radical analyses of pleasure and danger were sidelined. Straight men as a group never challenged the snares of masculinity; like others, they got what the activist sex therapist Leonore Tiefer calls "permission without real knowledge, real understanding, like people have in other domains of their life."

So much of what we call sex, Tiefer says, is actually "about training, common sense, *attention*. Sex glamorizes things that are everyday. It makes something the best or worst experience, but the doing of it and the script in your head make it so. It's not the thing itself, it's the meaning of the thing. It exists in consequences of actions. It exists in interpretation. So, when does coercion come in? As opposed to persuasion, as opposed to opportunity. It's not so easy. If we could figure that out without calling it sexual we'd be getting somewhere."

It has been a long time since we've practiced what the sexologist/cultural polymath Dr. Herukhuti calls "grassroots organizing in [the] bedroom." Since we've dug into the sensual. Since we've studied songs of freedom. So much of the culture teaches us to be afraid or ashamed, instead. Sex can't be abstracted from that culture, any more than sexual violence can be abstracted from other systems of violence. Consequences of action, all of them, matter. The politics of good and evil leaves only righteousness and shame. Complex humanity evaporates in shame, and we're back in the Garden, stitching fig leaves into garments.

(2018)

3

A Boy's Life

"When I think of how fragile men are," a dominatrix once said to me, "I feel so much pity. All that fear, all that self-mutilation, just to be 'men.' When I heard that those guys in Laramie took Matthew Shepard's shoes, I was so creeped out. I mean, shoes are so symbolic—'walk a mile in my shoes' and all that. Why did they take his shoes?"

From the beginning there was something too awfully iconic about the story. Matthew Shepard—young, small, gay, a college boy in the cowboy town of Laramie, Wyoming, a kid who, his father says, didn't know how to make a fist until he was thirteen—lured out of a bar by two "rednecks" ("trailer trash," "drop-outs," every similar tabloid term has been applied), kidnapped to a lonely spot outside of town, strung up like a scarecrow on a buck fence, bludgeoned beyond recognition and left to die without his shoes, his ring, his wallet or the $20 inside it. With that mix of real and fanciful detail, it has been called a trophy killing, a hate crime, a sacrifice. Press crews who had never before and have not since lingered over gruesome murders of homosexuals came out in force, reporting their brush with a bigotry so poisonous it could scarcely be imagined. County Attorney Cal Rerucha says death by injection is the just response. At the site where Shepard was murdered, in a field of prairie grass and sagebrush within eyeshot of suburban houses, a cross has been laid out in pink limestone rocks. In crotches of the killing fence, two stones have been placed; one bears the word *love*; the other, *forgive*. The poignancy of those messages has been transmitted out and beyond via television; it is somewhat diminished if one knows that the stones were put there by a reporter, whose article about the murder for *Vanity Fair* was called "The Crucifixion of Matthew Shepard."

Torture is more easily imagined when masked in iconography but no better understood. Perhaps it all will become clear in October, when one of the accused, Aaron McKinney, goes on trial for kidnapping, aggravated robbery and capital murder (his companion, Russell Henderson, pled guilty on April 5 and avoided death with two consecutive life terms), but that seems unlikely. The story passed into myth even before the trials had been set, and at this point fact, rumor, politics, protective cover and jailhouse braggadocio are so entangled that the truth may be elusive even to the protagonists.

What is known, though somehow elided, is that in the most literal definition of the word, Matthew Shepard was not crucified. His hands were not outstretched, as has been reported by all manner of media since October 7, 1998, when the twenty-one-year-old University of Wyoming student was discovered near death, but rather tied behind him as if in handcuffs, lashed to a pole four inches off the ground. His head propped on the lowest fence rail, his legs extending out to the east, he was lying almost flat on his back when Deputy Reggie Fluty of the Albany County Sheriff's Department found him at 6:22 p.m., eighteen hours, it's believed, after he was assaulted. It was Shepard's diminutive aspect—Fluty thought he was thirteen—and the horrid condition of his face and head, mangled by eighteen blows from a three-pound Smith & Wesson .357 magnum, that most compelled her attention.

Shepard had encountered McKinney and Henderson, both also twenty-one, at the Fireside Bar on October 6. They exchanged words that no one heard, then left the bar and got into a truck belonging to McKinney's father. There, Shepard was robbed and hit repeatedly. Out by the fence came the fatal beating. Shepard must have been kicked too, because he was bruised between his legs and elsewhere. Amid the blows he cried, "Please don't." He was left alive but unconscious, as McKinney and Henderson headed for an address they'd got out of him. En route they ran into two local punks out puncturing tires, Emiliano Morales and Jeremy Herrera, and started a fight. McKinney cracked Morales' head open with the same gun he'd used on Shepard, coating the weapon with still more blood. Herrera then whacked McKinney's head with a stick. Police arrived, grabbed Henderson (he and McKinney had run in different directions) and found the truck, the gun, Shepard's shoes and credit card. Police wouldn't put the crimes together until later, so Henderson was cited for interference with a peace officer and released. Henderson then drove to Cheyenne with his girlfriend, Chasity Pasley, and McKinney's girlfriend, Kristen LeAnn Price (both later charged as accessories after the fact), to dispose of his bloody clothes. McKinney, dazed from the gash in his head, stayed home in bed, and Price hid Shepard's wallet in the dirty diaper of her and McKinney's infant son, Cameron. Six days later, on October 12, Shepard died.

Those are the facts as disclosed by court records and McKinney's confession. (He has pled not guilty.) In response, the Equality State—which enfranchised women long before anyplace else, which struck sodomy laws from the books in 1977—has disowned McKinney and Henderson as monsters. So has the rest of the country.

And yet, McKinney and Henderson appear to be young men of common prejudices, far more devastatingly human than is comfortable to consider. They acquired the gun a few days before the murder in a trade for $100 in methamphetamine, drug of choice among white rural youth, cheaper than cocaine and more long-lasting, more relentless in its accelerating effects, more widely used in Wyoming, per capita, than in any other state. McKinney, says the friend who traded him for it, desired the gun for its badass beauty—eight-inch barrel, fine tooling, "the Dirty Harry thing." The trade occurred, I was told, while these three fellows and their girlfriends were on a meth binge. Before it was over they would smoke or snort maybe $2,000 worth of the drug. By the time they met Matthew Shepard, says the friend, who saw them that day, McKinney and Henderson were on the fifth day of that binge. They had not slept, he says, since before October 2, payday, when the partying had begun.

Those previously unreported facts—to the extent that anything can be factually determined in Laramie these days, with everyone involved in the case under a gag order[1]—may tell more about the crime, more about the everyday life of hate and hurt and heterosexual culture than all the quasi-religious characterizations of Matthew's passion, death and resurrection as patron saint of hate crime legislation. It's just possible that Matthew Shepard didn't die because he was gay; he died because Aaron McKinney and Russell Henderson are straight.

"If you're telling your feelings, you're kind of a wuss." Brent Jones, a heterosexual who went to high school with McKinney and Henderson, was guiding me through the psychic terrain of a boy's life.

"So what do you do when things hurt?"

"That's why God created whiskey, don't you think? You get drunker than a pig and hope it drains away—or you go home and cry."

"Is that true for most guys, do you think?"

"Yeah, pretty much."

"So secretly you're all wusses, and you know you're wusses, but you can't let anyone know, even though you all know you know."

"You could say that."

"Can you talk to girls about this stuff?"

"Unless you know this is the one—like, you're going to get married, and then you're in so deep you can't help yourself— but if not, if you think she might break up with you, then no, because she might tell someone, and then it gets around, and then everyone thinks you're a wuss. And you don't want people to think you're a wuss, unless you are a wuss, and then you know you're a wuss, and then it doesn't matter."

Among the weighty files on the proceedings against McKinney and Henderson in the Albany County Courthouse is a curious reference. The state had charged, as an "aggravating factor" in the murder, that "the defendant[s] knew or should have known that the victim was suffering from a physical or mental disability." The court threw this out; Judge Jeffrey Donnell, who presided over Henderson's case, told me he assumed it referred to Shepard's size (5' 2", 105 pounds) but was legally irrelevant whatever its intent. In a sense, it is sociologically irrelevant as well whether the prosecution regarded Shepard as crippled more by sexuality or size, since by either measure he was, in the vernacular of Laramie's straight youth, a wuss.

Wussitude haunts a boy's every move. It must have haunted Aaron McKinney most of his life. McKinney, too, is a little thing—not as little as Shepard, but at 5' 6", 145 pounds, he doesn't cut a formidable figure. George Markle, who roomed with him after they both dropped out of high school, describes McKinney as having "tiny arms, a tiny, tiny chest, no definition in his body." He affected a gangsta style—droopy jeans, baggy shirt, Raiders jacket, gold chains, gold on all his fingers. He'd ape hip-hop street talk, but "he couldn't get it going if he tried." His nickname was Dopey, both for his oversized ears and for his reputation as a serious drug dealer and user. His shoulder bears a tattoo of the Disney character pouring a giant can of beer on his mother's grave, an appropriation of a rapper's common homage to a fallen brother: "Pour a forty ounce on my homey's grave."

The prosecution contends that Shepard was lured out of the bar on a sexual promise. Before the gag order went into effect, county public defender Wyatt Skaggs said that neither Henderson nor McKinney ever asserted that they came on to Shepard. And in his confession, McKinney said Shepard "did not hit on or make advances toward" him and Henderson, according to Sheriff's Detective Sgt. Rob DeBree. Perhaps McKinney said something different when he came home that night and wept in the arms of Kristen Price, or perhaps, presuming homophobia to be an acceptable alibi, she thought she was helping him when she told the press that he and Henderson "just wanted to beat [Shepard] up bad enough to teach him a lesson not to come on to straight people." But once at the Albany County Detention Center, McKinney seemed to take up the pose of fag-basher as a point of pride. At least five prisoners awaiting trial or sentencing have asked their lawyers if the things he's said to them might be leveraged to their own advantage. "Being a verry [sic] drunk homofobick [sic] I flipped out and began to pistol whip the fag with my gun," McKinney wrote in a letter to another inmate's wife. He didn't mean to kill Shepard, he wrote; he was turning to leave him, tied to the fence but still conscious, when Matthew "mouthed off to the point that I became angry enough to strike him more with my gun." Even then, he insists, his attitude toward homosexuals is not particularly venomous, and the murder was unintentional.

McKinney's mother was a nurse; she died as a result of a botched operation when Aaron was sixteen. Markle says there was a kind of shrine to her in his house, but Aaron rarely spoke of her, and then only superficially and only when he was high: "He was always happy then. Once, on mushrooms, he said that if he would slide backward down a hill, he could see his mom in heaven." According to probate records, McKinney got $98,268.02 in a settlement of the wrongful death lawsuit his stepfather brought against the doctors and the hospital. "After he got the money, he had a lot of friends," Markle told me. He bought cars and cracked them up, bought drugs and became an instant figure in town. He was engaged at one point—"she got the drugs, he got the sex; I guess it worked out for a while"—until the girl found a more attractive connection. "He wasn't a babe magnet," Brent Jones says. He might make a good first impression—he's funny, I was told, though no one could explain how—but he couldn't keep that up. Women were *bitches* and *hos*, just like other men, who might also be called *fag, wuss, queer, sissy, girly man, woman,* the standard straight-boy arsenal, which McKinney employed indiscriminately, says Markle, "about as much as anybody— you know, joking around—he never mentioned anything about hating gays." He talked about marrying Price, who is eighteen, but, according to more than one person who was acquainted with them, he wasn't constant and didn't seem even to like her much.

He loves his son, I'm told. And what else? Blank. What did he talk about? Blank. What did he fear? Blank. Who is he? None of the boys can really say. Interior life is unexplored territory. As for exterior life, "Actually, when he wasn't high he was kind of a geek," says a guy who's done drugs with him since high school. "He wasn't the sharpest tool in the shed. He always wanted to seem bigger, badder and tougher than anybody," says Jones, a strongly built fellow who first noticed McKinney when the latter hit him from behind. "He usually didn't pick on anyone bigger than him. He could never do it alone, and he couldn't do it toe-to-toe."

Markle says nothing much mattered to McKinney in picking a fight except that, if he started to lose, his friends would honor the rule they had among themselves and come in to save him. A stock media image of McKinney and Henderson has them counting out quarters and dimes with dirty fingers to buy a pitcher of beer at the Fireside. It is meant to indicate their distance from Shepard, who had clean hands and paid for his Heinekens with bills, and to offer some class perspective on the cheap. *They were poor, they were losers, they lived in trailers, for God's sake!* McKinney, as it happens, didn't live in a trailer, though he had when he was younger—a nice double-wide with his stepfather, until recently program director at KRQU radio. His biological father is a long-haul truck driver whom he was heard to call "Daddy" only a few years ago, and in Aaron's childhood the family lived on Palomino Drive in the Imperial Heights subdivision. As teenagers he and his friends would drink and get high in the field behind it—"quite the hangout," according to Markle—where McKinney had played as a boy and where he would later leave Shepard to die.

Henderson spent most of his childhood in the warmly appointed ranch house where his grandmother runs a day care business and to which his late grandfather would repair after work at the post office. At the time of the murder, Russell lived with Pasley, a University of Wyoming art student, now serving fifteen to twenty-four months, in a trailer court no uglier than most in Laramie and with the same type of late-model cars and trucks parked outside, the same proportion of people pulling in and out wearing ties or nice coats or everyday work clothes, and probably the same type of modest but comfortable interiors as in the ones I visited. No matter, in the monumental condescension of the press, *trailer* always means failure, always connotes trash and, however much it's wrapped up in socio-culturoeconomico froufrou, always insinuates the same thing: *What can you expect from trash?*

McKinney and Henderson were workers. At the end of the day they had dirty hands, just like countless working men who head to the bars at quitting time. Dirt is symbolic only if manual labor is, and manual laborers usually find their symbolism elsewhere. The pair had drunk two pitchers of beer at the Library bar before going to the Fireside; no one remembers anything about them at the Library, presumably because they paid in dollars. Maybe they resented a college boy's clean hands and patent-leather loafers and moneyed confidence; they wouldn't have been the only people in town who did, though acquaintances ascribe no such sentiments to them. UW is a state school, the only university in Wyoming. It stands aloof from the town, but no more than usual. Poll a classroom, and about a fifth of the students are from Laramie, and half say their parents are manual workers. Shepard, originally from Casper but schooled abroad because his father is in the oil business, didn't need a job; Pasley, like most students, did. There's nothing unique here about the injuries of class. In a month at Laramie Valley Roofing, McKinney and Henderson each would gross around $1,200, roughly $7.50 an hour. With rent payments of $370 and $340, respectively, they were like a lot of people in Laramie, where the median household income is $26,000, the average monthly rent is $439 and the average family works two jobs, maybe more.

It's said that McKinney squandered the entire hundred grand from his mother's settlement, and in his application for a public defender he listed $0 in assets. Before moving to his last address, he and his family briefly lived rent-free in a converted indoor stable with no shower, no stove, no refrigerator and, in some rooms, a cloth ceiling and cloth walls. But everyone I spoke with who was openly familiar with him through drugs was skeptical about the poverty story. To finance his recreation, I was told by the guy tweaking with him in the days before the murder, McKinney would often be fronted an eight ball of meth (three grams, an eighth of an ounce, street price about $300; for him, wholesale, sometimes as low as $100), keep two grams for himself, double the amount of the remaining powder by cutting it with vitamin B, sell that, and have $200 and enough crank to keep two people awake for practically a week before he'd paid a cent. At one point a few years ago, according to a friend now monitored by an ankle bracelet, McKinney was buying an eight ball every few days.

Maybe he miscalculated the costs of his binge in that first week in October. A few days before Shepard would be tied to the fence, McKinney and Henderson walked into the Mini-Mart where George Markle works, and McKinney, agitated, shouted that Markle owed him $4,000 and that he needed it. Years earlier, Aaron had bought George a used Chevy S-10 low-rider truck. First it was called a gift, then a loan, then no one talked about it, Markle says, and after the friendship broke, he didn't intend to pay anything back. That day in the Mini-Mart, Aaron threatened to kill George. He had threatened him once or twice before within the previous few weeks, always with Henderson in tow. Markle told his boss, but neither of them thought much of it. "I'm gonna kill you"—it was just how people talked, just Aaron pretending to be big and bad. It was his way, like his exclamation on entering the store and seeing George: "Oh, look at that. It's my favorite little bitch, my favorite little whore."

"Things are good enough for me to stay for now," Elam Timothy, a writer, gardener and handyman, was telling me just before we decided what his pseudonym would be. "I have a relationship, I'm out at work and to as many people as I care to be, but I'm not looking through rose-colored glasses. They're demonizing those boys so they don't have to look at themselves. Yes, this could have happened anywhere, but it didn't. Can we please look at it? That whole 'live and let live' myth—in my mind that boils down to one sentence: if I don't tell you I'm a fag, you won't beat the crap out of me."

"Have you ever been hurt or threatened here?"
"No."
"Do you know anyone who has been?"
"No, but I don't know many gay men, either."
"So, what is it that's dangerous?"
"What's scary is just hearing people use the word faggot *all the time. It makes me feel like a pig at a weenie roast. Danger*

*isn't palpable, but I keep myself in safe pockets. I wouldn't
expect to find safety in the Cowboy [bar], but Coal Creek
[coffeehouse], yeah, that's safe."*

Laramie was founded on sex and the railroad, in that order.
Women created the region's first service industry, and soon
after the town's establishment, in 1868, it was associated with
some thirty saloons, gambling houses and brothels. Before any
of that, it was associated with death. Around 1817, a French-
Canadian trapper named Jacques LaRamie was working these
parts with his mates. As the story goes, he was young and
handsome, and in winter took his beaver traps upstream on
what is now either the Big or the Little Laramie River. In spring
he failed to return, and Indians told his erstwhile companions
that he'd been killed by other natives and stuffed under the
ice of a beaver pond. His headstone thus became the plains, a
mountain range, two rivers, a fort, a county, a railroad termi-
nal and, ultimately, the city.

From the foothills of the Laramie Range, the high prairie
where the city is situated stretches out, scored by steel tracks and
pocked by late-model houses defiant of the city's already shaggy
boundaries. From the right vantage point those are obscured,
and all that's in sight is the plain and, to the west, the Snowy
Range and what, against reason, seems like infinity. People may
swoon about Wyoming's mountains and river valleys, but the
power is all in the wind, which has shaped the plains like a pair
of enormous hands playing in a sandbox of soft soil and red
clay, massaging the earth into fine overlapping layers and fluid
hollows. Such subtlety is the profit of eons. Over spring break
a student from the university left his truck out in an open field
while the winds blew thirty, forty miles an hour; within two
weeks, the windward side of the truck had been sandblasted
down to bare metal.

Laramie, a pleasant place of liberal inclination and some
27,000 people, is not a railroad town anymore. Freight lines rush

through but are marginal to the city's economy. It's not a sex town, either, though in the history-charmed buildings abutting the rail yard along First Street, shopkeepers will happily show off narrow cubicles in an upstairs flat, or a slotted box in a side door, where nighttime ladies deposited their earnings under the madam's gaze and key, their work organized as on a sharecrop, with ledgered debt always exceeding income. Carol Bowers, an archivist at the university's American Heritage Center, recounts a history in which the town elders seesawed between plans for eradication and regulation, usually recognizing the superior benefits of the latter. (In one nineteenth-century city record, all but $20 out of $240 in fines and fees collected one month came from prostitutes.) So, the women were harassed, corralled, controlled by periodic raids, punished for any venture into legitimate civic life by threats to their licenses—but tolerated. "The town didn't want them to go away," Bowers says. "The town wanted them to be invisible."

A hundred years later, sex is almost totally in the closet. Only the truck stops off I-80 are visibly worked, by mobile squads of women or by men, who also work the rest stops. For every other unspoken desire there's The Fort, a rambling warehouse south of town that has survived prosecutor Rerucha's tireless efforts at suppression. There men, mostly men, stop in (all classes and tendencies, all night on weekends), nervous and chatty—about a practical joke or a bachelor party or the wife—before surveying the aisles, then scuttling to the checkout with a strap-on dildo or a Miss Perfection "port-a-pussy" or a sexual banquet of videos. A tall, lean man of the muscular outdoors type crouches before a display and comes away with the Sauna Action Pump, guaranteed to improve an erection beyond any natural capacity. Now and then one man is followed a few minutes later by another, under the red light and into the video booths in back.

In the best of times, sex is playground to the imagination, the place where what *is* need not be what it seems, where strength and weakness swap clothes, and the thin cry *This is who I am, this is who I dream of being ... Don't hurt me* finds rest. Laramie happens now to be associated with sex in the worst of times, sex boxed and squared in the unexamined terms of the "natural" course of things or the unexamined terms of "identity." Many in town are irritated by this association and by all the talk of hate since the murder attracted national attention. McKinney and Henderson, it's said, are "not Laramie." Before his death, Shepard was surely "not Laramie," either, if only because he took risks that other gay men in town might not have. Laramie, it's said, is not censorious about sex, homo or hetero—*We're just tight-lipped. We don't go there. We believe "live and let live"*— and it's certainly not hateful, just as most of the country is not, just as, perhaps, even McKinney and Henderson are not. If they all were, everything would be much simpler.

Hatred is like obscenity—hard to define, but you know it when you see it. On the morning before Russell Henderson pled guilty, the Reverend Fred Phelps of Topeka, Kansas, brought his flock to the county courthouse with signs declaring GOD HATES FAGS, FAG GOD=RECTUM, PHIL 3:19, SAVE THE GERBILS. Under prodding, Phelps cited scripture as his guide for most of this (the Bible says nothing about gerbils): "Thou shalt not lie with mankind, as with womankind: it is abomination" (Leviticus 18:22). I asked if he also subscribed to Moses' suggestion a bit further on, in Leviticus 20:13: "If a man also lie with mankind, as he lieth with a woman, ... they shall surely be put to death." He said he thought all civil law should be based on biblical code but added, "It's never going to happen. I'm a pragmatist, a visionary."

"So, if you could, though, you would execute homosexuals?"

"I wouldn't execute them. The government would execute them."

His only audience were police, press and a ring of angels— counterprotesters dressed in white robes, their great wings sweeping up before his gaudy placards. The next day the university's student newspaper covered the day's events, running in enlarged type the observation of freshman Kristen Allen that "they have no business using the Bible verses out of context; God hates the sin but loves the sinner." On campus, where Phelps later moved his protest, onlookers expressed disgust at his message and invoked "tolerance."

Before it came to signify the highest state to which straight society could aspire, tolerance was something one had for a bad job or a bad smell or a nightmare relative who visited once a year. In its new guise, tolerance means straight people know of gay men and women, but there is no recognizable gay life, no clubs except a tiny one on campus, no bars or restaurants or bookstores flying the rainbow flag. It means the university might institute a Matthew Shepard Chair in Civil Liberties but has no anti-discrimination policy that applies to homosexuals and no employee benefit policy that extends to domestic partners.[2] It means the public school curriculum does not say teachers must "avoid planning curriculum promoting perversion, homosexuality, contraception, promiscuity and abortion as healthy lifestyle choices"—the policy in Lincoln County, Wyoming—but it also does not include *homosexuality* among vocabulary terms for sex ed classes at any grade level, and mentions the word only once, for eighth grade, under "Topics to Be Discussed ... particularly as they relate to [sexually transmitted diseases]." It means a father tells his lesbian daughter, "If you have to do this you should do it in the closet," and the mother tells her, "Let's just pretend I don't know, okay?" It means her brother "tries to be as supportive as he can be—and he is—but if a man hit on him, he'd beat the shit out of him. He wouldn't beat up someone for another reason, and he thinks that's an accomplishment—and it is." It means Chasity Pasley's mother won her custody battle, overcoming the charge that as a lesbian she was unfit, but her children had to call her partner "Aunt." It means if you're gay and out and attend a company party with your boyfriend, the sense in the room is *We know you're gay and that's okay, but do you have to bring your boyfriend?* It means Fred Dahl, the straight head of UW's Survey Research Center, accepts the university's expression of outrage over Shepard's murder but tells a social work master's candidate named Shannon Bell that her project to poll Wyoming residents on their attitudes toward homosexuality might amount to harassment of straight people, and anyway, "One good rodeo season and Wyoming will be back to normal."

In one graduate class discussion of the case, the high-minded talk was all of tolerance as students challenged a woman who had said she abhorred violence, but, still ... homosexuality, it's immoral. Amid the chatter, a cowboy who'd been silent said plainly, "The issue isn't tolerance. We don't need to learn tolerance; we need to learn love."

There may be, as the song goes, a thin line between love and hate, but however many twists it takes, it is life's defining line. What keeps that line so strong, like strands of the clothesline used to tie Matthew Shepard's wrists, are all the little things of a culture, mostly unnoticed and unremarked, like the way in which the simplest show of affection is a decision about safety, like the way in which a man entwined with a woman is the stuff of everyday commerce but a man expressing vulnerability is equivalent to a quaint notion of virginity—you save it for marriage.

"Masks are no longer as protective as they used to be," the filmmaker and pioneer in gay media John Scagliotti was telling me. "If you're gay, no longer can you hide, because straight people watch TV, and they see how people hide. And also this has changed straight culture, so all the little things you do might make you question whether you're straight, or straight enough. Your own suspicions are suspicious.

"It gets even more complicated now that all these things that represent maleness are very attractive to both gay and

straight men. The downside of this, in a way, is that straight male bonding, and male bonding in general, especially in rural places, is going to be a very confused thing. Already at gyms eighteen-year-olds don't take showers anymore—or if they do, they take all their things in with them, like modest little things. You're confused, you're eighteen, and you really like this guy; he's your best buddy, and you'd rather spend all your time with him than with this girl. And you are *straight, but now you're worried too."*

The Henderson trial was to have begun on the first Tuesday after Easter. At the Harvest Foursquare full-gospel church that Sunday, people wore nametags and expressed a serene camaraderie. Then they sent the children downstairs to play during the "illustrated sermon"—a dramatization of Christ's Passion. It was a stunning performance, beginning with the Jesus character racked with sorrow in the Garden of Gethsemane. The narrator said Jesus suffered like any man. Then, departing from the script, he said: "Every time I see an image of a feminine Jesus, it makes my blood boil. Jesus wasn't a weakling. Jesus was a man. If Jesus was here today, he could take on any man in this room." Later, when the Jesus character was tied to a post, flogged by two men soldiers who, we were told, took "sensual pleasure" in every fall of the whip, the narrator said: "Jesus didn't cry out for mercy … Jesus was a man. Jesus was a man's man." The Jesus character writhed in agony. After he stumbled offstage with the cross, and the only sounds were moans amid the pounding of nails, the narrator described the tender caress of the hands now ripped by sharp iron. In the congregation, men were moved to weeping. By the end, they were all singing, swaying, proclaiming their weakness before the Lord.

Time was when "a man's man" could mean only one thing, and in the romance of the West, that meant cowboys. In reality Laramie is as contradictory as anything liberated from caricature, but in symbolism its outward identity remains hitched to the cowboy. Wild Willie's Cowboy Bar anchors one corner downtown; a few feet away is The Rancher. Farther up the same street is the Ranger Lounge and Motel; down another, the legendary Buckhorn Bar, with its mirror scarred by a bullet hole, its motionless zoo of elk and deer and prong-horned antelope, bobcat and beaver and buffalo, a two-headed foal, a twinset of boar. Around the corner stands the Cowboy Saloon, its façade alive with locomotives and thundering horses, lightning storms and lassos, portraits of grand old men who'd graced the town in history (Buffalo Bill Cody) and in dreams (Clint Eastwood). A wall inside the courthouse bears the silhouette of a bronco buster, whose figure has also appeared on Wyoming license plates since 1936. The university's symbol is the rodeo rider; its sports team, the Cowboys (or -girls); its paper, the *Branding Iron*; its mascot, Pistol Pete; its recruiting slogan, "It's in our nature."

For the men of Laramie who didn't grow up on a ranch riding horses and roping cattle—that is, most of them—the cowboy cult appears to be as natural as the antlers affixed to a female elk's head hanging on a wall at the Buckhorn. It all seems to fit, until you look closer and realize that this buck is actually Bambi's mother butched up. For those who did grow up to be cowboys, the rituals and vestments may be just as they were for their fathers and grandfathers—like going to the dance hall on a Saturday night, scrubbed and polished and wearing one's best hat and boots—but the meanings have changed, or at least got ambiguous. In a different setting, the waves of men kicking it up to "Cotton-Eye Joe" at the Cowboy Saloon would be high camp, just as the beautiful, guileless cowboy explaining the rodeo to me, undulating in imitation of the art of bull riding, could as easily have been auditioning for a spot with The Village People.

Camp flies under the radar of straight Laramie: heterosexuals didn't wink when the golden anniversary commemorative booklet of the university union featured a sailor flanked by two gamesome cowboys, circa 1940s, with the caption "Come alongside cowboys ... let me tell you a sea story ..." But the rodeo rider doesn't need to know he's a gay icon for such things to tinge his identity, any more than he needs to know he's a Western icon. He grows up on a ranch but takes a degree in civil engineering, forsaking the land but not the culture. His children then trade in the heels and pointy toes for something else, or they perfect the look but with a suspect authenticity. Their grandfathers' world is still theirs, but now in nostalgia.

The cowboy was not part of Wyoming's conscious image until after he had ceased to exist in the form later to be romanticized. In 1889, the governor's appeals for statehood contained none of the heroic references adorning the front of the Cowboy Saloon; instead, he imagined Wyoming as a magnet for industrial capital, a dream that would not be fully abandoned by state planners until 1997. As detailed by Frieda Knobloch, a UW professor of American Studies, the state's history in this regard can be read as a continual longing to be what it is not—first, in anticipation of a factory economy growing up on the shoulders of vast oil and mineral reserves; then, in advancement of the Wild West as a tourist attraction just as the enclosure of the open range was complete. Central to the latter project were artists from the East (Frederic Remington, Owen Wister) whose work was financed or seized upon by local promoters. By 1922, Wyoming's governor was urging citizens to put on "four-gallon hats" for the benefit of experience seekers from the East at a Frontier Days celebration. In 1939, even as the state's Department of Commerce and Industry was lobbying investors with forecasts of a manufacturing dawn, its head man was again reminding locals to dress up as cowboys to "give our guests what they want." Perhaps some in Laramie bridled so at the presence of the national press on the Shepard case not only out of their own defensiveness and justified anger at reporters' arrogance—jamming the door when Henderson's grandmother declined comment, blustering over being barred from the courtroom when they hadn't reserved seats, mistaking cottonwoods for oaks in print—but also because of some deep vibrations of that old tradition of outside gawking and self-exploitation. I was taken to task for making note of this history and its vestiges, even as the town flaunts the imagined cowboy. A heterosexual lawyer named Tony Lopez chatted with me for a long time, but nevertheless let me know, "This is home, and you're an uninvited guest."

Now in front of the small ranches on the edge of Laramie, the third vehicle might be a school bus, which the rancher drives to make $300, $400 a month in the off-season. No small spread survives just on cattle. In fewer than ten years the price of a calf has fallen from well over a dollar a pound to sixty cents. The profit margin for these ranches, never fantastic, according to Brett Moline, the University Agricultural Cooperative Extension educator for Albany County, is now "squeezed so tight one financial mistake can be enough to wipe you out." Most ranch owners are in their late fifties or early sixties; younger ones have either inherited the land or are carrying so much debt from buying that they won't be in business long. Without a lot of money to live on and huge assets all tied up in land, the only way to realize the value of what they have is to sell it—usually to housing developers or to out-of-state gentility, who might pay three times the land's worth to set up a ranchette.

Wyoming, with 480,000 people, still has the lowest population density in the country, and where there's space there is a kind of freedom. The state has no income tax, no motorcycle-helmet law, no law against openly carrying a gun, no open-container law on the interstates (meaning you can drink without worry unless you're drunk); there's a seat-belt law, but it's not enforced (police take $5 off the fine for another violation—say, speeding—if you're buckled up). Until last year children didn't have to go to school before the age of seven and didn't have to stay in school past the eighth grade. Unless there's a weapon involved, Laramie police say they prefer wrestling a suspect to the ground to other kinds of force, and in ten years they have killed only one civilian.

"This is the last frontier," says Laramie police officer Mike Ernst, with a wink. After the university, the government is the biggest employer, and after the bars, the most striking commercial establishments are bookstores and restaurants and, near UW, the fast-food strip. On the fringes of town rise some enormous houses, but elsewhere some people have no running water or refrigeration, so in summer the soup kitchen substitutes peanut butter for meat in takeaway lunches. Most people, though, live in bungalows in town, trailers and suburban houses a bit farther out. Except for Mountain Cement and the sawmills, there's little manufacturing work, mostly only retail and service jobs, maid work at the motels, short-order cooking and rig washing out at the truck stops, telemarketing for the hippie kids, and temp work from construction to computers, but none of that pays more than $8 an hour.

McKinney and Henderson were roofers. Construction has a short season in Wyoming, intensifying even normally intense work. An eight-hour day can stretch into ten or twelve hours of fitting a shingle, banging a hammer, fitting and banging and banging bent over, on a grade, on your knees—bang, bang, bang. "I hurt a lot every day. I'm only twenty-one," Brent Jones told me. "My back shouldn't hurt." Jones works for a competing roofing company. "It's not bad if you use a nail gun, but if you use a hammer—eight hours of that and you can't even turn a doorknob. … You just work through the pain. Sometimes you take a bunch of Advil. You go to bed at night and just pray that when you wake up you don't hurt so much."

Sometimes you drink—"booze, the cause of and answer to all of life's problems," Jones says. Drinking is a pleasure in its own way in Laramie and a curse in all the usual ways. Officer Ernst said that if alcohol somehow disappeared, Laramie wouldn't need three-quarters of its police force. *The Boomerang*'s daily police blotter is dominated by DUI and domestic disturbance calls, and not by coincidence. News of murder is rare, but it's ugly. In the year before Matthew Shepard was killed, fifteen-year-old Daphne Sulk was found naked in the snow, dead from seventeen stab wounds; eight-year-old Kristin Lamb, while away visiting her grandparents in the town of Powell, was kidnapped, raped and thrown into the garbage in a duffel bag. Six years ago the body of a gay UW professor, Steve Heyman, was found dumped by the side of a road in Colorado. Law enforcement and university administrators alike simply sidestepped that murder. Memory appears to be elusive. After hearing of Shepard's beating, state senator Craig Thomas declared, "It's the most violent, barbaric thing I've ever heard of happening in Wyoming."

There are 14,869 women in Albany County, according to the 1990 census, and 1,059 extra men. Stefani Farris at the SAFE Project, a haven and advocacy center for people who've been abused or sexually assaulted, thinks "people in this town would be spinning if they knew how many times women were beaten by a husband or boyfriend." The state recorded 163 incidents of domestic violence in the county in 1997, nine rapes and ninety-nine aggravated assaults. In its 1997–98 report, though, SAFE notes 3,958 phone calls, almost all from women, reporting battering, stalking, sexual assault and other physical or emotional hurts, almost all committed by men. It notes 1,569 face-to-face sessions; 1,118 individuals served; 164 individuals sheltered for 2,225 total days. SAFE doesn't spend much time analyzing perpetrators, Farris explained. "When you see that women are being battered, their children are being abused, their pets are being killed, you see a woman who comes in and we've seen three other women before come in who were in the same situation with the same guy—it's hard to have any sympathy for what the man went through."

The court remands some batterers to the ADMI Program at the Southeast Wyoming Mental Health Center for re-education, but the project's director, Ed Majors, says that all he can deal with is behavior, not psychology. "I can't find a dime for services, [so] the deep issues are still not addressed. If you eat chocolate and use Clearasil, you're still going to have problems."

"Such as?"

"When it's fear or hurt, which is typically the primary emotion at work, when you can't say, *I'm scared shitless*, most hurt and fear will come out in the only vehicle men are allowed. It comes out crooked. It looks like anger, it's expressed as anger, but it isn't."

"Here's a joke for you," an amiable guy at a bar offered. "What do you get when you play a country song backward? You get your car back, you get your dog back, you get your house back, you get your wife back ...

"Here's another one: You can have sex with a sheep in Wyoming, just don't tie the shepherd to the fence.

"Oh God, now you're gonna think I'm an inbred redneck asshole."

There was no trial for Russell Henderson in the end, so what drama his story could arouse had to be fitted into one early April hearing. According to his testimony, Henderson had disagreed when McKinney suggested robbing Shepard, but when they all left the bar, McKinney said drive, and he drove. McKinney said go past Walmart, and he proceeded; stop the car, and he stopped; get the rope, and he got it; tie his hands, and he tied them. Henderson never hit Shepard, he said. "I told him [McKinney] to stop hitting him, that I think he's had enough." McKinney then hit Henderson, who retreated into the truck with a busted lip. Finally, again McKinney said drive, and Henderson drove.

Henderson offered nothing more. How is it that Shepard left the bar with them? Why did they beat him? Why were they going to Seventh Street—supposedly to rob Shepard's house—when he lived on Twelfth? Why would they stop to pick a fight with Morales and Herrera? When Henderson and Pasley and Price drove to Cheyenne to throw away the bloody clothes, why didn't they take McKinney and little Cameron with them and keep on going? Such questions have to wait for McKinney.

At the hearing Henderson looked like a man numb from combat as Cal Rerucha and Wyatt Skaggs—men whose names appear on court documents involving Henderson since childhood—went through the legal motions, as Judy Shepard told the court of Matthew's sweetness and ambition, of his mounting achievements, of the horror of his last days and the depth of her loss; as Henderson's grandmother, Lucy Thompson, the woman who raised Russell, told of his own sweetness and disappointments, of his expectations for his GEDs, of the inexplicability of his actions and the breadth of her grief. When Russell told the Shepards, "There is not a moment that goes by that I don't see what happened that night," he spoke as one does of a bad dream half-remembered, hopeless to resurrect the rest. When Mrs. Shepard told him, "At times, I don't think you're worthy of an acknowledgement of your existence," he did not flinch. In a proceeding marked by sobs and tears suppressed, the only figure who flinched less was Mr. Shepard.

Henderson was transferred to the Wyoming State Penitentiary. The word around town, originating with a prison guard, was that the inmates had held an auction, or perhaps it was a lottery, for his services and those of McKinney. Prosecutor Rerucha says he expects the only time Henderson will leave the pen is as a corpse for burial. Only death would have been a harsher sentence. The tumbrels are rolling for McKinney.

It should be easier for the state to cast McKinney's trial as a contest between good and evil: to caricature Shepard as a child-saint, because to think of him as a man evokes a sexual experience no one wants to know; and to caricature McKinney as a devil-man, because to think of him as Laramie's, or anyone's, child sits harder on the conscience. In this respect Henderson's was the more difficult case, because from the beginning he emerged as that stock character in the country's rerun violent drama: a quiet boy, kept to himself, "the most American kid you can get," in the words of his landlord.[3]

Judy Shepard told *Vanity Fair*, "I believe there are people who have no souls," and others have told me they believe some people are just "born bad," but Russell Henderson was born like any child of a young mother in bad trouble—premature, sickly, poisoned by the alcohol in her blood. Cindy Dixon was nineteen when she had Russell, and, as Wyatt Skaggs remembers, "she was the sweetest, most considerate, loving person when she wasn't drinking; when she was drinking, she was abusive, obnoxious, every single adjective you could think of for an intoxicated person." On January 3, 1999, at forty, she was found dead in the snow about eight and a half miles from town. Early reports had her somehow losing her way after leaving the bars on foot, in light clothing, on a night so frigid and blustery that Elam Timothy and his boyfriend turned back while driving on the road where later she'd be found. Her death from hypothermia was finally determined a homicide: Dixon was bruised, her underwear torn, there was semen; and now a man named Dennis Menefee is on trial for her murder. Somehow the fact that Russell lost a mother—and Mrs. Thompson, a daughter—through another murder, a sex crime, never counted for much in all the stories about Laramie.[4]

"I don't like my place in this town," Henderson said to an old girlfriend, Shaundra Arcuby, not long before Shepard's murder. "Part of it," she said, "had to do with his mom and what people said about her. The thing about this town is that who you are is kind of set in stone. It's not that easy to remake yourself."

Shaundra fell in love with Russell when they both were in high school (he a sophomore, she a senior) and worked at Taco Bell. She was confused about an old boyfriend, who was bullying her to get back with him. "Do what makes you happy,"

Russell said. "That was the winning point with me," she recalled. "Someone's giving me an ultimatum and someone's telling me to be happy; there was no question what I'd choose." They'd hang out, watch movies; he always came to the door, spoke to her mom. He made her tapes—Pearl Jam, the Violent Femmes. They went to her prom; friends thought they'd get married. Then she dumped him: "I was the first female in my family to graduate high school and not be pregnant," she said. "I just couldn't think of marriage. It scared me, so I ran away." Not long after, she would get married, disastrously, and then divorce.

Most of the guys who knew McKinney in high school didn't know Henderson—"he was a little too good." He collected comic books and baseball cards, loved scouting, even beyond making Eagle Scout. He pumped gas, fiddled with an old Corvair. He played soccer—the "fag sport," as some Laramie youth call it. He had fantasies of being a doctor but was headed for Wyoming Technical Institute for mechanics until he was told, days before he was to celebrate high school graduation, that he wouldn't get a diploma because he had missed a paper. He was prayerful in the Mormon tradition. About homosexuality, Lucy Thompson says, he believed "everyone has a right to their own free agency." Until he was fifteen, he helped Lucy with the dialysis machine that kept his beloved grandfather alive, and watched as the old man's life drained away. Bill Thompson never let on how he suffered. Neither did Russell. "He never ever talked about the hurt that was inside him," Lucy told me. "He'd say, 'That's okay, Grandma; don't worry, Grandma.'" She told the court, "When my husband, his grandfather, passed away, so did a part of Russell."

Brent Jones remembers Henderson as "kind of an asshole," less of a troublemaker than McKinney, but "his elevator didn't go to the top floor, either." He had some juvie trouble. A judge once told Cindy Dixon she'd have to choose between Russell and her boyfriend. Dixon was not in good shape that day and said, "Oh, that's easy," with a nod toward the boyfriend.

It's said that over the past forty years Lucy Thompson has raised half the kids in Laramie. She is a woman of profound serenity. Russell was in his grandparents' care from his birth to the age of five, when they thought he should be in the nuclear family. Cindy was married then, with two little girls. Three and a half years later the Thompsons again got custody. In the intervening period Russell took a physical and emotional battering from his mother's partners. Years of police reports follow Cindy's own familiarity with violence. Once Russell told his grandparents about a harrowing beating he had watched his mother endure. Why didn't he call them? "When that happens, I just freeze, and when I do something about it, I just get retaliation," Lucy remembers him saying.

The standard description of Henderson is that "he was a follower." At work he was the leader, says Joe Lemus of Laramie Valley Roofing. Both boys are nice, friendly people, Lemus says. Sure, they'd talk *fag, wuss, sissy.* "In grade school, you call people fat, stupid. When you get older, this is just what you say; it's like calling someone a retard." Everybody does it, even college kids (one of whom scratched KILL THEM under the title of the UW library's copy of *How to Make the World a Better Place for Gays and Lesbians*), even the straight-boy cub reporter at *The Boomerang* who went on to intern at *Rolling Stone* after helping to cover the Shepard murder. According to police accounts, when McKinney and Henderson came upon Morales and Herrera, it was Henderson who called them "fucking bitches."

"Why the fuck are you calling us bitches?" Morales said, and McKinney hit him from behind. Police Commander David O'Malley testified that in questioning Henderson about the fight, Officer Flint Waters told him they'd have more to talk to him about if police found someone with a bullet: "Mr. Henderson laughed and said, 'I guarantee that you wouldn't find anybody with a bullet in them.'"

Lemus says that in the period leading up to the murder, Henderson was downhearted; Chasity had cheated on him.

McKinney was excited; he'd just bought a gun. They were working between eight and eleven hours a day. Henderson had recently turned twenty-one and was eager to go to a bar. It was new for him, though I'm told he was not a stranger to drink and had his own sources for crank as well. When he was younger, a doctor had told him that because of the circumstances of his birth, alcohol (and presumably drugs) could affect him very badly. His grandfather asked Russell if he understood what that meant. "Deeper than you think," he answered, gesturing to his mother's photograph.

"Certain things make sense only if you're out of your mind," an experienced woman told me. "On meth, you would know what you were doing, but in that moment it doesn't matter. We used to have the rankest, most foul sex when we were on dope. Men don't get erections too well on speed, so already that's bad, but then there's the two-hour blow job, because when you start something, you just have to finish, only you can't finish because he won't get an erection and he won't have an orgasm, and you'd really like to stop but you just can't."

Maybe Wyatt Skaggs is right when he says "drugs were not involved in this case," or maybe he's just being lawyerly. Rumors abound about what set that night in motion—love triangles, revenge, a mob-style debt collection. Reality is usually less baroque. Matthew Shepard smoked pot and had at least tried methamphetamine, according to people who knew him; McKinney dealt drugs and used them with Henderson; they all had a mutual acquaintance who regularly carries a police scanner, whose feigned ignorance about drugs is transparent, and whom every drug user I met recognizes as a link in the drug trade. Those things are not rumors but maybe just coincidence.[5] And maybe Skaggs is more right when he adds: "That's not to say [meth] couldn't have been used sometime before; you don't need to take it that night to feel the effects." McKinney and Henderson were never tested for drugs.

History is one long quest for relief through chemicals, more powerful substitutes for endorphins, released when you cry so hard you run out of tears, but it is difficult to imagine a more unappetizing recipe for relief than methamphetamine. It is made from ephedrine or pseudoephedrine, extracted from over-the-counter cold and asthma medicines, then cooked up with any of a variety of agents—lye, battery acid, iodine, lantern fuel, antifreeze. A former user says it tastes "like fake crab sea legs marinated in cat piss," but its medicinal benefits, especially for its large constituency of construction workers, is that "nothing hurts anymore; you're wide awake; you seem to accomplish what you set out to accomplish. Only later do you understand that you've been up for two days"—and that, depending on how much you smoke or snort or shoot, euphoria morphs into hallucination, which morphs into paranoia, which morphs into God knows what.

According to the state's Methamphetamine Initiative, Wyoming's eighth-graders use meth at a higher rate than twelfth-graders nationwide, and among juvenile offenders in its correctional institutions in 1997 at least 50 percent had a history of meth use. Albany County is not one of the state's top three target zones, but drug sources in Laramie volunteer that meth is everywhere. Maybe McKinney is lying and maybe he's not when he says Shepard "mouthed off," prompting him to the fatal frenzy of violence, but one crank-head told me that he once almost wasted someone just for saying "Hi." "You're so paranoid, you think, 'Why is he saying Hi? Does he know something? Is he a cop?'" And maybe all the meth users I met were lying or wrong or putting me on in saying they immediately took the murder for a meth crime because it was all too stupid and, except for one heinous detail, all too recognizable.

None of this is a defense for what happened, but it complicates the singular picture of hate crime. Why did they kill him? "That was the meth talking," I was told. But why did they pick on him to begin with? "Because he was a fag." So why do you think they didn't kill him because he was gay? "They were regular guys, and then they beat up the Mexicans." And, anyway, "what kind of a man beats the shit out of a wussy guy?"

Ask around for impressions of Matthew Shepard and you find as many characters as there are speakers. A charming boy, always smiling and happy; a suicidal depressive who mixed street drugs and alcohol with Effexor and Klonopin; a good listener who treated everyone with respect; "a pompous, arrogant little dick" who condescended to those who served him; a bright kid who wanted to change the world; a kid you'd swear was mentally defective; a generous person; a flasher of money; a good tipper; a lousy tipper; a sexual seeker; a naif; a man freaked by his HIV status or at peace with it; a "counterphobic" who courted risk rather than live in fear; a boy who, his father said, "liked to compete against himself," entering races he couldn't win and swimming contests he'd finish "dead last by the length of the pool" just to prove he could do it; a boy never quite sure of his father's approval; a gay man; a faggot; a human being. Any one of those Matthew Shepards could have been set up for death; the only constant is that he'd still be dead, and McKinney and Henderson would still be responsible. Gay men are killed horribly everywhere in this country, more than thirty just since Shepard—one of them, in Richmond, Virginia, beheaded. Gay and straight, male and female, some 40,000 individuals have been murdered since Shepard; the only constant is that they are dead, and most of their killers are straight and most of them are men.

Among those who advocate hate crime laws, it's always the sexuality of the victim that's front and center, not the sexuality of the criminal or the everyday, undifferentiated violence he took to extremity. Among the tolerance peddlers, it's always the "lifestyle" of the gay guy, never the lifestyle of the straight guy or the culture of compulsory heterosexuality. Even among those who argue that the victim's sexuality is irrelevant—that Shepard died just because a robbery went bad or just because McKinney and Henderson were crazy on crank—the suggestion is that the crime is somehow less awful once homophobia is removed, and what is brewing inside the two men bears less attention. "The news has already taken this up and blew it totally out of proportion because it involved a homosexual," McKinney's father told the press. Eighteen blows with a .357 magnum—murder happens.

During an exercise at Laramie High School a few years ago, students were asked to list the best things about being a boy or a girl. The boys' lists typically noted no breasts, no period, no pregnancy, no menopause and one other scourge of femininity that the guidance counselor who told me this story had been too stunned to remember. I was at the school, flipping through yearbooks, noticing that the class of '96, Henderson's class, had identified its number two "pet peeve" as "skinny wimps who complain about jocks." The previous day, Dylan Klebold and Eric Harris had killed their classmates at Columbine High School, 140 miles away. Through that crime ran a cord from every high-profile school shooting over the past two years. Springfield, Pearl, Paducah, Jonesboro, Conyers—in each case the boy murderers or would-be murderers had been taunted as a wuss, a fag, a loser, or had been rejected by a girl, or was lonely and withdrawn, or had written harrowing stories of mayhem and slaying. Two of them had killed their pets. All of it, like the meanness of the jocks some of them despised, was regarded as just boy play—*Oh, Fluffy's in the trash can? Boys will be boys.* And by the logic of the culture, it was just boy play, like McKinney's brawling, like Henderson's admonition out by the fence, "I think he's had enough." Only when it turned to murder did it register, and for that there's prison, the death penalty, more violence.[6]

For any of these boys—for any boy—what does it take to pass as a man? At Henderson's hearing, Judy Shepard memorialized the number of languages Matthew spoke, the friends he'd had and books he'd read, the countries he'd traveled, the promise life held. As she spoke the courtroom heaved with her agony. But in the story writ large, it's almost as if Matthew's death counted for more than it might have if he had been just a wuss, a fag, her son; if he had been found in a ramble, with his pants down, with a trick (as have so many murdered gay men, whose cases have never been exploited by presidents to win points or by big, polite gay groups to raise dollars); if he had been killed simply because he was tiny and weak; if anything about the murder or its aftermath had forced a consideration of sex and freedom, instead of only tolerance and hate.

Since Shepard's death, the talk is all of hate crime laws. But as Rita Addessa of the Lesbian and Gay Task Force in Philadelphia, who nevertheless supports such laws, admits, they "will have no impact whatsoever on addressing the causes of anti-gay violence." They matter only to the dead or the maimed. For even if Wyoming were to become the twenty-third state with a hate crime law including anti-gay violence, and even if a federal law were to pass, the little Matt and Matty Shepards would still grow up learning their place, because for them in all but eleven states discrimination is legal, and everywhere equality under the law is a myth. It's said that hate crime laws symbolize a society's values. If that is true, it means gay people are recognized only in suffering, and straight people are off the hook. It means Shepard may stand for every homosexual, but McKinney and Henderson stand just for themselves. It means nothing for life and, because its only practical function is to stiffen penalties, everything for death.

In her interview with *Vanity Fair*, Judy Shepard said she thought that her son would probably approve of the death penalty if he could know this case, if it had been his friend and not himself beaten at the fence. And in her conclusion at the hearing, she told Henderson: "My hopes for you are simple. I hope you never experience a day or night without feeling the terror, the humiliation, the helplessness, the hopelessness my son felt that night." Not just that night. As a gay man in America, Shepard must have sensed all of those things just around the corner, and not just in violence, not just in blood. Looking back on Henderson's biography, and on McKinney's, I wonder if, in different measure, they aren't already too well acquainted with such things; if perhaps the injuries of terror and humiliation aren't already too well spread around in this season of punishment and revenge.

"If a guy at a bar made some kind of overture to you, what would you do?"

"It depends on who's around. If I'm with a girl, I'd be worried about what she thinks, because, as I said, everything a man does is in some way connected to a woman, whether he wants to admit it or not. Do I look queer? Will she tell other girls?

"If my friends were around and they'd laugh and shit, I might have to threaten him.

"If I'm alone and he just wants to buy me a beer, then okay, I'm straight, you're gay—hey, you can buy me a beer."

(1999)

4

The Wonder Years

Since this is going to be a story about sex and children, let's start with a bit of groping in the priest's chamber.

I must have been twelve. My confederates and I, all suited up in our little scout uniforms—demure blouse, ribbon tie, sash of merit badges across the chest, jaunty tam-o'-shanter—were mustered in the rectory, there to be investigated on our knowledge of the Blessed Virgin. This was the last step toward our achieving an honor called the Marian Award. I remember the word *investigated*. I remember, too, sitting on the long bench, looking at the heavy draperies, the carved legs of the long dining table, waiting my turn in the half-dark, feeling the gaze of the stripped and suffering Jesus behind me while, at the head of the table, our resolutely unmortified investigator began asking first one girl and then another such questions as "Where do babies come from?" "What do you have between your legs?" "What do you have here?" laying hand on breast, and so on like that. Hmm, I thought, these were nothing like the sample questions in the manual I'd been reviewing for days. And what *was* he doing easing my friend up across his tumid belly and onto his lap? I'd never liked this priest. He was florid and coarse, with piggy eyes, a bald head and thick fingers that he'd run along the inside of the chalice after Communion, smacking his lips on the last drops of the blood of Christ. My mother didn't teach me about sex—

I don't count the menstruation talk—but, without quite saying so, she taught me to regard authority figures as persons who had to earn respect. Obedience was rarely free, never blind. Time has stolen what this priest asked me, where, if anyplace, he touched me; I remember him stinking of drink is all, and myself standing schoolmarm straight and reciting, with the high-minded air my mother had instructed me to affect when challenging adults, the statement I'd been preparing: "Father, I fail to see what that question has to do with the Marian Award. Girls, let's go." We escaped in a whirl of gasps and choked giggles, rushing to telephone our scout leader. I had no inclination to tell my mother, but the other girls told theirs, and forthwith the priest was relieved of child-related duties. We got our Marian medals without further investigation, and before long the priest dropped dead in the street of a heart attack. Even now, as middle-aged men weep about the lifelong trauma inflicted by an uninvited cleric's hand to the buttocks, I consider my own too-close brush with the cloth as just another scene from childhood.

There were very different scenes, many more in fact, that I could just as easily summon now and file under the heading *sex and childhood*, though at the time I thought they had no more to do with sex than our encounter with the priest or, for that matter, my mother's subtle lessons in self-possession. They contained, rather, the bits and pieces of a sensual education that would be put into some recognizable pattern only later. And because, at least in my school at that time, official silence about sex meant we were also spared punishing lectures ("Thou shalt not commit adultery"? Who knew?), what was left to us was indulgence in the high-blown romance of the church: Gregorian chants and incantatory Polish litanies; the ecstasies of the saints; the intoxicating aroma of incense, of hyacinths at Easter and heaped peonies in June; the dazzling brocades of the priests' vestments and the Infant of Prague's showy dresses, which we girls pawed through when cleaning the church on Saturday; and the dark, severe beauty of the nuns.

There is a parallel in my ordering of childish memories here and the public reaction to Judith Levine's *Harmful to Minors*.[*] Levine spends a large portion of the book advocating for candid, comprehensive sex education in schools, something many of my generation never had. But the spirit that animates the book is a less programmatic, polymorphous appreciation of the sights and smells, the sounds and language and tactile delights that make a person—adult or child—feel alive in her skin. Levine's central preoccupation, running like a golden thread through the book, is the pursuit of happiness, the idea that kids have a right not just to safety and knowledge but to pleasure too. And pleasure here means the panoply of large and small things that constitute *joie de vivre*, including the satisfaction of relating deeply with others in the world. Knowledge means more than facts and technical skill; it is the ability also to understand the prompts of body and mind—to recognize "When you can't not have it," as one woman quoted by Levine answered her daughter's "How do I know?" question—and the wherewithal to decide when it's time to get out of the rectory.

In another age and country this might be called reasonable, everyday stuff. Dissecting the various sexual panics of the past couple of decades, Levine marshals a catalogue of what, in the scheme of things, should be reassuring studies and statistics to show that satanic ritual abuse is a myth; child abduction, molestation and murder by strangers (as opposed to family members) are rare; pedophilia (an erotic preference of a tiny portion of the population) typically expresses itself in such hands-off forms as voyeurism and exhibitionism; child sex offenders have among the lowest rates of recidivism; child porn is almost nonexistent, and what's out there (less reassuringly) is reproduced and distributed chiefly by cops; sexual solicitations aimed at children over the internet, while creepy, do not automatically result in actual assaults; and "willing encounters" between adults and

---

[*] Judith Levine, *Harmful to Minors: The Perils of Protecting Children from Sex*, University of Minnesota Press, 2002.

minors do not ruin minors.[1] Although Levine has noted in interviews that as a teenager she had a sexual relationship with an older man, she never mentions it in the book, nor does she delve too far into this last taboo. She relegates to a footnote the fascinating, difficult story of Mary Kay Letourneau, the thirty-five-year-old Seattle-area teacher convicted for having an affair with a thirteen-year-old former student, who impregnated her twice and insisted to the press, "I'm fine."[2] Levine's most detailed discussion of age-of-consent laws involves the more easily comprehended story of a precocious thirteen-year-old who asserted she was exercising free will in running away with an emotionally immature twenty-one-year-old, the fellow ultimately locked up for statutory rape. More than once Levine states, for anyone suspicious enough to wonder, her unswerving opposition to every form of forced, coerced or violent sex, and to sex between adults and young children. It shouldn't be necessary for her to assert, for instance, that just because kids have a far greater chance of dying in a car accident than at the hands of a sex offender that doesn't mean sexual abuse isn't a problem, but she does. Yet, for all that, her book is being blasted by the heavy guns and light artillery of the right-wing sex police as a child molester's manifesto.

One reason is timing. The priest scandal has raised a hysteria against which any rational line on youthful sexuality has about as much chance as that student facing the tank in Tiananmen Square. Even without that, nothing seems to make the blood boil like the suggestion that it's possible for teenagers to emerge unscathed or even enriched from consensual sexual relations with adults. Some leftist friends recoil, even as I ask, What about X, who says it was like an answered prayer when his parents' thirtyish friend initiated him sexually at thirteen, when for months afterward at the end of the school day he would politely kiss his same-age girlfriend (now his wife of decades) and then rush to this experienced woman's bed? What about Y, who seduced her married teacher when she was seventeen and he forty-five, and who, thirty years later, has with this same man one of the most egalitarian unions I have ever seen? What about Z, who as a youth regularly sought out the company of older men because, apart from a sexual education, they offered him a safe place for expression, a cultural home, a real home? The priest scandal, which forecloses any attempt to separate vicious crime from pervy nuisance from consenting encounter, has further limited the possibilities for thoughtful discussion on the real things people do and feel, the causes and effects and complex power exchanges of a human activity that does not, and will never, operate according to the precepts of a textbook or law book.

Another reason is that Levine's most bombastic critics had not read the book before damning it. On the radio, Dr. Laura Schlessinger, who called on the University of Minnesota Press to stop its release, took her cues from Judith Reisman, who declared Levine an "academic pedophile." A longtime zealot in the trenches of the anti-pornography cause, Reisman huffed to *The New York Times*: "It doesn't take a great deal to understand the position of the writer. I didn't read *Mein Kampf* for many years, but I knew the position of the author." Tim Pawlenty, the Minnesota House majority leader, did not read the book but equated the publisher's role with "state-sanctioned support for illegal, indecent, harmful activity such as molesting children." Robert Knight, a spokesman for Concerned Women for America who urged the university regents to fire those responsible for this "evil tome," said he "thumbed through it." Knight, whose organization is dedicated to bringing "Biblical principles into all levels of public policy," might consider what, at a practical level, that might mean, starting with Moses' commands to his warriors in the Book of Numbers: "Kill every woman that hath known man by lying with him. But all the women children, that have not known a man by lying with him, keep alive for yourselves."

Still, I think Levine would be pilloried by Dr. Laura and her ilk even without the priest scandal and even if she had ignored the subject of sex across the age divide. For the pleasure principle she enunciates challenges the decades-long organizing strategy of the right. Ever since Anita Bryant first demonstrated the political advantages of attacking homosexuals, the right has exploited real anxieties about sex, love and family to constrain the liberatory spirit, whether expressed by sexual preference, divorce, abortion, contraception, women's freedom or teen sex. This has not managed to send queers back to the closet, lower divorce rates or "protect the children." US teenagers have about four times the pregnancy rate of teens in Western Europe. Those receiving Abstinence Only education still have sex, and are about half as likely to use protection as kids who've got broader sex information. Even with abortion rights severely curtailed, US teenagers have abortions at about the rate they did just after *Roe v. Wade*. One in four has had a sexually transmitted disease; one an hour is infected with HIV; and, not incidentally, among American children one in six is poor.[3] That notwithstanding, the sex panic strategy has succeeded in the only way it had to, creating a power base—with all the institutions, electoral heft, law-making capability, grassroots presence and funding that implies— to advance an agenda for everything from bedroom snooping to global dominance. Levine's critics are part of that project, and since she butts against it almost from her opening pages, they are striking back.

What is more telling is who isn't rushing to the defense. While a group of free-speechers, pro-sex feminists and radical gay activists have generated support for Levine and her publisher, there has been silence from mainstream feminist organizations and the liberal sex education and child health establishments. That may be because they too have felt Levine's sting. Rather than build a countermovement to insist on sexual freedom, she writes, such heavyweights as Planned Parenthood, the National Campaign to Prevent Teen Pregnancy, ETR Associates (the largest US sex ed publisher), the National Education Association, the Health Information Network and a host of progressive sex educators tried to appropriate the "family values" rhetoric of the right, joining in "a contest to be best at preventing teen sex."

"The Right won," she writes, "but the mainstream let it":

> Comprehensive sex educators had the upper hand in the 1970s, and starting in the 1980s, they allowed their enemies to seize more and more territory, until the Right controlled the law, the language, and the cultural consensus. ... Commenting on its failure to defend explicit sexuality education during an avalanche of new HIV infection among teenagers, Sharon Thompson [author of the engrossing book on sex and love among teenage girls, *Going All the Way*] said, "We will look back at this time and indict the sex-education community as criminal. It's like being in a nuclear power plant that has a leak, and not telling anybody."

Throughout the Clinton era those forces largely stood by as the most sexually reckless president in memory signed a sheaf of repressive legislation, acts with names like Defense of Marriage, Abstinence Only, Personal Responsibility, and Child Pornography Protection. The last on that list, capping a legal trend that, as Levine says, "defined as pornography pictures in which the subject is neither naked, nor doing anything sexual, nor ... is even an actual child," was recently struck down by the Supreme Court. The second to last, also known as the welfare bill, is up for reauthorization this year, along with its enhancements of penalties for statutory rape and its policing of teen sex, motherhood and marriage. As part of that bill the Clintonites insisted that minors were too young to consent to sex with an adult, while in criminal law they eased the way for prosecuting minors as adults and jailing them as adults—in which circumstance, consent usually isn't an issue. To grasp the effect of liberal silence about Levine, it is perhaps enough to recall one name: Dr. Joycelyn Elders, sacked by Bill Clinton as surgeon general in 1994 for saying that masturbation is part of childhood and it doesn't hurt to talk about it. Elders has written an eloquent foreword to *Harmful to Minors*. Back when Elders was twisting in the wind, ABC's Cokie Roberts called her "a sort of off-to-the-left, out-of-the-mainstream, embarrassing person"; now *The Washington Times* insinuates that Elders is soft on molestation. From self-abuse to child abuse in eight years, one absurd charge prepares the ground for the other.

Beyond right-wing lunacy and liberal retreat, what the brouhaha also signals in its small way is a failure of the left. In organizing around issues of sex, love and family, the right has surely been cynical but at least it speaks to the deepest questions of intimate life. Its answers are necessarily simplistic and straitened. The family is falling apart? It's the homos. Marriage seems impossible? It's the libbers. Sex brings suffering? Just Say No. Love seems distant? Jesus Saves. Except among those queer and pro-sex radicals, to the extent that such questions are even entertained on the left, the answers tend toward a mixture of social engineering and denial: there's nothing wrong with the family that an equitable economy, divorce or gay marriage won't fix. Marriage isn't alienating; equality is the key. If sex ed were better and condoms free, teens wouldn't get pregnant and wouldn't get AIDS. If abortion is painful, you've been propagandized. If sex is painful, you're doing it wrong. If love is painful, find a new lover.

Levine is too sensitive to the complexities of human relations to be characterized as advocating happiness-through-policy in the area of childhood sexuality. But if her putting *children* and *sex* together in the same sentence can be read by the right as license, her heavy emphasis on the pleasure-enhancing possibilities of sex education may encourage readers on the left to believe that kids can be protected from bad sex, mediocre sex, regret, risk, danger, pain. And they can't, any more than adults can. They can't because, in matters of sex, desire is a trickster. What you see isn't always what you get, much less what you want, though it may be what you need. In matters of the heart, intimacy means vulnerability means daring to bet against pain. As with all bets, sometimes, often, you lose.

Levine makes this point, but she so wants kids to have better information, better experiences—and she argues so well and hard for those—that somehow it gets lost. Citing a study showing that 72 percent of teenage girls who'd had sex wished they had waited, Levine wonders whether this regret isn't really about romantic disappointment and asks, "Might real pleasure, in a sex-positive atmosphere, balance or even outweigh regret over the loss of love?"

Can we know pleasure without pain? one might ask in return. Can regret over lost love, at any age, be so easily balanced? Even sidestepping those twisting lines of inquiry, isn't the promise of "real pleasure" as much a romantic ideal, as much an invitation to disappointment, as the promise of true love, especially for the young? However wished, it's not so easy to disentangle sex from the hope for love, to revel in pure, transporting sensuality without letting expectations, not to mention clumsy technique, get in the way. It doesn't have to, and it doesn't always, but sex *can* rock your world, and not always in the best way, even with the best will in the world. We are weak, after all, and life's little joke is that in that weakness lies the potential for our ecstasy and our despair.

This isn't to discount the lifesaving value of open education about sex, condoms, desire, freedom. It surely isn't to discount joy. But rather than promise kids a world of good sex—like promising a world of happy marriages, monogamous fulfillment, self-sustaining nuclear families—maybe it's more helpful to explain sex as the sea of clear water, giddy currents, riptides, sounding depths and rocky shoals that it is. You learn to navigate, find wonder in the journey, scrape yourself up, press on anyway and survive. And sometimes, sometimes, you experience a bliss beyond expression.

The political job is to expand the possibilities for such experience, to free people to navigate, help them survive the hurt, or not hurt so bad. Maybe if we could be honest about sex, we could be honest about marriage and monogamy and family.

Maybe if so much didn't hinge on an outsized faith in pleasure and fidelity and romantic love—if for people in couples or families, everything didn't depend on the thin reed of love, and for people on their own, coupledom wasn't dangled as the apex of happiness—all the talk we hear about community might actually mean something. The great virtue in Levine's book is its hope that children might learn to find joy in the realm of the senses, the world of ideas and souls, so that when sex disappoints and love fails, as they will, a teenager, a grown-up, still has herself, and a universe of small delights and strong hearts to fall back on.

(2002)

Pictures from an Exhibition

Madonna
Madonna, Material Girl
Madonna of the desperate search
Madonna most mutable
Marilyn incarnate
Lucky star
Virgin unlikely
Virgin defiled
Boy toy
Siren
Sensor of the heavenly deal
Blonde inquisitor
Mirror of truth
Vessel of daring
Maverick
Venus of the radio waves
Bane of censors
Queen of the underground
Queen of charts
Mistress of sex

Down the years the headlines, the insignias, the monikers, have merged in my imagination as a kind of profane litany. The sensuality of my childhood faith transfigured: Madonna, as she frequently reminds interviewers, is, after all, a Catholic girl. And that girlhood Catholicism—at once repressive and voluptuous, forbidding and prone to contradiction, to extremity and a sense of naive liberation—haunts her every exhibition.

Behind the woman now photographed standing nude in a pizza parlor, or exposing herself in a window, or being bound and gagged by skinhead lesbians there lurks, back in time, the *Do I dare?* of a teenager giggling with her girlfriend as they kneel in church naked under their overcoats, of a little girl about to flip back on monkey bars to reveal bright red panties beneath her school uniform, of a child captivated by thoughts of the nunnery. Unpretentious, common urges distilled from their particularity and stylized into art. *How about you?* she seems to shout—you with your hungers and secrets and glorious confusions. With that simple solicitation, she has pricked the consciousness of the culture.

But Madonna an artist? Instead, she has come to be seen as something of a religion herself, her incarnations recalled like a mystery. There are zealots of the faith (Camille Paglia); high-priest interpreters (postmodernists speaking obtusely in academic texts); apostates (mainstream reviewers who, having presented the credential of onetime adherence, now condemn her). That last group has been particularly active since the publication of her book,* and was best represented by Caryn James in *The New York Times Book Review*, who criticized *Sex* for being humorless, unimaginative, unsexy, cautiously geared to the middle class. In short, Madonna "signed a $60 million deal with Time Warner and became an institution instead of an iconoclast"—which, coming from the *Times*, is like the Holy Roman Empire faulting the faithful for abandoning the catacombs.

---

* *Sex*, Warner Books, Maverick and Callaway, 1992.

Rather than draft Madonna into political service (as Paglia does, calling her "the future of feminism") or excavate her arts-theory intentions (to the extent she has any, they only work against her) or defend her work against inane charges of commercialism (this is popular culture), I'd like to offer some notes from the sensualist's receiving end.

1.

First, the package. There are two, really: the combined release of an album, *Erotica*, the oversize picture book, *Sex*, and a video; and the package-within-a-package—that is, the presentation of the book, which is wrapped and includes a CD single of the album's title track and a funk-trash bind-in comic book.

Sex, which can be bought only by adults, comes in a Mylar prophylactic, vacuum sealed; inside, "Erotica" rests in a mini version of same, which opens and closes like a Ziploc bag. The book is thin, sleek, spiral-bound between sheets of aluminum, stamped with SEX in small sans-serif type on the cover and a serial number on the back. It looks like a scrapbook of someone who is conscientious about preserving what's inside. Cool as a rejection, the metal outer leaves are nevertheless inviting to the touch, though if you're not careful you might hurt yourself on the cut-out X between parentheses on the back cover.

The Mylar wrappers have caused consternation in bookstores. Packaging in all but the metaphoric sense has lost its allure; the ravishing object, like the mundane, comes mostly unsheathed, with no dallying promise of something wonderful inside. *Surprise me* requires ever more strained feats, as the space between presentation and revelation narrows to nothingness. And so Madonna's playful clothing of *Sex* is abhorred as an infringement on the consumer's right to see what he wants and see it now.

2.

The CD begins with the sound of diamond scratching vinyl—a track being cued up, memento of the DJ's art—and then plummets into heavy synthesized beats, sucking you to the depths of the bass line as if through a tunnel to some sinister club. The first time I heard it, the pure drive of the sound reminded me of the beat from giant boom boxes blasting beneath my window in summer, or from cars that cruise by in the night with outrageously rigged amps—annoying at 3 a.m. but strangely thrilling all the same. A Lower East Side sound, rough with a graceful edge. The song's infernal rhythms and its lyrics about pleasure/pain remind you why Tipper Gore got so worked up about rock and roll. In the background, animal noises from human voices; in the foreground, eerily disembodied, Madonna's snarly, commanding tones.

Every mainstream review I've seen of *Sex* has said nothing about "Erotica," as if it were the bad eyeshadow in a promotional Gift With Purchase at cosmetics counters. Yet Madonna has made a career out of marrying sound and light, transforming the rock video, and concert, into an occasion for spectacle. Killjoys argue that her songs would be nothing without their accompanying visuals, but that is nonsense and manages to ignore both the dialectic of rock art and the wild freedom of dance music. Disco came and went too soon before the music video caught fire, but its attraction was inseparable from the gaudy stage of the dance hall, the overt come-on and courtship of the dance. People trashed disco then, as they do Madonna now, guarding against any moment when their sex might take over where they think their head should be.

Sex and "Erotica" do not function together as do pictures and music in a video (the "Erotica" video uses the images in rapid cuts that, like a tease, considerably heighten their individual power to agitate). Their packaging as a unit, though, provides a clue to the book. Where every image might be a still with a soundtrack there is the contradiction to Literature. Also to the Book of Photography, which normally enlists one as a connoisseur.

3.

Madonna begins *Sex* with a disclaimer: "Any similarity between characters and events depicted in this book and real persons and events is not only purely coincidental, it's ridiculous. Nothing in this book is true." Yet the book *is* like a scrapbook, less a showcase for pictures than a souvenir. Crisp black-and-white studio shots (the photographer, Steven Meisel, is famous for his stark images in *Vogue*; the art director, Fabien Baron, is from *Harper's Bazaar*) appear along with contact proofs, with average or even poor quality pictures torn around the edges and stapled or taped to the page, with snapshots accompanied by scrawled words and punk-style stories in cut-out. Color is mostly bilious and rudely interspersed. Bits of writing course riotously throughout: on phone sex, sex with a younger man ("Probably the most erotic sex I ever had. But he gave me the crabs. ... So you win some and you lose some"), sex in the morning, sex with a fat man, sex and a language barrier ("Sometimes when you can't speak it kind of frees you up. They're whispering all this shit in your ear and they could be talking about the theory of relativity for all you know. They could be calling you a cunt bitch whore from hell. They could be saying, 'As soon as you come I'm going to kill you,' and you're yelling, 'Yes! Yes!'"). Here, a set of lyrics from "Erotica"; there, some typewritten notes on abuse and power. The one, stripped from the music, seems silly; the other, slapdash in its observation that upper-class women especially "must be digging it," tiresome. Here, a lathered-up story about licking a strange woman on the beach; there, a dialogue between Madonna's alter ego, Dita, and her psychiatrist; here and there, letters of ridiculous longing.

What is a scrapbook but testament to the chaos of remembering? Assembled piecemeal in the privacy of hours, it is free space for yearnings, for happiness preserved, for ideas that have yet to find full expression and maybe never will or should, for loves and losses and embarrassment. Dishonesty betrays the scrapbook's essence, but artifice—all the tricks one plays with oneself while ever conscious that *this is not how I really feel*—is as natural as the contradictions of character, and as intriguing. For sex as subject matter, the scrapbook is the perfect medium.

But *Sex* is not "true," so of what is this scrapbook a souvenir? Not of experience. Not even of desire, exactly. Madonna bills it as a catalogue of her fantasies, but even those cannot be discretely hers; they are too stylized. It's a souvenir of performance.

4.

Pictures from an exhibition I: Leather mask (one size). Black leather peek-a-boo bra with silver-tone studs and matching high-cut bikini and wrist straps (chains optional). Thigh-high boots, midriff halter with gold-tone chains (both in black patent leather). Cupless leather lace-up teddy. Sheer Lycra halter bodysuit (also customized models). Necklace, medallions, rings—for nose, ear, eyebrow, finger and nipple—all in sterling silver. Zip-leg rubber pants with lacey crotch insert (black only). The motorcycle boot. Black fishnets (pantyhose or stockings). Leather harnesses (for men or women, with or without chains). The motorcycle cap (sizes for men and ladies). The new toe shoe, black leather on a chunky vertical platform.

5.

Pictures from an exhibition II: Madonna reflected in a stand-up mirror, the room behind her bathed in light, her hair unkempt, her lipstick perfect, the pose of an insolent teenager who has been studying Hollywood and nude sculpture. "My pussy is the temple of learning." A portrait of curves from shoulders down; her right hand holds her breast, her left hand catches the light across her tummy and is lost in the shadow between her legs; her jeans crumpled around her ankles. A portrait of curves from the hips down and from behind; her right hand clutches her cheek, her left hand holds the waist of a pair of cut-off jeans; her legs like a kid's in ankle boots. A man with a face like a fox, sitting up in bed with hands behind his head, a mirror against his left breast and in it the reflection of a woman's left breast. The same man in the same bed (with the same cigarette?) holding his hair away from his face while the same woman holds his chin, inspecting the lipstick she has just carefully applied to his mouth. Portrait of a woman's ass in yellow and red, light of a Mexican summer, a man's hand dusting talcum powder on her fleshy dome. Madonna reflected in the wall mirror of what looks like a tacky motel but could be anywhere—maybe Miami?—naked except for a short-sleeved pale blue sweater pulled up to reveal her breasts, which she holds while looking sulky and a little sluttish; her hair unkempt, her lipstick perfect.

6.

"She should have done real trash or high art," a friend said after looking at *Sex*. Instead, she made the liberal compromise. There's nothing mutually exclusive about real trash and high art if by the former one means the total transgression of every accepted standard and norm. Susan Sontag makes the most persuasive case for this in "The Pornographic Imagination," describing the way in which the extreme or "deranged consciousness" is transmuted into art. But Madonna makes no pretense of being "a broker in madness," and she hasn't constructed *Sex* as an explicit turn-on. She is a popularizer, a manipulator of recognizable surfaces. Her concession to the supposed middle class may be more audacious than it seems. It says sexual fantasies are everyday stuff, no "truer," sicker, more or less exalted if the fantasist is in an xxx booth or an artist's studio or her own room, daydreaming at home.

It's easy enough to dismiss the s&m pictures, which constitute less than a quarter of the book. Gianni Versace has domesticated black leather and bondage, and in less posh quarters a shop somewhere sells leather bustiers and studded dog collars, if not the hardest gear. Madonna has always had a knack for recognizing the commercial possibilities in common longings, glammed up. A friend told me the other day about spending Christmas once with relatives in a small Northwest town, stunned to see the bright packages with Santa wrap disclose vibrating dildos and leather accessories. Perhaps it is no coincidence, then, that especially in those pictures that bear Meisel's signature style, one half-expects to see a designer's name superimposed in cool, thin type.

Sex never commences without advertisement of some kind; what's striking about these particular pictures is how completely sex is subordinated to advertising, how flesh is as if subtracted from the scene, leaving merely the elaborations of a sexual idea. Is this just Madonna trying to shock her daddy—and let's not get all ho-hum about the sight of someone on a rack—or is there something disturbing, in a less familiar sense, about this playing out of the desolations of sex in the age of AIDS? She herself may not know. It's only because popular conceptions of pornography lag behind the reality of the truly forbidden that s&m still has power as an evocation of danger. Surely, an ultimate, destructive obsession exists on society's margins, but as ritually practiced in bedrooms and commercial parlors, s&m is about the safest sex around. Today, the most dangerous sexual activity is love, its threat to the body joining its traditional potential for annihilating the spirit. Love invites trust, which could invite death. The eroticism of s&m is so diminished because, by contrast with love, s&m has become an idle passion.

7.

I don't think I'd like the bondage pictures better if Madonna had displayed conviction, but what's irritating about them as photography is that, unlike, say, the s&m pictures of Robert Mapplethorpe—extreme ideas allowed the luxury of their excess—they inspire no speechless wonder, only a series of questions to determine *What does she mean?* Sex withers under such scrutiny. As Van Morrison sings, "It ain't why, why, why. It ain't why, why, why. It ain't why, why, why. It just is." Madonna's best pictures just are—artful as fabrications of the intimate impulse or reflections of an extravagant spirit, and ineffably, unapologetically pleasurable.

8.

Intimate photography as practiced by lovers is part of love's act; the gestures, poses, looks, even the decision to pick up and aim the camera, are more important than the final object. Once the thrill of first inspection is past (even then, it is the contact sheet, the cascading sequence of images, that most excites), the photos are laid aside; later the camera is raised, and the game begins again. This is why photographs found among a betrayer's things are so much more devastating than a detective's snapshots. *I caught you in the act*—which is to say, the play of love, not the act of sex.

Nudity in such pictures retains its erotic charge as in almost no other situation. One is stripped—not for art or science or to make a political statement but for a lover's eyes, for sex.

(Also, as Madonna recognizes better than most, for fun.) And as befits such a game, the subject is a kind of mirror, reflecting the lover back.

Whose is the reflection in Madonna's most entrancing pictures? For whom is she smiling so joyously as, decorated only in bunny tail and long black gloves, she straddles a happy dog? Herself. Yourself. Another friend asked me, "Would anyone care if these pictures were of anyone but Madonna?" Of course not; whatever their voyeuristic interest, the private photos of others are always exclusionary. But in this act Madonna has cast the whole world as her accomplice. She makes a good joke adopting the alter ego Dita—from Dita Parlo, the prisoner's escape into love in *Grand Illusion*.

9.

Late last year, in what initially seemed the ultimate commodification of a hallowed image, Saks Fifth Avenue devoted three windows to a tableau of nuns. Normally the mannequin is an affront, the body as clothes tree. But here these artificial representations of women who in their actuality renounce all ordinary representation of their sex were oddly distracting. Neutral, beautiful, revealing nothing in the way of flesh or form or personal history, the nun of my childhood recollection —her habit dark, her face and chest swaddled in white slabs of starched linen—was as close as one could get on Earth to the saints whose icons lined the church walls. And like those saints, about whose apparitions and gracious favors we were taught in school, she alone possessed the secret of herself.

It's different today. Unless they are cloistered, most nuns have been forced out of their concealing habits and into dowdiness, allowed neither mystery nor the self-expression of style—the church thus accomplishing in the guise of freedom what a thousand years of tradition could not: the eradication of their allure.

And yet, and yet ... Seen from another angle, perhaps the habit of heavy cloth and wimple, once it became an archaic costume and not simply a variation on ordinary women's clothing, was merely a kind of social armor protecting what was really most alluring about nuns, and still is: their radical habits of being, their lives beyond the boundaries of commerce and feminine convention. That obstinate dignity resists appropriation, even in a Saks window.

I came upon this scene at a time when I was reading a slew of biographies of Madonna, each one intent on defining her: control freak, workaholic, incorrigible exhibitionist, Marilyn wannabe learning the hard way that "it's lonely at the top." Nothing so maddens the second-rate critic as a subject who isn't fixed and clear, and Madonna is the supreme stylist of image. "She has never, in any public forum, let herself go," lamented Caryn James of the *Times*, as if "letting go" were a virtue in a business dedicated to hurling unguarded individualism beneath the steamroller of commerce. Looking at the pictures in which she is most triumphantly naked—hitchhiking, arched against a fountain, hoist in the air from a T-frame suspension—I thought, Madonna has made her body her habit. She herself can't be commodified because she so enthusiastically commodifies whatever image she adopts.

"Ah, but," a friend cautions, "there is always a deeper oppression." True enough, but just as the overwhelming strictures of religious life do not negate the strength of women who preserve their essence, so Madonna's self-creations ought to be measured against the overwhelming demands of superstardom. Talk of liberation, of "being yourself," is always constrained, and those who most energetically proclaim themselves liberated are often the most deluded. Madonna gets into trouble whenever she explains herself as a revolutionary; much better her performance, which, even at its freest, whistles with ambiguity.

And impatience with ambiguity, the lockstep of convention, is behind all the criticism that *Sex* isn't sexy. "The newsstand right near my house sells a lot hotter stuff than that—and you can look at it for free," wrote Andrea Peyser in the *New York Post*, quoting a male editor at the paper. From a different standard of taste, "It looks like the same tired old porn," wrote Robert Hofler in *Newsday*. (Hofler was furious that "the hetero Madonna" should portray herself disporting with women, while poor lesbians, "who have no choice in the matter," are stuck only with themselves.) Whichever way you cut it, the difference between *Sex* and skin magazines is the difference between Madonna and Vanessa Williams posing for porno when that was the least-bad job: sexual subject versus sexual object. Madonna's cavort with Isabella Rossellini and her unbound embrace with the two skinhead women—in a picture that evokes both the sweet shudder of a kiss to the neck and the pleasure of the one who plants the kiss—are performances of desire. Williams' photographs with another woman, which logically cost her the Miss America title in 1984, were a boss's act of possession.

10.

On this matter of sexual subjectivity, my friend Dennis Selby, whose novel *Sanctity: or There's No Such Thing as a Naked Sailor* is a whirl of sexual psychedelia, recently compared Madonna's effect on American culture to that of Andy Warhol: "What Warhol was doing, and what Madonna is now doing, is the conscious, artful manipulation of hip. Hip is (and always will be) the medium of the true genius. ... Warhol's universe made being gay hip, and it can never be unhip again. And how did he make gay hip? He spread the gay appreciation of cock into the hetero culture through his art, in different media (meantime making even artistic facility hip). Madonna's world is the world of cunt, as openly ravenous as Warhol's gay dick world. No one will ever be able to avoid the existence of hungry cunt again. That's art!"

I hate to spoil the purity of this comparison, but Madonna's is also the world of a hungry heart—something Warhol's wasn't, at least overtly—which is what makes her such a supremely popular figure. She flaunts sex but hopes for love and, like Dita Parlo's winsome adventurer in *L'Atalante*, is wild about both. This can make things messy; the lover always risks being unhip.

11.

Madonna dreamed of being a nun as a child. It was a common fantasy among Catholic schoolgirls in the 1960s, especially girls in working-class or earnestly middle-class neighborhoods. I dreamed of being a saint, and, reckoning that the surest route to sainthood was martyrdom or miraculous occurrences, I spent a lot of time on my knees at an outdoor shrine praying for a vision. I later came to understand that this longing for sainthood, for the habit, had less to do with holiness than with the wish to be special. For in abnegation, even the humblest holy woman was ostentatious; thus does naive piety mature into exhibitionism.

And how does exhibitionism mature into art, into something that expresses an authentic wish for self-possession, body and soul? There is an infantile naughtiness to some of the pictures, particularly those of Madonna writhing and preening with Big Daddy Kane and Naomi Campbell, all of them looking like bad actors in a B movie that's not bad enough to be camp. *Let's break the rules*, those pictures say, and you hear the echo of the little-girl laugh, proud and at the same time guilty for having got away with something. Where the pictures don't talk about rules; where the laugh is just a laugh, the expression of exuberance; where Madonna tears through public streets neither self-conscious in her nakedness nor self-satisfied like figures in nudist colony brochures, whose breasts and penises disown their function as magic playthings—there *Sex* is irresistibly exhilarating.

In the passage from shock to daring, irresistibility is the key. Shock is simple and, in an age where all the barricades have been charged at least once, redundant. Daring is more subtle, because the obstacles are more refined. In the realm of sex, all manner of preferences have been noted and named. What disturbs is the suggestion that they might not stay neatly in their boxes, that sexuality might be something that is not always fixed and whose expression might ring with contradictions. Daring courts freedom; it knows that calculation has to risk embarrassment.

(1992)

Grand Guignol, American-Style: Convicting Woody Allen

In November 1992, *Vanity Fair* published an article about the bitter breakup of Mia Farrow and Woody Allen which concluded: "A gripping courtroom drama may be in the making, one that would undoubtedly give tabloid TV its highest ratings ever. Or things could be settled overnight. Left unresolved, however, is the healing process." The timbre of that conclusion, a combination of hoped-for salaciousness and therapeutic cliché, is typical of its author, Maureen Orth, a journalist breathless for the lurid detail, the tearful confidence.

Ordinarily, an overgrown gossip column with pretensions wouldn't matter, except that this one, "Mia's Story," was angled to popularize a claim of child sexual abuse against Woody Allen; and now, more than two decades later, its gossip, innuendo and selective quotations have been presented as the evidence-never-entered in the criminal-trial-that-never-was by writers, bloggers and Twitterers hungry to play prosecution.

I will not play defense, because there is no defendant. What there is, amid the shards of human experience on display, is a confrontation with malleable memory, with love and cruelty, with suffering as public spectacle, and our own tenuous attachment to something without which any of us would sink in an era hot for punishment: the benefit of the doubt.

This winter, as Allen was being honored for lifetime achievement by the Golden Globes, his reputed biological son, Ronan
Farrow, took to Twitter to call him a child molester. Ronan's
older sister Dylan then wrote an open letter describing her life
of pain as a result, she says, of an assault by her adoptive father
when she was seven. Nicholas Kristof, a friend of Ronan and
Mia Farrow, exploited his *New York Times* platforms to broadcast the letter. He called it news. A few months earlier, Orth,
again in *Vanity Fair*, had spoken to Dylan, now twenty-eight,
but the daughter's disclosures were eclipsed by her mother's
suggestion in the same article that Ronan might actually be
the son of Frank Sinatra. A reported friend told *People* that
Dylan felt "overshadowed," and that this, coupled with the
Globes tribute, spurred her to further action. The *Times*, pervy
as any tabloid but without the honesty, then gave Allen space
to argue his innocence—something that, were this a real trial,
would require no proofs.

To a society jacked on the politics of personal indictment
and the pastime of instant opinion, this modern Grand Guignol
has been like catnip to Fluffy. Websites have run interactive features saying "Do You Think Woody Allen Is Guilty? [Yes] [No]
VOTE," and hordes of people, knowing little, mistaking more
and presuming much, have weighed in, mostly to damn Allen.
The techno age meets the eleventh century, when verdicts were
determined by which side mustered the most supporters to court.

And yet, outside the clattering sound machine, Dylan's and
Woody's statements read as testaments of the aggrieved. It is
possible that they both are.

The original allegation arose as Farrow and Allen, who had
always lived separately but shared legal parenthood of three
children—Moses, Dylan and Satchel (now Ronan)—were in the
midst of dissolving their affairs following the discovery that
Allen was romantically involved with Farrow's daughter Soon-
Yi Previn. On August 4, 1992, days before they were to sign a
custody agreement, Allen is said to have molested little Dylan

in an attic of Farrow's Connecticut country house. The next day Farrow called Dr. Susan Coates, a child psychologist in New York, to say Dylan had begun to complain that Allen abused her. "I was puzzled, because in that conversation [Farrow] was very calm," Dr. Coates later testified. "I did not understand her calm." Within a week, Allen sued for custody, a bold or naive action for one under suspicion of a hideous crime.

The only legal forum for the airing of accusations was the custody trial. Allen lost. The court's opinion—Judge Elliott Wilk was "less certain" than the state-appointed investigators that Dylan hadn't been abused, but regardless there was no merit to Allen's bid for custody—now pops up online as proof of Allen's criminality. Records of the 1993 trial are sealed, and sworn testimony reported contemporaneously provides only patchy light.

Of relevance, though: Dr. Coates testified that, before the allegations were made, she had warned Allen that Farrow's extreme animus presented "a really dangerous situation" and advised him not to visit the country house. Allen did not heed the warning. About the day in question, one nanny said later that she'd lost sight of Dylan for fifteen to twenty minutes; another nanny said she'd seen Allen with his head in Dylan's lap while watching TV; a tutor said she'd noticed at some point in the day that the child was not wearing underpants. None of that testimony was "consistent" with Dylan's accounts of being abused, contrary to later press claims that it was. None told Farrow at the time that she had noticed anything unusual; nor did Farrow notice anything wrong with the child that day or the next morning, when Dylan and Satchel sat talking to Allen. Later, Dylan said nothing about an assault to her pediatrician, who found no physical evidence of sexual abuse. Farrow proceeded to question the seven-year-old on videotape over the course of at least twenty-four hours. In a sworn deposition which was mysteriously withdrawn before trial, the Farrow children's longtime nanny, Monica Thompson, who hadn't been at the house on August 4, stated: "I was present when Ms. Farrow made a portion of that tape outdoors. I recall Ms. Farrow saying to Dylan at that time, 'Dylan, what did Daddy do ... and what did he do next?'" Thompson added, "Dylan appeared not to be interested, and Ms. Farrow would stop taping for a while and then continue."[1] After a six-month assessment, the investigating team from Yale New Haven Hospital's Child Sex Abuse Clinic concluded that the child had not been molested; in a sworn deposition the head of the team stated that Dylan had "a rehearsed quality" in interviews. One of Farrow's experts criticized the Yale New Haven report as unreliable. Coates and another therapist who was seeing the Farrow children criticized the videotaping as potentially manipulative.

"We will probably never know what occurred on August 4, 1992," Judge Wilk concluded, but the issue at hand was custody. Allen could not name his children's friends, doctors, pets or dentist, had no experience bathing or dressing them or even spending the night in their home, and lacked "familiarity with the most basic details of their day-to-day existence." He was a useless father and a "self-absorbed, untrustworthy and insensitive" man, who was dividing the family. Dylan needed to be protected. At the same time, the judge agreed with therapists that "Mr. Allen may be able to serve a positive role in Dylan's therapy" and ordered that a process for clinical visitation between father and daughter could be initiated in as little as six months. Looming over the proceedings and influencing the judge's rhetoric was the figure of Soon-Yi, whose own person and particularity were spectral and who was made a symbol of exploitation.

A few months later an investigation by New York State's Department of Social Services concluded in the case of Dylan Farrow: "No credible evidence was found ... that the child named in this report has been abused or maltreated."

Obviously, there could be no criminal case. In formalizing that, Connecticut prosecutor Frank Maco nevertheless emboldened those who wished to try Allen by other means. In an extraordinary five-page statement, he declared that he personally "view[ed] the Wilk decision as vindicating the child's complaint and the corresponding activities of the mother to memorialize the complaint." In fact, Maco said, there was probable cause; he just wouldn't act on it, for the sake of the child. William Dow III of the Connecticut Bar Association's Criminal Justice Section remarked later, "It leaves [Allen] a convicted child molester without the benefit of a trial."

From this stew of fact and assertion the laptop prosecution picks what morsels suit it to construct a neat, uncomplicated story. *We just want the truth* has been the refrain. The truth is, beyond the straight-up mischaracterization of Judge Wilk's decision, there is no neat story. And there is nothing high-minded or radical or feminist in pretending otherwise. There are, however, principles.

History matters. Suspicion about children in peril was swirling through the culture when this family drama began. *The Courage to Heal: A Guide for Women Survivors of Child Sexual Abuse* had inspired therapists, self-help groups, crackpot theories, accusations, numerous trials and family ruptures from the time it was published, in 1988. Incest, as feminist psychologist Janice Haaken has observed, became the name for women's many problems that "had no name"—to borrow Betty Friedan's 1963 phrase—and that still don't have names enough. Recognizing this does not diminish the reality of child abuse, sexual or otherwise; it is simply a social fact.

In 1990, when the infamous McMartin satanic ritual abuse case finally ended in acquittals of day care teachers in Los Angeles, dozens of women and men elsewhere were in jail for fictional abuse. The first accusation in what would become the satanic panic was made in 1983 and grew from a root ball of marital collapse, money troubles, grievous family loss, addiction and mental illness. It was a mother, not a child, who claimed a McMartin teacher had done terrible deeds. It was a self-described therapist who then prodded children to confabulate. As the panic spread, the children's wild tales obscured a social substratum of fears, economic insecurity, cultural obsession with sexual danger, and a grotesque quasi-therapeutic network and media to exploit it all. In 1992 the False Memory Syndrome Foundation was established to support families and individuals falsely accused and to study the ways memory may be manufactured and then overwhelm a person. The Pulitzer Prize for fiction that year went to Jane Smiley's *A Thousand Acres*, which pivots on memories of father–daughter incest.

We don't know if Mia Farrow was influenced by any of this. We do know that when she told Dr. Coates that Allen was "satanic and evil" because of his relationship with Soon-Yi shortly before Dylan made her allegation, the time was rife with sexual fears about children. Often, as detailed in Debbie Nathan and Michael Snedeker's masterful book, *Satan's Silence*, "what came from the mouths of babes were juvenile renderings of grownups' anxieties."

Memory matters, and isn't a tape recorder. It is, as Elizabeth Loftus explained in a TED talk, "more like a Wikipedia page— you can go in there and change it, but so can other people." Loftus, a renowned psychologist and memory researcher, has conducted many striking experiments that have implanted false memories in subjects, who later recall them with the same conviction, detail and emotion as people with real memories. Years after the McMartin case, a research psychologist in Texas called James Wood did an experiment employing the interview techniques (though not the subject matter) used on kids in the day care case, encouraging his child subjects toward fantasy rather than fact. Within minutes, Debbie Nathan reported, "the kids started to make up bizarre stories." In the day care cases, children were encouraged to invent abuse stories by adults who refused to take no for an answer. The children suffered grievously for their false memories, which don't disappear with age.

We know Dylan Farrow's memories are real to her, and harrowing. Beyond that, nothing. It's possible, Loftus says, that "the seeds of suggestion were planted before August 4, and then watered afterward," when her mother questioned her lengthily, and investigators compelled her to repeat and repeat.

Love matters, and isn't simple. Soon-Yi is Mia Farrow and André Previn's daughter. Allen had ignored her (as he had all of Farrow's older children) until he didn't. It was unloving for Soon-Yi to take up with her mother's companion when she was in college in late 1991. It was unloving for Woody to take up with his children's sister—and selfish not to foresee the bomb it would drop in the family while he was still part of it, albeit unconventionally. In honesty, though, anyone who has known love's madness must pity all three in this triangle.

People behave badly; they all did. It was unloving for Mia to invite the other children into her pain; to rage openly against Soon-Yi and Woody from January 1992, as her estranged son Moses describes; to make the family an emotional armed camp. It was unloving—twisted, actually—to infantilize Soon-Yi, the eternal child at twenty; to speak of her relationship as incest and to hang a sign saying "child molester" on a door of the room where Woody slept at the country house when visiting in July 1992 to celebrate Dylan's birthday.

Heartbreak is a howling plain. We don't know how Farrow's suffering blew back on Dylan; surely, we must pity the child. How does a child who sees her mother's agony, who wants to please her, love her?

The head of the Yale New Haven Hospital team testified that although Dylan's many accounts of abuse had some major contradictions, there was one "very striking" consistency: she connected it with "one, her father's relationship with Soon-Yi, and two, the fact that it was her poor mother, her poor mother," who had lost a career in Allen's films.

Children matter. Orth et al. follow the lead of prosecutor Maco by imputing to Judge Wilk more than he said about Allen's "inappropriately intense" behavior with Dylan. The words are a fragment of testimony by Dr. Coates. While treating their son Satchel, Coates had been talking to both parents. Her relevant quote about Allen's behavior, from the judge's decision, is: "I did not see it as sexual, but I saw it as inappropriately intense because it excluded everybody else, and it placed a demand on a child for a kind of acknowledgement that I felt should not be placed on a child." Playing favorites among children is not good. Attaching the whiff of sex to it is worse.

There is a creepiness to the way so many who write about this case luxuriate in suffering, hang on every insinuation, wring from it the dirtiest conclusion. This too is the legacy of moral panic: in the guise of defending the child, children were sexualized. They could not be looked at naked, photographed in the bathtub, kissed all over, without raising alarms. Adults could be arrested for that, and have been, with the result that every child's body, no longer innocent in delight, became a potential crime scene.

Farrow testified that she had complained to Allen, back when Dylan was two or three years old, that he looked at the child "in a sexual way": "You look at her when she's naked." We don't know what, if anything, was in Allen's glance, his head, his way, when looking at his toddler daughter naked. Because this has been quoted to support arguments that he is a child molester—and assumes the reader will naturally agree that, yes, it is true, a child in her birthday suit is pornographic—we know, or should recognize, its chilling logic.

We don't know if it was sinister that Allen let Dylan suck his thumb, or read to her in bed in his undershorts, or rested his head on her lap. We know how those ascribed actions were interpreted by others who believed, or had heard for months, that he was a sicko for loving Soon-Yi. Invited to attack the sicko and rally to the victim, we are left little space to imagine ways that children might be better considered, raised up, loved and finally protected when the grown-ups' world around them decomposes.

Doubt matters. Something horrible happened to Dylan, but there are many ways to horrible. A mother who uses her children as a weapon is not admirable. A prosecutor who drops a case but convicts by press release insults justice. Doubt is not the refuge of monsters. It is the enshrined right of all, who tempt fate believing they shall never need the benefit of it.

(2014)

7

Triangles

It's hard loving a married man. One who is far away, with a life structured by family and history and expectation, who dreams of freedom but needs the chains. It's hard being that needed chain, the wife, icon of the known world, blameless victim whose sympathizers nevertheless cannot help daubing with the colors of failure: *Poor thing ...*

It's not supposed to be hard being the married man with the lover and the wife and the life. *That's the life!* Until he gets caught. Then the slurs come swiftly, predictably: narcissist, cheater, hypocrite, pig.

In the latest political sex scandal, which isn't a scandal at all but a circumstance as old and common as time, South Carolina governor Mark Sanford, Jenny Sanford and María Belén Chapur have provided an edifying example of pain as a condition of life, love as both a drowning pool and sustaining spring, adultery as the monogamy system's disowned twin. And all that liberals can talk about is what a fraud he is. No sooner had Mark made his forced confession that he was not hiking the Appalachian Trail but canoodling with María in Argentina than the knees of the righteous, in this case Rachel Maddow, Maureen Dowd and legions of Democratic water-carriers-cum-bloggers, snapped in unison. "Hypocrite!" they didn't quite thunder. Christians thunder; liberals sneer, but it amounts to the same thing, counting sins.

They got quite a lot wrong. Contrary to what's been asserted, Sanford is not known as a "Bible thumper" in South Carolina politics, and he recently irritated those who are by not signing a bill that would have blazoned I BELIEVE on the state license plate. He wasn't elected governor in 2002 by pushing family values; he ran as a vague libertarian and was elected because a lot of Democrats, black voters in particular, abandoned the incumbent, Jim Hodges, who got into office powered by their votes and then engineered an immense transfer of wealth from the poor and black to the better-off and white via his education lottery. Sanford didn't "lead the charge" against Bill Clinton in the Monica Lewinsky affair; he said Clinton had lied (he had) and, like a dutiful low-level congressman in a party of discipline, voted for impeachment (along with five Democrats). He is no more of a right-wing, hate-filled moralist than most anyone in the party of Barack and Bill, the party of "Don't ask, don't tell," the Defense of Marriage Act, and Personal Responsibility in the form of punitive welfare reform, lectures to teenagers, lectures to poor single mothers, lectures to black men on Father's Day and laws that make life harder for them all. He could not, as has been said, "embarrass" the State of South Carolina, itself an embarrassment since slave times, enabled quite effectively in that condition over the years by politicians regardless of party or avowals of faith.

None of this says much for Sanford, but it says a lot worse for his liberal scolds. They profess to be cosmopolitan, above religious mumbo-jumbo, vanguardists for self-determination—to know better, in other words, all the while arguing the case for compulsory monogamy and just punishment for sexual sin more vigorously than the religionists they laugh at. "The travel partners of infidelity are shame, deception, embarrassment, hurt and heartache—ugly, negative, soul-diminishing feelings," intoned Mark Lett, executive editor of *The State*, in explaining why it was so vital for South Carolina's main newspaper to publish private communications between the governor and his lover. "There is no joy among responsible journalists in telling stories about infidelity and its seat mate, personal failure."

Of course, there is terrific joy among journalists. Nothing sells papers like a good sex scandal. But it isn't just business or just the general degradation of the political culture that has encouraged so many in public life to seat themselves in moral judgment. It is also the resistance—forty years after Woodstock and Stonewall, forty-plus after the Summer of Love and the long debates on liberation and desire—to look love and marriage plainly in the face as the often embarrassing, sometimes tragic, reckless, ecstatic, devastating, delightful, humdrum human endeavors that they are.

It is as if so many years of self-help, so many versions of *Men Are From Mars, Women Are From Venus,* so many couples counselors and Oprah shows, so many exhortations that *Yes, you too can be happy; you just have to want it,* have rendered many people stupid, believing in tidy happily-ever-afters, if only one works hard enough at it.

Into this multiply reinforced delusion, the Sanford affair has arrived as a clarifying wind. Like most men, the governor didn't think the years of correspondence with Chapur, a journalist, the regular exchange of views and observations, the small change of life passing between them, meant anything. Who knows what had become of conversation between himself and Jenny, bounded by concerns for the children and the property, politics and the next campaign? And who knows if his pen pal didn't actually help the marriage work for a time, like a release valve, allowing the homely business to prosper. *He and Jenny always seemed so happy,* people have said. Maybe they were. Maybe María had a part in that. If Jenny had had a boyfriend at arm's length, maybe it would still be working.

As the governor tapped those innocent emails, the ones written before he "crossed the ultimate line," he probably believed distance was a prophylactic. But it was a leaky one, because by the time he and Chapur consummated their affair, they were longtime intimates—"the heart," as he said, making its insistent claims—and all that was left was to negotiate the terms of surrender or renunciation.

Clearly Sanford thought those were the only options, as once returned to South Carolina in the summer of 2008 he mounted his heavy equipment and went about digging holes on his plantation in a frenzy of frustration. On the one hand there was love, on the other the life; maybe he needed both, and could imagine no way to reconcile the two. Now Mark's friend and spiritual adviser Cubby Culbertson says that the Sanfords are no longer linked by feelings, that they persist in their marriage "out of obedience instead of out of passion." It is easy enough to scoff at that, easy enough to say one or the other should walk away, and maybe they should, maybe they will. But what is compelling about this story is its familiarity. People are foolish sometimes, or wiser than they know; sometimes they're trapped, or fearful, often both. People who should walk away never do, and sometimes their reasons can't be contained in a word or glib phrase. Only a misanthrope would damn them with irony and condescension.

It would be nice to say that there is some political solution for all the Jennies and Marks and Marías, some variant on self-help in the form of open marriage, polyamory and the like. Some answer. Some sexual accommodation that vanquishes the possibility of pain. And there is, sometimes. But not always. Sometimes sex does change everything.

(2009)

8

Sin, a Story of Life

Fall 2002. As a child I tried to imagine what a day, a year, a life-time of hearing confessions must be like for the common parish priest. It was said that the sainted voluptuary of suffering Padre Pio would spend seven hours a day in the confessional. Did pilgrims seeking absolution burden him too, I wondered, this stigmatic bleeding from hands and feet and side, with the same paltry crimes that I and my little confederates heaped upon the patience of our mostly unremarkable priests, Saturday after Saturday? *Bless me father for I have sinned ... disobedience, lies, a broken fast in Lent, a taking of the Lord's name in vain, impure thoughts, impure deeds ...* Events in search of a narrative; acts with no history or complicating context, no personality caught between good and evil; generic sins from tykes who could not but be generic sinners. It was only later, with age, that I understood sin as a story of life, and confession as neither moral audit nor ransom from hellfire but, in truest form, something altogether more human, a talking cure, the poor man's psychotherapy. If such homely characterizations now seem profane it is doubtless not in the usual sense of the word. For once again in human affairs, the confessional looms as a symbol of dank mystery and corruption.

In the sex scandal enveloping the Catholic church it stands as emblem of clerical secrecy, site of criminal accusations, source of indignation among old-timers who said a lifetime of mea culpas believing that divine grace depended on the purity of priests. Its representative virtue, forgiveness, has been supplanted among churchly concerns by zero tolerance. To its suspect privacy has been counterposed a different kind of talking cure, the public recollections of people who say they were abused by priests. Those recollections have been conveyed in countless press reports and public forums. However valuable the airing of old secrets is for the speakers, as shaped and deployed in the press their stories have somehow left them behind.

It has become meaningless whether those speaking up were four or thirty-four, whether they saw a priest naked or were raped, whether they always remembered or have unearthed fantastical recovered memories, whether they felt pain or, harder to divulge, guilt because of an uninvited pleasure. They are generic victims now, of generic abuse committed by generic "pedophile priests." Their stories have merged into "the story," one that everyone and no one knows. Its favorite themes are sin and betrayal, but the words have become like Catholic kitsch, colorful and empty, the spirit of camp snuffed and, in its place, the whiff of the invert. Sex as a social fact, part of the jangled, needy, contradictory culture of humans, not gods or monsters, has disappeared in the wash of words about sex. The society of grown-ups has picked up childish things, and it doesn't look as if it's going to put them away soon.

1.

Faith, fear, emotion aside, there is only one story we know with complete confidence. That is that one self-righteous institution, the press, has got another self-righteous institution, the church, on the run over a subject that both think about obsessively and rarely, if ever, deal with intelligently. The church is responsible for the scandal; the press, for raising it to the level of panic.

A fraternity of personal injury attorneys, newly arrayed in righteousness, has assisted. Each has a motive to dissemble: the church, because it distanced itself from human suffering and covered up; the lawyers, because there's money to make, and some had abetted the cover-up; the press, because it has fashioned itself as part policeman, part lurid carnival barker, and contradictions get in the way. In outline the story goes like this.

The setting is Irish-Catholic Boston. By January of 2001, eighty-four civil lawsuits were pending against John Geoghan, a sixty-six-year-old defrocked priest, for alleged sexual abuse of minors over his thirty-four-year career. He was also facing criminal charges. The church had already paid up to $10 million to settle fifty civil suits against him. On March 23, 2001, the *Boston Phoenix* published an investigative report by Kristen Lombardi detailing the case that twenty-five accusers were also making in a civil suit against Cardinal Bernard Law, archbishop of Boston, for allowing Geoghan to continue parish work until 1993. Court records had been sealed, but Lombardi interviewed plaintiffs who asserted that as long ago as 1973 they or their families had begun telling church officials, though never police, that then-Father Geoghan was molesting children. Law became archbishop in 1984 and so, they said, he knowingly endangered children for nine more years.

This was the first such negligence case ever brought against a US cardinal, and Lombardi was the first to ask, What did the cardinal know and when? She would go on to file several more dispatches in 2001, and her paper would editorialize that Law "must come clean." To hear the story told now by the *Boston Globe*'s Spotlight Team—a kind of priest-sex SWAT unit of reporters—no one had a clue that this all might be bigger than Geoghan until its investigators stumbled on "a routine court filing" in this anything-but-routine case. Likewise, the world would now be innocent of "horrific childhood tales" of abuse had it not been for the *Globe*'s first article on the subject, in

January of 2002, and the nearly 300 stories that followed over the next four months under the banner "Crisis in the Church," often positioned opposite another popular feature, "Fighting Terror."

Scandals are meat for the newspaper business, and among big-daily editors, longing for Pulitzer opportunities, nothing is so desired as the fragrant "internal document." In the priest scandal the *Globe*'s editor, Martin Baron, was fortunate to have as his target a centralized command-and-control institution whose workers' near-vassal condition lends itself to surveillance, hence files, hence many thousands of documents.[1] That aforementioned routine court filing was an admission by Cardinal Law in July 2001 that he had received a letter in 1984 alerting him that Geoghan had been accused of molesting seven boys in one extended family. The *Globe* filed a motion to unseal the Geoghan papers, including church personnel and medical records. Within months it was in receipt of some 10,000 pages.

The stories were rolling. On January 31 the *Globe* reported on confidential settlements the archdiocese had made over the past ten years involving seventy priests. Under the title "The Convicted and the Accused," it listed twenty-four names. Although an accompanying report stated that beginning in the early 1990s "the archdiocese was so eager to keep victims from going public or taking claims to court that it even paid some dubious claims," there continues to be no clarity on what was valid and what was dubious. The *Globe* appended a hotline number, soliciting readers' stories.

The dramatic frame of each story to follow recapitulated that of Geoghan's: (a) a priest had molested children; (b) he had been found out; (c) rather than report him to police, his superiors reassigned him, often packing him off first to church-run therapy; (d) the priest molested again. Prosecutors began getting itchy. The archdiocese passed them the names of ninety priests whose files going back to the 1950s included any sex-related complaint. To Catholics, Law apologized and said that accused priests would be plucked from ministry. To plaintiffs in the eighty-four Geoghan-related lawsuits, he authorized a settlement of up to $30 million.

"And the diocese knew" became the money line. By April, 500 people had retained lawyers and were making claims against the archdiocese and its officials. The number of Geoghan's accusers in civil complaints rose to 130. In May, the archdiocese Finance Council announced that, due to additional liabilities, the $30 million would have to be renegotiated. Letters in the press predicted that plaintiffs would become suicidal. Outside the Cathedral of the Holy Cross, where Law said Mass on Sundays, protesters carried signs saying SELL THE CHANCERY, PAY THE VICTIMS and chanted "Caiaphas, Caiaphas" over a bullhorn. The *Globe* polled readers as to whether Law should resign; 65 percent said yes. There was a scent of payback. In 1992, during a scandal involving a former Massachusetts priest, James Porter, eventually imprisoned for abusing twenty-eight girls and boys, Law had thundered from the pulpit: "We call down God's power on the media, particularly the *Globe*!" Now the roles were reversed. "The documents," noted the Spotlight Team, "produced a sea change."

Other newspapers and bishops around the country followed Boston's lead, the synergy of personal injury lawyers and editors forcing the release of more documents, consequently generating more stories, more tort claims and more criminal investigations. Between January and June, some 250 priests and three bishops nationwide would resign or be sacked. More than a dozen would be arrested. Three would be shot, two of them killed. Two would commit suicide. Almost all would be mute: *Father X did not return phone calls.*

In Boston, Geoghan would get up to ten years in prison and lifetime probation for squeezing the buttock of a ten-year-old, either while teaching him to swim or lifting him out of a pool in 1991.[2] The Massachusetts Legislature would pass a bill shepherded by Mitchell Garabedian, attorney for the Geoghan plaintiffs, requiring clergy to report any suspicions or allegations of child maltreatment—just like every other professional working with children. Unlike other professionals, however, clergy would be required to trawl their memories for anything they might ever have suspected. Because the Department of Social Services investigates only reports current enough that the child in question is still a child, older memories would be referred to the local DA. That part of the bill was thus an invitation to a fishing expedition. No loud warnings would be raised about the potential for prosecutorial excess. Disdain for the power of the church would clothe the power of the state in unearned benevolence.

In Dallas, meanwhile, the US Conference of Catholic Bishops would declare that "for even a single act of sexual abuse of a minor—past, present or future—the offending priest or deacon will be permanently removed from ministry" (though not necessarily defrocked); that any future accusation will be reported to police and result in the suspension of priestly faculties; that accusers will receive immediate pastoral care, and priests will be encouraged to get a lawyer.

"No second chances," the conference president, Bishop Wilton Gregory, exclaimed, emphasizing public relations over principles of the faith, but the bishops would still be criticized for excessive lenience. One man who had received a priest's unwanted attentions as a teenager told me he opposed this scythe-like leveling that equated one wrong with many, defined all wrongs the same and foreclosed the possibility of redemption. Being somewhat prominent in victim circles, however, he was hesitant to speak out: "It makes me feel like I'd let down the side." The *Boston Herald* said defrocking of the accused "ought not even be debatable," and "there is no such thing as going too far to protect this state's children." Cardinal Law raised a problem, though; even after being ousted, accused priests "still exist." At some point along the way, scandal had tipped into panic.

"What is it, like 80 percent of priests are accused now?" a media-savvy Boston friend asked this summer. It was just a deduction—all those stories, the numbing succession. Estimates of priests accused of sexual abuse (from verbal harassment to touching to rape, of children, teenagers and adults) since 1950 range from 1.7 to 4 percent.[3] Because one would be too many, numbers aren't really the point. Priests aren't supposed to have their way with anyone, least of all children, but neither are children supposed to be harmed by mothers, fathers, grandfathers, stepfathers, mothers' boyfriends, uncles, aunties, brothers, stepbrothers, family friends, foster parents. And yet they are. According to the annual federal "Child Maltreatment" report, out of about 3 million complaints to state child protective services in 2001, there were 903,000 substantiated cases of maltreatment by relatives or caretakers; 10 percent were classified as sexual abuse. The suffering child is terrible, whatever the cause, but there's no payoff in shattering the illusion of home, no journalism prizes, no hefty lawyers' fees for bringing the family to its knees. The child who says *Daddy raped me* has little to look forward to besides Daddy behind bars. The act is a crime, assuming the charge is true, too common for scandal.

In the church, sex is a scandal whether or not it's a crime, whether or not the charge is true. Since the 1980s, when sexual abuse was recognized as a major issue in the US, the Catholic church, by general estimate, has paid out between $850 million and $1 billion in settlements and related costs.[4] The vast majority of cases are said to have involved teenage minors between the 1950s and 1980s.

A striking misrepresentation here is the transformation of those past payouts—which proliferated after the Father Porter scandal—into not only incontrovertible evidence of guilt but proof that *Nobody knew.* Lawyers negotiated those deals, and the profusion of claims once checkbook justice had been established in the 1990s was no secret. Perhaps most claims were legitimate, but not all. Now the considered thought goes wanting. How church bureaucrats, human beings, might have behaved under stress of scandal; how the store of 1990s documents reflects the archdiocese's chaotic attempt to address the problem; who might have been falsely accused; how detectives and prosecutors might be propelled by ambition—such matters evade scrutiny. It's unseemly to place the church's failings and sexual dishonesty alongside every other institution's failings and desire to avoid bad press. It's unseemly to mention money as anything but the church's weapon or just punishment. We are asked to believe that money could not also be an inducement to accusation, as if in this one area of life the urge to make a buck is inoperative. We are asked, thus, to abandon skepticism, to be stupid and inert, avid for depravity and, worse, satisfied that if one claim is true then so must they all be.

The case of Father Gordon MacRae indicates the murk around old settlements. MacRae was abandoned by the church and convicted in 1994 of crimes entirely unsupported by evidence. His accuser based his claims on repressed and recovered memory, discredited now by serious psychological researchers. Prosecutors offered MacRae a deal of two years in prison if only he'd say he was guilty of molesting a teenager. MacRae refused, and got sixty-seven years. The accuser, whose brothers had already received checks by making civil claims against MacRae, collected $200,000.[5]

No particular formula seems to have governed most of the church's payments. The Boston archdiocese reportedly paid $400,000 to settle a claim that Geoghan had made lewd phone calls to the children of one family. Phil Saviano of the Survivors Network of those Abused by Priests, or SNAP, settled for $12,500 in the 1990s after alleging that a priest forced him to perform oral sex beginning at age eleven. Saviano never promised silence. Lately some people who did enter confidentiality agreements have started talking. Whether they sought a quiet deal initially, or were cowed into it by the church or their own lawyer, or spotted an opportunity for shakedown (like the boyfriend of Minneapolis archbishop Rembert Weakland, who got a "Dear John" letter and then wangled $450,000 for his discretion), all have been treated with equal sympathy by reporters. Beginning in January, Boston lawyers who for years had made nice gains off confidential settlements—generally 30 percent—started denouncing the archdiocese's "hush money," calling the church a "racket" and Law "despicable." More was to be gained now from regular face time in the news as the voice of the voiceless. For balance, the *Globe* ran one story pointing out the lawyers' complicity. The story served the same purpose as the placing of *alleged* before the words *victim* and *pedophile priest*, and was as easily ignored.[6]

Now comes Father Paul Shanley before the bar in Cambridge. Once famous as Boston's "street priest," a political radical who ministered to runaways and spoke out for gay rights, he is a man upon whom all the fears and frenzy of the moment have converged. By the time he was indicted on charges of child rape, indecent assault and battery, on June 20, it was evident that if the Catholic church was running a racket, it wasn't alone. At her press conference District Attorney Martha Coakley thanked reporters and personal injury lawyers for their help in the "struggle" to bring criminal charges. The night before, her office tipped off television stations so they could pre-record the reaction of the family of Gregory Ford, an accuser in the case and Boston's best-known victim. "She understands TV," said a producer for Boston's Channel Five, whose legal commentator until recently, Roderick MacLeish, had negotiated dozens of secret settlements with the church and now represents Shanley's accusers in civil actions.

MacLeish told the *Herald* that the Fords' decision to go public and the release of 1,600 pages of documents from Shanley's personnel file marked "the major turning point in making this a national crisis." Indeed, Shanley's story—as told by his accusers—has captured the national imagination. Back in April, MacLeish put on a dramatic press conference, broadcast live and timed to give print reporters a tight window to meet late afternoon deadlines. His PowerPoint featured cunningly selected excerpts from the documents, which have been quoted ever since. Some reporters wept. The *Globe*'s editorialist declared Father Shanley "a depraved priest." The *Herald*'s called him "quite possibly one of the most depraved men ever to don a clerical collar." No charges had yet been brought; it would be almost a month before Shanley was arrested, more than two before he was indicted. In June those papers' reporters were among the scribblers crying, "Martha, Martha" as Coakley deadpanned, "Paul Shanley is innocent until proven guilty."

2.

It has been reported that the Shanley documents reveal a thirty-year pattern of boy-ravaging, cover-ups, guilty transfers from parish to parish. They do not. That they contain an admission by him of rape and a psychiatric evaluation showing that "his pathology is beyond repair"; they do not. That they prove that both the archdiocese and even the Vatican knew of abuse accusations against him in the 1970s; they do not. That they show he left his pastorate in 1989 because of sex abuse charges; they do not.

What the documents do contain relevant to sexual abuse is:

§ one hearsay allegation from 1966 or '67 (undated, unsigned, written in two different hands), which Shanley forcefully denied and whose subject never made a claim, though MacLeish tells me he has "found the boy" and they are talking;

§ a 1988 report about a man in a mental hospital who had made "a passing reference to sado-masochism" in a conversation with Shanley and then thought the priest "was coming on to him";

§ a set of incoherent notes from a Chancery worker's 1992 conversation with a woman who said that a decade earlier

Shanley gave a ride to a fifteen-year-old who jumped from the car after the priest said the boy "could sleep with both men and women";[7]

§ four allegations made in 1993–94 (following the Porter scandal), involving male teenagers dating back about twenty-five years. One may have been from a blackmailer who harassed church workers by phone. Another involved a purported deathbed confession. Documents generated in the 1990s as a result of these allegations are also in the file. Shanley was finished with parish work by this time and near retirement.

When the documents were released the claims from 1993–94 were long settled; one or two others were pending. As media attention has escalated so have the claims.

Paul Shanley may be as rotten a man as some say he is, but the four accusers in the criminal case say they themselves didn't know they had been abused until the scandal erupted, and we have heard nothing from the defense.

Gregory Ford, twenty-five, "recovered" his memories of rape and abuse, according to court papers, after being shown, first, the *Globe*'s January 31 article (to which he didn't react) and then a photograph of himself receiving First Holy Communion from Shanley (upon the sight of which, his parents have said, he fell to the floor in tears). Ford has had a hard time in life, having cycled through seventeen mental institutions or halfway houses. Paul Busa, also twenty-five, has said, according to court papers, that his memories "began flooding back" after he learned of Ford's claims. Anthony Driscoll, twenty-five, met with Ford and MacLeish in March, according to a sworn statement by Ford, and said he "wasn't sure if he was molested." In April, after seeing the same psychiatrists as Busa and Ford, he was sufficiently certain, so MacLeish filed a civil lawsuit for him. About the other accuser, thirty-two, little is known, except that he too immediately forgot being abused, made his accusation after Ford went public, and has the same lawyer.

All Prosecutor Coakley will say is that each man has "memory issues." Those memories, monstrous in the clipped syntax of the indictment—"unnatural sexual intercourse," "penis in child's mouth," "child's penis in mouth," "penetration of child's anal opening"—are nearly identical for Busa and Ford, who spoke on the phone while reconstructing their memories. Both say Shanley pulled them out of religious instruction classes almost every Sunday between 1983 and 1989, so as to sodomize and otherwise abuse them in the pews, the rectory, a bathroom, the confessional. The boys would have been six when it began; Shanley, fifty-two. No one is on record as having noticed anything amiss then.[8] Not their parents. Not the several women who taught catechism at St. Jean L'Evangeliste in Newton, where Shanley was stationed from 1979 to 1989. No adult remembers Shanley pulling kids out of class.

In the universe of accusations against Catholic priests, the foregoing are far from the most compelling, dependent as they are on "memories" that weren't even memories—much less gossip, whispered confidences, allegations, criminal complaints or testimony—until the scandal made them so. When Shanley was arrested in May, New York's local ABC-TV affiliate bypassed intermediate definitions and translated "memories" directly as "crimes too horrible to imagine." But most reporters have followed MacLeish's lead, arguing for the soundness of those memories by linking them with the gossip, whispered confidences, hearsay confessions and allegations of others.

Some of those stories, related most wantonly in *Vanity Fair*, are on the order of the Catholic grotesque: filthiness accessorized with crucifixes, rosaries and threats of burning in hell. Shanley himself, according to family members, admits to past "sexual misconduct." In a January 31 letter to friends, he wrote that "it was never with a child but with a highly sexualized adolescent, never with an 'innocent,' and was so non-traumatic then that some of the victims returned. And it was never repeated in the thirty years since that I have tried to make up for my wrongs."

He has pleaded not guilty. On the advice of attorneys, he has otherwise been silent.

To be skeptical of the criminal charges is to be immediately suspect. "I know exactly the story you're going to write," attorney MacLeish said to me in a stormy interview: "The Case for Father Shanley." MacLeish has affidavits and lie detector tests, the evaluations of paid therapists and the promise that clients will cooperate with criminal prosecutions if those are possible. He says he has turned away hundreds of people whose claims didn't seem credible, and his worst fear is that someone will be falsely accused. Thus armed, he is confident that the truth is exactly what his clients say it is.

It would be comforting to say, Let's wait for trial, but it's unlikely that court proceedings can reveal much. To the extent that the case turns on memory, there are no criteria for assessing one narrative of the past against another if all "memories" are judged to be equal. In the instance of Gregory Ford, was he brutalized by the priest and thus from the age of eleven or so began to fall apart, drinking, eventually turning violent upon himself, his family and others, experiencing nightmares of dislocation and grief? Or is this unhappy condition a mystery that didn't make sense and now only seems to? Ford's father told the *Newton Tab* that after reading the *Globe*'s January 31 article, "I knew from that moment on that I was going to have all the answers."

It is in the nature of things that people want their suffering explained. The rape narrative seems to provide a reasonable explanation. Reasonableness, a subjective quality, doesn't make it true, nor does it prove that Shanley was the rapist. To the extent that the case turns on every other objection to Shanley, it is a case about sex. And "sex," as the writer and radical activist Amber Hollibaugh says, "is the first place we lie to ourselves."

Shanley certainly lied to himself. In the documents there is a haunting entry. It is handwritten, dated March 3, 1994, and appears to be notes from a conversation between a church worker and someone from the Institute of Living, a clinic that evaluated Shanley after the allegations arose in the 1990s. Although rejecting the version of events that the archdiocese ultimately settled on, he is said to have admitted to the "substance of complaints—sexual activity w/ 4 adolescent males and w/ men and women" going back many years:

Observation about self—
—ashamed—embarrassed—wished I had found the gay community
—gay

In all the writing about all the accused priests in Boston, only Shanley is gay. Others may be homosexual, labeled as such by therapists. They may be ambisexual, like Geoghan and Porter and Father James Birmingham, cruel updates on the demented priests of nineteenth-century anti-Catholic pornography, dirty old men compulsively copping a feel, cornering children in closets and sacristies, pawing them in the family home. Repellent as they are, the abuses of such men can be filed in the folder marked SICKNESS. Shanley's is a harder case, not because he did nothing wrong but because he also had adult relationships; because some people have upset the dyad of victim–victimizer by saying they were willing sex partners; because an accident of birth placed him in the pre-Stonewall/post-Stonewall transition, between the closet and coming-out-but-not-quite. He has not formally come out to his family. He did, however falteringly, find the gay community, and the history of that community, which is also a history of sex in the late twentieth century, is now on trial with him.

One need only read the civil complaint MacLeish filed against Law, two former auxiliary bishops and the Archdiocese of Boston for negligence and infliction of emotional distress. The defendants, it says, knew or should have known that Shanley was a child molester as early as 1984. Why? Because of Shanley's "deviant beliefs"; also, because of "indications that Father

Shanley was a founding member of NAMBLA," the North American Man/Boy Love Association.

Shanley was not a member of NAMBLA. He never spoke at a NAMBLA conference or at a conference of what would become NAMBLA. The claims have been widely circulated as fact because the NAMBLA connection figured large in the lawyer's PowerPoint extravaganza that made the priest a monster.

MacLeish is a clever man. NAMBLA is to sex in the 2000s what the Communist Party was to politics in the 1950s, a tar baby upon which the fears of the age have adhered and association with which is enough to get one fired, shunned, suspected of the worst beastliness. Born in Boston at the tail end of a gay sex ring panic in the late 1970s, NAMBLA is now accursed in mainstream lgbtq circles, barred from Pride parades, refused meeting space, denounced lest failure to do so is interpreted as going soft on pedophiles. The same has happened to Shanley. Boston's largest circulation gay paper, *Bay Windows*, has editorialized, "He deserves whatever the criminal justice system has in store for him." *The Advocate* calls him "the indicted pedophile who posed as a gay activist." And at the level of individual consciousness, a gay man after Mass at the Jesuit Urban Center shuddered at the mention of Shanley's name—"the NAMBLA guy"—and said that although he could weigh whether the state had proved its case in a murder trial, even if he secretly felt the defendant had taken a life, he could not be an impartial juror in Shanley's case. "It's just too awful."

Like NAMBLA, the deviant beliefs upon which Shanley is being judged also originated in the 1970s. Let us, then, travel back a bit, to that very different time, when the drinking age was eighteen and bars were thick with teens passing fake IDs and grinding to songs from *Sticky Fingers*; when runaways converged upon Boston by the tens of thousands, begging, tricking, dying; when police were entrapping gays in the Fenway, and *Fag Rag* was publishing articles like Charley Shively's "Cocksucking as an Act of Revolution." The Vietnam War was over, almost. It had come home in the form of drugs and broken vets, a generation turning to spiritualism and mystic cults. In the Catholic church, priests and nuns were leaving for love. Others stayed in, questioning celibacy and the subordination of women, articulating a theology of liberation, hoping that the spirit of Vatican II and its "preferential option for the poor" might overcome centuries of authoritarian identification and change the church, change the world. In Washington, then-congressman Father Robert Drinan offered the bombing of Cambodia as grounds for impeaching Richard Nixon; in South Boston/Roxbury, Father Jack White had been the first official candidate for Congress to call for impeachment. "Social sin," the US bishops' Catholic Campaign for Human Development wrote in 1973, applies to "structures that oppress human beings, violate human dignity, stifle freedom, impose gross inequality." Yet in Boston, white Catholic gangs were stoning black children. And at the Chancery, Father Shanley's personnel file grew fat with letters of condemnation and a few of praise for reported statements like "You can't be anything in the Catholic church if you are openly gay," and cheeky arguments that Kinsey's research on the prevalence of homosexual experience "should be good news to straights as well as gays: it means a man who sits all day watching football and 'Gunsmoke' does not then have to go beat up a queer for Christ."

On June 17, 1973, the first issue of *Gay Community News* appeared in Boston. Under events on page one it listed: "Fr. Paul Shanley ... has been working with younger gays and bisexuals, to overcome the negative conditioning of the Catholic church. For raps and counseling ..." He had a roving ministry between 1970 and 1979, and his name and number would appear every week for years in the paper's Quick Gay Directory, along with those of Good Gay Poets, Dignity, *Fag Rag*, Red River Dyke Collective and my friends Littlejohn and Andy Kopkind, who hosted "The Lavender Hour" on WBCN radio. To review the archives of *GCN* now is to witness a community putting itself together. Along with self-defense tips and news, sex and politics were discussed regularly and without restraint. Lesbian feminists and male transvestites fought it out over performances of femininity. "The View from the Closet," by A. Nolder Gay, called on readers "to build a new, yet very old model" of intergenerational relationships. Everybody in, nobody out was the paper's message, because "any attempt to formulate a single conception of gay identity is simplistic and self-righteous."

"For me it was the Golden Age," says John Mitzel, who worked on *Fag Rag* and *GCN*, "before AIDS, before the right wing dismembered the victories of the sixties, and Reaganism convinced everyone Greed Is Good." At seventeen he had run away from Cincinnati, where his mother had mistaken sexual precocity for mental illness. "I've always been interested in older men, and I was sexually active from about the age of twelve. I would follow hot-looking men onto the bus—twenty-, thirty-, forty-year-olds—then get off where they did. My technique was rather crude. I'd just say, 'Can I blow you?' Of course, they ran off in horror. They don't teach you how to be a sexual predator at age twelve." *Fag Rag* would be a storehouse of desire, home for fact and fancy, including sexual memoirs recounting adolescent seduction of older men, with headlines like "Tailor's Tongue Cools Off Sweaty Youth in Damp Jockey Shorts" and "I Was a Street Boy." (*Boy* and *youth* were idiomatic, designating anyone from adolescence to early twenties, sometimes older.) The grittier edge of such sexual negotiation was to be found at Park Square and bars like The Other Side, where a man who asked to be called Wayne Hay worked from 1974 to 1977.

"That's where I met Paul," Hay recalled. "It was a couple blocks from the Greyhound station and a big hustling loop in Bay Village. The place was full of teenagers. He'd come around every night. Mostly he was looking for someone he already knew was in trouble. These were people abandoned by their family because they were gay—throwaway kids, really. I know how destructive that life is emotionally and physically. It's a wheel down the road. I saw it all the time. I saw Paul take people who had no place to go but under a bridge or who were looking for a trick at 3 a.m. so they'd have a place to sleep."

"With him?"

"In the bar world everyone was gossiping about who they slept with. I heard it all, and I never heard in all those years anyone gossip about sex with Paul. All those thousands of kids, not one ever said, 'I had sex with Paul Shanley and he was great or he was awful.'"

Others did hear things, rumors that they shrugged off or didn't believe. "I thought, all you need is one kid who's not getting what he wants," said George Mercier, a founder of the gay Catholic group Dignity, and in those years Shanley was surrounded by teenagers. Since the scandal erupted, a few former street kids have said help came in exchange for sex. One reports he was raped at thirteen; another that he was too wise at fourteen to let things go too far; a third that at fourteen-fifteen he felt "lucky" to be with the priest.

If, as now stated, some people were suspicious of Shanley's sexual behavior in the 1970s, they either didn't make their concerns known then or their complaints didn't make it into Shanley's file.[9] What did get filed constitutes a broken narrative of the life of a man moving uneasily between two cultures, one of calcified authority, the other of liberation aborning; and between two churches, one of condemnation, the other of love. These cultures, these churches, clashed most dramatically over sex, and the 1970s documents, while providing nothing on the priest's deviant behavior, are replete with his deviant beliefs. It is a mark of which side won that those thought crimes are now entered as evidence of sex crime, and that the bilious churchladies (and a few men) who reported Shanley's fag-loving heresies to the Chancery should be upheld as models of Christian virtue:

> As a Christian who believes homosexuality is a "Sin" against every plan God has for men and women …

The inference that Father now intends to speak publicly advocating sex education ...

He said, "Homosexuality is a gift from God and should be celebrated ..."

He stated that we as teacher's [sic] and people should accept these people [homosexuals] as normal individuals ...

I was appalled ...

I am incensed ...

We think he should be silenced immediately.

Such letters were occasioned by talks Shanley had given around the country or over the radio. Reporting on a speech he gave to Dignity in Rochester, New York, in 1977, one Dolores Stevens wrote: "He can think of *no* sexual act that causes psychic damage —'not even incest or bestiality'"; in "non coerced" sexual relations between adults and minors "the adult is not the seducer —the 'kid' is the seducer and further the kid is not traumatized by the act per se, the kid is traumatized when the police and authorities 'drag' the kid in for questioning."

"No rational person could defend such beliefs," MacLeish said to me. In deposing Monsignor William Helmick, a secretary to Cardinal Law, he referred to a '70s-era article quoting Shanley and asked, "Was it any part of the teachings of the Roman Catholic church ... that it was appropriate for priests to discuss sexual relationships between men and boys?" After some throat-clearing and further prodding, the monsignor finally agreed that "it would be appropriate to condemn" such relations, and also agreed when MacLeish demanded: "Paul Shanley is making statements [e.g., 'homosexual acts are not sinful'] that are contrary to the doctrines of the Roman Catholic church; is that not correct?"

An attorney for the archdiocese might have asked Helmick about another assertion by Shanley in the file, this in the priest's own words: "We can say some things without question: any sexual act with the same or opposite sex is sinful if it is rape.

Or if it involves the seduction of children." Shanley's accusers would no doubt argue that whatever he said proves nothing about what he did. Of course, they would be right.

Consider, though, what a "rational person" might have concluded from Shanley's comments on teens, sex and trauma at the time they were spoken. Nineteen seventy-seven was another year of sex panic in America. Anita Bryant's "Save Our Children" campaign overturned an antidiscrimination ordinance in Dade County, Florida, and spread fears of homosexual "recruitment" across the country. Prosecutors and politicians were making their names in a frenzy over "kiddie porn," a campaign that would later be discredited but that also attracted a gaggle of mainstream feminists and other liberals and took aim most directly at gay men. In Chicago, articles by the *Tribune* linking child abuse, kiddie porn and homosexuals spurred increased police harassment of gay clubs and cruising sites. In Seattle, police recruited hustlers in order to bust gay bars. In Michigan, an eighteen-year-old blew his brains out after being questioned by police and exposed in the press following the arrest of an older man with whom he'd been involved. And in a town just outside Boston, the arrest of Richard Peluso for having sex with teenagers led to a dragnet that would ultimately involve twenty-four other men and sixty-three youths in what became known as the Revere Sex Ring Scandal.

There had been no complainants, no victims, in the Revere case until police successfully threatened Peluso with consecutive life sentences if he refused to name names. Likewise, the thirteen youths who cooperated did so under pressure from police, psychiatrists and priests. The mother of one sometime hustler was coerced into signing over legal custody to the state, which promptly locked her son in youth detention until he talked. Another youth told a lawyer that he loved some of the men with whom he'd had sex but was afraid of what the police would do if he didn't talk. The DA's office solicited anonymous tips, and its hotline, promoted by Boston's major media, became a relay for innuendo about countless gay men. In March 1978, 103 men perceived to be gay were arrested in the Boston Public Library after being propositioned by undercover cops. The message to gay youth was: *Here's your future—aggravation, humiliation, incarceration.* Out of meetings held at *Fag Rag* and *GCN* there emerged a fightback.[10]

In the end charges were dropped or greatly reduced, none of the men served time, and the DA responsible for the scandal was swept from office. At a conference afterward on sex between men and teenage boys, Shanley spoke, along with ethicists, psychologists, writers, lawyers, nuns, teenagers, youth advocates, feminists, the president of the local Daughters of Bilitis and a researcher for the sex-abuse theorist David Finkelhor. It is impossible to imagine such a meeting occurring today. A 1979 magazine account noted: "At the end of the conference, 32 men and two teenagers caucused and formed the Man Boy Lovers of North America." It was this sentence that MacLeish projected at his press conference. But Shanley was not part of that caucus, as I learned from a Catholic priest and a Protestant minister who were.

"The problem is whenever you're talking about sex, you're also talking about fear; and wherever there's fear, there's also the possibility of exploitation," the gay media pioneer John Scagliotti (Littlejohn in the '70s) says, looking back on that time. "Sex panics are all about exploiting people's fears, but Shanley had a fear of sex too. Those ads saying 'Gay, Bi, Confused? Call Father Shanley'—if he'd added one more sentence, 'Want to have sex with an older, handsome priest?' I'd have no problem with it; in fact, I would have been there too. One could get moralistic about it and say that's a bad thing, but what's really immoral is the whole homophobic reality that made it so hard for people to be honest.

"What you have to understand is there was a void then for young gay people. Some got into gay liberation; a lot of them got to the only gay person they knew who was out or sort of out, and he was usually older. Most gay adults who really understood these things were afraid shitless of dealing with youth. It's different today; the community has developed. Back then, though, a lot of the people who got into 'helping' also did it because they liked the young things. They didn't even have to have sex, but it was a turn-on. It's no different from straight men hanging on every silly thing that comes out of the mouth of a pretty teenage girl. But gay life is a tough one, tougher then. Kids needed places of protection, and there were these guys who knew it, and who probably had those feelings once themselves. Everyone was a little vulnerable, don't forget. But it was also kind of a scam, and the kids knew it was a scam. It's like the Mafia ran gay bars; thank God for the Mafia. You understand it, but do you like the Mafia?"

Paul Shanley was into helping from the time he himself was a kid, organizing boys in Dorchester to protest a ban on evening softball, teaching crafts, planning dances and hayrides. His scrapbook is a catalogue of boyish enthusiasm before homo-social physicality raised a wary eyebrow: pictures of him as a teenage camp counselor tumbling smaller boys in gymnastics; sensitive shots of sensitive boys his own age, neatly dressed, arms akimbo; here a quote from Oscar Wilde, there a photo of Rock Hudson; yearbook photos (beside his, "To err is human, to forgive divine"); and before long, men in black cassocks, playing basketball, pushing a lawn mower, featured in the newspaper at ordination like so many brides of Christ.

He entered the seminary in 1954 and was ordained in 1960, at twenty-nine. At St. John's Seminary, I was told, discussion of sex presumed a suppressed interest in women and was conducted in Latin. Another priest, slightly younger than Shanley, who has spent decades trying to reconcile dedication to his vows with attraction to younger guys, told me that when he entered the seminary at seventeen, he equated celibacy with bachelorhood, and that didn't seem to be much of a sacrifice. Sex didn't yet exist for him, not consciously. About Shanley so much is unknown in this respect. His best friend, Father Jack White, says Shanley was a great listener but didn't talk about personal things. Most men didn't. It's a commonplace that only in the priesthood is a young man transformed from tyro to sage, the elders who once corrected him suddenly seeking his advice. And only in the priesthood, pre-Stonewall, could a gay man with no particular courage escape the prying questions, the life with Mom stretching into old bachelorhood, and be admired.

Reading Shanley's file, I kept asking myself, Why did he stay once there were options? It's a too-easy question today, asked with a too-hetero confidence and a too-distant appreciation for vocational attachments. In the language of Boston's attorney-media-accuser trinity Shanley was simply evil—"just like Ted Bundy," one of his accusers told me—planning his every move for predation. Jack White says a commitment to the social Gospel kept Shanley going: "He helped people through the worst moments of their lives, saved many people, especially young people, from committing suicide. Whatever else is alleged, true or not, he has a pastor's heart."

People seldom make a lie of their entire life, but seldom meet their own ideals, either. Shanley's examination of conscience is in the realm of the unknown, but his ideals for Catholicism could be breathtaking. In the files he worries about the limitations of an ad hoc ministry of one. In a 1973 letter to Boston archbishop Humberto Medeiros he proposes the church become, effectively, an annex to the gay movement, providing community centers and free clinics, specialized addiction programs, employment counseling, housing projects, legal aid, prison ministries and halfway houses, a "zap group of pickets" to exert pressure for equal rights, liaisons to curb police violence, education for straights, suicide hotlines, a farm retreat for gay couples to build enduring relationships, and of course the Mass. That now seems as naive as a group naming itself a Man/Boy Love Association and not expecting to be reviled. If Medeiros replied, it is not in the file. But people were taking down a president; anything seemed possible, even Christianity in the image of Christ. Jesus, as Shanley reiterated, says nothing about homosexuality but much about charity, "the Queen of virtues."

Shanley is said to have had "a silver tongue," and he preached on "Brother Jesus," turning out the moneychangers, dividing loaves and fishes, hailing the Good Samaritan: "Love one another," "Love thy neighbor as thyself" and, hardest of all, "Love thine enemies, do good to them that hate you." Officially, his was a Ministry to Alienated Youth. On the street, his typical schedule began at 6 or 7 p.m., touring the Common, the red-light Combat Zone, the squares and transit stations, finding kids lost, strung out or pre-boarding for a fall. Today lawyers and journalists pronounce breezily upon what Shanley should have done.[11] But "imagine yourself, a social worker newly arrived in town," he wrote in a 1972 newsletter. "There is—no ADC, no Children's Service, no Mental Health Center, no Legal Aid, no Social Security, no Blue Cross, no Family Counseling, no Guidance people, no Red Cross, no TB wagon—nothing. You are all alone, buddy." It was a crime for a minor to run away from home, a crime to take in an underage runaway. Until Sister Barbara Whelan, Shanley and others started Bridge Over Troubled Waters and bought a Winnebago to provide free, confidential medical care, street people had no realistic health option. Bridge and Shanley would be accused of abetting delinquency. More than 150 pages in his file constitute a memoir of the period. It has been pronounced arrogant. Shanley was vulnerable to the snares of pride, but more striking is the need—of youths starved for purpose and affection, some in such extremis that the greatest immediate assistance anyone could provide was a clean needle and advice on the dose that wouldn't kill them; of a priest so acquainted with grief that his own privileges seem at once shameful and inadequate:

Holy Week 1972

Midnight. Somewhere on Route 78 ... searching for a place to sleep. I am overwhelmed with loneliness, ashamed at my pleas to God to find a way out for me. All my prayers should be for my people for whom there is no way out. How many 16 year olds are also lonely tonight on the road, on the run? Is it really so important for me to go on? The Letters say so. They warn: "If you give up so must we. You are our hope." People shouldn't put such hope in a mere man, any man. It's almost sacriligious [*sic*]. If they knew the madness in me, festering below the surface, they would join the ranks of my accusers.

O God, why has Thou forsaken these lovely, gentle people!

My thoughts run to that beautiful whiskey priest of Graham Greene's novel, the last one left in Mexico, underground, no good, yet he cannot leave. How the people use him, then push him out. For me it is not like that. These kids can't even use me. They ... have no need nor inclination to turn to the power structure that is the established church in America—my Sacraments are worthless to them.

It is not frequently that anything can bring me down. I know I'll be up tomorrow. But today again I met this kid who haunts me, who is everywhere across the land—the candidate for heroin addiction. ... It is as if some kind of human defoliation program had decimated the country's youth.

When Shanley wrote those words, he had been seeing a man named Arthur Austin for three years. Their involvement would continue until 1974. Austin was twenty when he first went to see the priest, heartsick from his first break-up and distraught that his longing and pain, proof of faggotry, meant a future of shadows. In high school Austin, a fragile soul, had fantasies of joining the priesthood. "I loved the idea of Jesus," he told me, "all those images of kindness and gentleness and peace and loving people. I grew up pretty tough working-class, and my father was extremely tyrannical. I thought I could go into the priesthood and all of this stuff would go away. I had this vivid image of Christ putting his arm around me, with my head on his shoulder and just being loved because I existed. It was magical thinking, and certainly when I was young, very confused magical thinking."

Austin can recite the old prayers, and as a kid he had basked in "the whole Roman extravaganza," the litanies and echoing chants, "all this beauty and safety." When, near the end of their first meeting at a rectory in Braintree, Shanley, according to Austin, told him, "I want to give you access to my body to ease your pain when it becomes too unbearable," Austin "was spellbound." *Vanity Fair* reported that the priest stripped him right there, but Austin told me that Shanley's ultimate manipulation was to say: "I want you to think about this."

"So I go home and think about it: I'm a faggot. No one knows. He's the only one who understands me—and I'm going to walk away from this? Now he's not just holy, he's Jesus."

Today when Austin speaks publicly, as he did at MacLeish's press conference—adult regrets showcased to validate accusations of child rape—he draws on hoary cadences, calling on Almighty God to smite "foulness and treachery." He told me Shanley made him his "sex slave," used him when "I just wanted him to talk to me and that didn't happen, or listen to music with me and that didn't happen." In hindsight everything that passed between them is hateful. But once, he recalled, he told people, "In fifty years Paul Shanley will be canonized." For years Shanley would call up, ask for a rendezvous, and Austin agreed, sometimes buying a bus ticket to visit the priest out of town. "I could never say no. I was very, very afraid of him." He likened himself to a battered wife, but once Austin got a real boyfriend and an unlisted number, Shanley never called again. To Austin, the priest was more than a bad boyfriend or a bad priest, more than a man scarred, like him, by everything he'd ever heard about the disgrace of loving men, isolated by his secret, desperate for physical contact in a profession dedicated to forswearing it, and making all the wrong choices. He was, instead, "a sociopath." Austin is suing the archdiocese and Shanley for damages.

Bill McLean was twenty-one, a junior in college, in 1973 when he saw Shanley's ad offering counseling to people confused about their sexuality. He remembers the Beacon Street apartment, the sign on Shanley's desk—HOW DARE YOU ASSUME I'M HETEROSEXUAL—and the moment when his expectation that the priest would try to "talk me out of it" pivoted to relief that "I was not sinful, sick, evil; I was okay." They spoke of many things: "He was very sophisticated, and so political, I can't tell you, tying in the personal with the political, [which] was very cool to me." On their second meeting McLean pressed, "How do you ever know unless you have sex?" Shanley named some places to meet men. "No way I was going to do that. I didn't want to be outed. So, he said, 'Well, we could try some stuff here ...' I thought, Great. I was dying to have sex with somebody—a guy—because it was in my mind all the time. I really wanted to have sex with him the minute he alluded to it. I was so glad finally to find someone in whom I was confident it wouldn't leak out."

They had sex half a dozen times over the next year and a half. "He was as easy as could be with me. I thought he was incredibly gentle." McLean says that since the scandal broke, friends have told him, "You went to him for counseling and he took advantage":

> That is such nonsense. I never attributed whatever struggles I had in my life to Father Shanley. He was the only one I could go to. I liked talking to him, I liked having sex with him. After a while, I got kind of frustrated. I wanted a boyfriend. He was always encouraging me to find someone. But I wasn't going to come out in Boston. He told me about the world; he told me about San Francisco. A month after I graduated I was on a plane to California, specifically to come out.

Maybe they should have talked more, McLean sometimes wonders. Maybe they shouldn't have had sex, or had it so quickly. "To tell you the truth, the first three or four times, each time I was kind of a wreck afterward." What they had done was illegal, abhorred by polite society. And McLean had enjoyed it. It takes some time to appreciate that sexuality is social and personal, a story of maybes and should haves, or, often, shouldn't haves; a negotiation of yes-no-yes, well … which we talk about only in terms of yes or no, because how else to bring this unruly thing to rule?

John Harris at first didn't think he had a case against the archdiocese. MacLeish declined to represent him. Another personal injury attorney, Carmen Durso, thought otherwise. In 1979, Harris was lonely, twenty-one, uneasy having faced the truth about his sexuality. A professor suggested he see Shanley. He was surprised that the priest, handsome at forty-eight, came out to him. They talked and then Shanley left the room, where Harris, surprise again, found some soft-core porn. When Shanley returned, Harris, a nervous man, said he was feeling edgy. Shanley suggested a massage. Harris agreed, and with the lights turned low, the two stripped down and began rubbing each other with baby oil. This was all pleasant, if strange, Harris recalls. It was his first experience with a man. In the heat, he says, Shanley said, "I want to fuck you." Embarrassed by his own arousal, anxious about going farther but reassured that everything would be fine, Harris consented. When in the midst Harris said, "I think we should stop," Shanley, he says, said, "I'm almost finished."

This is not what Jesus would have done, not what the hero in a romantic novel would have done, not what the thoughtful lover would have done. But what men and women do carried away in the moment falls far short of the congress of angels, and Shanley is a man. A troubling aspect of the scandal is the erasure of a priest's humanness, and the way human fallibility plays out sexually. To speak only of power, as is customary, is to say this is not also a story about men, about the power sex exerts over men, about our queasiness and hypocrisy toward sex, especially sex between men. With sex simultaneously gorged upon and shrunk from, every bit of nonsense with respect to power can be indulged. "I thought he was God," one of Shanley's accusers told *Vanity Fair*. If true, that bespeaks not only a failure of theology but an alarming deference to authority, sex or no sex; yet the writer, Maureen Orth, never paused to reflect. Having indicted power, she hurried on to the next seamy tale of sex.

However much it figures in the rhetoric, power is not on trial in the priest scandal. If it were, every priest, every bishop, every teacher and parent who ever terrorized a child into fearing his fantasies, hating himself or his desires, would now also be in the dock. Every vituperative letter in Shanley's file would be read out as evidence of the construction of shame and the enforcement of sexual lying. Every elision of God's love with a sexual elect would be declared a crime against love, an abuse of power of the highest order. Every preachment, from what-ever quarter, that convinced children they were slaves of adult authority, mindless in obedience, without will or choice, would now be properly named child abuse. And every penny extracted from the church would be dedicated to broadening the options, inspiring independent minds and strengthening boys and girls, gay and otherwise. In the story of scandal, though, only sex wounds and destroys, paralyzes the will, bears the burden of conferring rosy happiness or, if not, despair.

"I didn't find romance," Harris told me. He said it earnestly, the way Austin mourned the absence of long talks with a lover— as if this were not elusive, rare, and as if second thoughts about sex were not life's circumstance. Like Austin, he has suffered depression, and like most people, his story isn't simple. His scene with Shanley concluded with climaxing in the priest's arms followed by tremendous confusion. A week or two later, he again called the priest. He didn't know whom else to call. They would not have sex, but Shanley acquainted him with the gay bars and the South Street Theater, a porno house with a popular back room. Harris disliked its sex-no-chaser anonymity, and Shanley escorted him out. "I know your type," Harris remembers Shanley saying: "You want the suburban house with the white picket fence."

It was true, but Harris understood it as an insult. Later in one of those bars, he met the man with whom he would share a life and a suburban home for twenty years, but not before steeling himself with whiskey sours. It was not the best relationship, Harris said. "I made choices too, but people need tools. As a gay person, as a closeted person, you don't have those tools." Shanley should have introduced him to other gay Catholics, should have made him feel better about himself, helped him to make better choices: "I didn't have a father. Where was my male role model? Who was there to guide me?" Instead, the priest introduced him to sex and showed him where to find more. It was bound to be a bumpy ride, but as the starting point for oppression, sex was also an on-ramp to the highway toward self-determination. And by then Shanley seems to have abandoned illusions that the church might offer anything more affirming.

The two never saw each other again. Shanley's long jousting with Archbishop Medeiros intensified. As 1979 closed, the ascendance of John Paul II meant ferment in the church would be resolved the old-fashioned way: critical theologians were silenced; Dignity was expelled from church property; Medeiros was congratulated by Rome for attacking "homosexual culture" and "weeding out overt or latent homosexuals" from the seminary. As for Father Shanley, "a troubled priest" because of those deviant beliefs, which, as Medeiros informed the Vatican, the priest told the media he "would continue to proclaim ... to the rooftops," he was disciplined with the humbling assignment of parish work.[12]

Of time's sway over judgement, Harris says: "Would I have described him as a monster five years ago? No, because I didn't know what he did to other people. Would I describe him as a monster now? Yes."

3.

Secrets, like scandals, flourish in gardens of embarrassability. The closet case, the closet culture, are uniquely assailable in this respect, which is why coming out is the single greatest achievement of gay liberation, and sexual denial the blackmail note waiting to be written for the Catholic church. But even among accusers of priests, there are some secrets too dirty to speak about openly in this season of no secrets. I have heard their confessions.

Now, you can't write this. It would kill my mother. My father sexually abused me for years when I was little ... My brother forced me to suck him off. How many times? Thirty? *... My father called me a worthless faggot. How many times? Constantly. I started giving blow jobs in the first grade. I once asked an older boy if that was the only reason he liked me ...* My husband beat me. He chased me across a cut field until my feet bled ... *My father was an alcoholic. There's alcoholism in the family ...* There's depression in the family ... *My father raped me ...*

According to psychiatric records, when he was nineteen and institutionalized Gregory Ford "revealed being sexually molested by neighbor and cousin(s) for about 3 years ages 7 to 9." Doctors considered this a breakthrough. His parents suspected one adult, but then Mr. Ford hurried to interview his son, and the family concluded it was all a misunderstanding. In a deposition, Gregory's sister said that a witness to his ravings as he was being taken to the institution had told her that Gregory "specifically said 'my father raped me.'" That was also probably a misunderstanding. But since these claims were never investigated, how can MacLeish be so confident, as he was with me, that when Gregory reportedly cried out, "I was raped!" he was retrieving a fragment of memory about Shanley?[13]

Sins of the family don't make sins of a priest any less bad or scandalous, but they do disrupt the one-size script of happy child–monster priest–ruined life upon which so much rhetoric, money and legal action depend. It is understandable that people might "come forward" about their sexual history only selectively, but so long as they do, the reality of sexual violence can never fully be known.

What cannot be said takes many forms, subtler forms. Among sex panic's distorting features is the subtraction of complexity from those labeled *victim* or *survivor*. They, too, are denied their humanness—perhaps in ways more profound than the accused, because the price of sympathetic attention is the amputation of experience. Shame and guilt can live on in other recesses because in the heat of scandal they need not be explored, merely asserted. But what sustains the shame and silences, and not just for any individual? What do we miss when we confine any life within the tight frame of accusation? Ignoring such questions means the reality of sexual vulnerability can never fully be known, either.

A man named Bill Gately thinks about those questions a lot. When a visiting missionary entered his bedroom and began stroking and kissing him at fourteen, he "became lifeless" not just because of the outrageous intrusion but also because of "my confusion about mortal sin and my shame about having an erection." This was in the mid-1960s, and young Bill's only referents to sex had been school lectures against self-abuse and his parents' warnings against premarital intercourse. "I remember making deals with God that I wouldn't eat Hostess cupcakes if I could only stop masturbating." Disinclined to petty bargaining, God said, No deal. But Gately, too, imagined being a priest, the highest calling in the view of his timid, loving father, who as the child of a violent alcoholic had found safety in the church, and as an adult opened his home to priests. The priests never seemed quite human to Bill. There was generosity in the home but "no sensual dance," and his parents treated their visitors as objects of obsequious respect. To this brew the priest who entered Gately's bedroom and would do so again until the kid was sixteen added a souring ingredient.

"The issue for victims of shame and guilt," Gately says, "is the knowledge that it felt physically good. Most people aren't going to admit this. That feeling has nothing to do with inviting it. It doesn't mean you liked it." The priest was not violent, but nor was he sexually attractive, yet there was young Bill with a hard-on. A different boy with a different background, maybe a different priest, might have responded differently. Augusten Burroughs has written of his "first excellent blow job from a Catholic priest" at fourteen as being akin to "a straight guy ... having one of the centerfolds from *Playboy* step out of the magazine and hand you a bottle of mineral oil." But for Gately, "In my little-boy mind I thought, I'm some sort of pervert. What he did, in a moment, was terminate any honest dialogue I'd had with my parents and siblings. All these things were much more debilitating than the act itself."

In public forums, Gately tells the simpler loss-of-innocence story that Catholic audiences have come to expect. Privately, he plumbs complexity in talks with hundreds of victims and some accused priests. About the latter he says, "I think sexual abuse isn't so much a sexual thing or a power thing but a deep desire to connect emotionally. A lot of these guys live this illusion of purity, enthusiasm and understanding. Nobody can be what humanity demands that they be. At some point they think, I hate this life. With Bernard Law it's the same problem. His addiction is to prominence, to power. This isolates but also protects him from his own loneliness. It's where he finds something like solace. Others find it in a rest area or a bar or in a kid's pants."

In the aftermath of Burroughs' encounter, the priest "sobbed and he shook and looked, there on his knees, like he was about to split into pieces. He, the priest, was vulnerable and ruined for

that moment. And I, the fourteen-year-old, felt kind of thrilled."
Gately was incapable of feeling thrill or power at fourteen,
and could no more enjoy the experience than he could tell the
priest to get out.

I didn't grow up with the notion of priests as saints. Many
ate too much, smoked like stacks, bet on horses and earned
our allegiance, or didn't, by the quality of their hearts. Saints
in any case were dead, and, as I came to realize, some weren't
even saints in the common understanding of the word. As if to
underscore that, in the midst of the scandal Pope John Paul II
canonized a man who not only wrestled with devils, flagel-
lated himself to bleeding and fasted to the point of collapse
as a novice, but later was accused of dallying with women,
pomading his hair, perfuming his body and faking the stigmata.
The Vatican once forbade St. Pio de Pietrelcina, as Padre Pio is
now called, from hearing confessions and having any contact
with his female devotees, who were known to lavish him with
kisses and fight for the chance to tell him their sins. Rome was
so unsettled by the extravagance of his cult and his ease with
fanaticism that twice it put him under investigation. His own
order bugged his cell, and perhaps his confessional—the tapes
contributing to Pope John XXIII's disciplinary restrictions. By
1968, when Pio died, his reputation and that of his cult had
been restored by John's successor.[14]

As Michael Bronski noted in a column on this in the *Boston
Phoenix*, saints are made as object lessons: in elevating Pio, the
pope reinforced the ancient Catholicism of miracle, mystery and
authority. And yet there is something oddly modern about it all
too, this example of colossal frailty, of ambiguity at the edge
of hysteria, holiness and accusation. The pope has insisted on
modifications in the US bishops' zero tolerance policy toward
accused priests, saying it did not allow for due process and
forgiveness. He expressed something as significant by offering
the troublesome figure of St. Pio for contemplation, reminding
Catholics that our embarrassment, our shame, is us.

At the Dallas meeting, Cardinal Anthony Bevilacqua of Philadelphia spoke of the need "to begin to restore the credibility of the church and moral authority ... so that once again our faithful, without any embarrassment, will be able to say, 'I'm proud to be a Catholic.'" Bevilacqua has advocated purging gay priests. Bishop John D'Arcy of Fort Wayne, Indiana, announced he would kick out "effeminate" seminarians, and later the pope ordered seminaries to reject candidates with "obvious signs of deviations." In New York a gay priest who asked to be nameless said that between the gathering threat against gays and the presumed-guilty policy toward anyone accused, "you can almost imagine Stalin's Russia: everyone fears the knock on the door in the middle of the night."

The targeting of homosexuals has outraged victims' groups, Catholic journalists, gay groups and reformers. They point out, rightly, that there is no statistical correlation between homosexuality and pedophilia, and that females and males have both been on the receiving end of unwanted attention.[15] They call for democracy, accountability, transparency. They, too, are embarrassed, and ham-handed responses—the bishop of San Jose evoking the peep show by ordering windows cut into confessional doors—only add to their chagrin. The acid irony is that liberals who have spent the past year fixated on every detail about priests and boys, or priests and men, are now in high dudgeon over the church's homophobia.

In a sense the reactionary churchmen are keener to the crisis than the liberals. Their solution has no more chance of working now than it did in the late 1970s, but their appreciation, even in disdain, of the challenge presented by gay liberation is far more acute than reformers acknowledge. That challenge, at its core, is a broadside against the regimens of sexual shame. It asserts that sexuality is central to humanity, not some "don't tell the children" unclean thing, not something dependent on marriage and the imprimatur of normalcy. It asserts that sexuality is born with us; that desire, pleasure, love, may be complicated, almost certainly will be, but people really do have the right to pursue such happiness; that they also have the right to pursue celibacy, chastity, abnegation, but, like the rest, those are sexual choices; and, among believers, that all of it is God's creation, and nothing God made can be bad, even if it often goes bad. Some utopians, renegades, hippies and free-loving feminists had always believed such things. Stonewall put it all out there. For more than thirty years the ethos of sexual freedom has been working its way through mainstream culture, moving forward, thrown back, diverted by commerce or expedience from its essentially moral root, surviving but not without a lot of dislocation. The essential questions—how to live honestly, mindfully? how, really, to love?—are the same as they ever were, and still hard. Revolution of the body is a lot easier than revolution of the mind, and for all the claims to liberation, we are still groping in the dark, still in a period of transition identified with the 1960s–70s.

Family, marriage, work, worship: the old forms are gasping; the new ones have yet to be fully invented; and maybe the best evidence is that no one knows what to do with the kids. In Massachusetts, one in five high school girls is mistreated by her boyfriend, one in ten kids needs some mental health service but only a fifth of those get it, one in thirty-eight witnesses violence in the home, one in forty-seven is him or herself neglected or abused, one in five is hungry. Boston Medical Center recorded a 45 percent spike in the ranks of hungry children treated there between 1999 and 2001. No Spotlight Team monitors such mundane suffering. The fact is, the most attention kids ever get is when they're hurt, dead or in the dock themselves for sleeping with their neighbor, killing their parents and sometimes both. The easy slur that anyone who advocates strengthening children is somehow "blaming the victim" only points to the chasm of social irresponsibility. Sex panics are a way for America to save the children, believe the children, where otherwise they're ignored.

The long winds of change that have unmoored secular relations have created a special predicament for the Catholic church, one not easily solved by introducing marriage into the priesthood, as reformers fancy. In parallel to organizing patriarchy and patrolling the ramparts of right loving—all religions do that—Catholicism has had, in the form of its priesthood, a queer culture for a thousand years. Whether individuals are homo or hetero is beside the point. Here is an institution removed from the everyday construction of straight masculinity: a community of men, living together, freed from admonitions to marry and multiply, engaged in ritual and performance, praising gentleness, wearing dresses and bound together in worship of a naked man on a cross. Body and blood, a heady mixture of rapture and camp, at once constrained and extravagant, mortifying and incarnational, that culture is now stripped and under attack.

For a long time no one thought about this much. Even the most flamboyant priest (like the most butch nun, requiring a separate discussion) was beyond sexuality. It was all part of the old world, and the churchladies loved the gay priests, the way they loved Liberace. No one who grew up in the church pre-Stonewall could miss the way the priest who organized the talent shows and liturgical pageants, who dressed just so and drank martinis, dazzled the women, and if in private he rued the deception of it all, we never guessed. With gay liberation came not just an uncloseting of sex but of identity, and eventually the straight world started to recognize the markers.

The problem for the conservatives is that they love the church culture of the marvelous but hate the sensibility that has largely sustained it. They may be able to suppress sexual practice among priests, but the transmutation of sensual impulse into spiritual expression and transporting faith has always been Catholicism's special grace, and it's too late now for a little purging to obscure suggestions of the homoerotic. The problem for the liberals is that, in their attachment to plain common sense and unforgivable sin, what they seem most to want is for the church to be American, which is to say, Protestant. Whiskered denunciations of licentious Rome, "the Whore of Babylon" in old Protestant tracts, politically corrupt and sexually dangerous, have their echo in the priest scandal, only now the most vigorous declaimers are Catholics—in Boston, Irish Catholics who, unlike their immigrant forebears, have "arrived" and no longer need the church for its consoling sacraments and mutual aid, for its mysteries as a light in hard times. More than once have protesting descendants of those old immigrants found themselves outside churches confronting Boston's new immigrants—Haitians and Vietnamese, Latin Americans and Africans, who, defying their co-religionists' attacks, have asserted support for the archbishop. If that support is mainly reflexive or born of need, it is also true that the countries to which these people remain culturally attached have not raised sex as the screen upon which to project all their desires and all their fears.

It's clear how Paul Shanley, a transitional figure between the homoerotic closet culture of the church and the audacious gay culture of post-Stonewall America, has become the emblematic figure of the present crisis. Whatever sins of the flesh he has committed, his failure of the spirit lay in his inability to free himself from the culture of secrecy and shame even as he strained to move the church from what he called those "historical abuses." To loved ones he confessed:

> I am sorry beyond telling for the wrongs of my life and for the sorrow and anguish of which I have been the occasion. How I envy those who say in their declining years: "if I had it to do over I would not do anything differently." For me it is the opposite: I would do many things differently. For one, I would never have become a priest and tried to wrestle with mandatory celibacy and the myriad consequences of that folly. But who knew?

Upon that one miscalculation followed another, a too-great optimism that Catholicism's contradictions of sensuality and sin, love and censure, freedom and authority, could be resolved within the terms of church structure. Shanley's defeat came long before his name was made tinder for scandal, and years before even the first serious sex claim was made against him. When he resigned his pastorship at St. Jean's in November of 1989, by his account because he would not take an oath committing pastors to give "internal assent" to the pope's position on any issue, his lifetime ministry of loyal opposition and prophetic witness was finished. As he wrote to Bernard Law: "I do not leave in protest, or for a woman, or from disillusionment. I leave the active priesthood in grief. Someone has said 'I could not love thee half so much, loved I not honor more.' To take this oath would dishonor the priesthood." From there his archdiocesan file traces his decline—ailing, estranged from the family of the church, full of doubt and disappointment though not without a brittle humor, finally accused.

Perhaps when he is tried there will be gathered outside the courthouse some of the Catholic demonstrators who earlier stood outside Boston's Cathedral of the Holy Cross, bearing images of Satan, screaming denunciations, brooking no opposition, casting the first stone. They are, they say, brokenhearted and betrayed. Having learned well only the Catholicism of condemnation, they are more compelling evidence of the church's failure than even Bernard Law or his disgraced priests.

(2002)

9

The Upside of Censorship

*My mouth drops at this incredible meal Jean-Pierre has come
up with and we eat humming and umming and ah yeah oui oui
great slurp and a li'l wine to freshen the spirit and cheese and
yogurt for dessert and after that we talk about bats and owls
and get into bed ... so fuckin' cold without the heater working
that the skin almost freezes to the sheets ... he undresses quick
and ouch ouch jumps beneath the sheets moaning at the freeze
of them and I undress and ... ah ... ah ... inch my way beneath
the covers and we rub and warm each other up breathing hot
breath on each other's bodies to chase the chill away and soon
that becomes frenzy and we're getting on in the heat of delicious
sexual contact the sheets go flying off it doesn't matter anymore
the heat has come up from the heart into the surface of flesh and
eyes glowing we roll back and forth and finally there is sleep ...
long restful uninterrupted smooth warm exterior interior sleep
where dreams chase the hedges and dogs wheel around the sky
and not a river or snake or any sexual image but the strongest
one of all and its rhythms of life itself ah yeah ...*
—David Wojnarowicz, diary entry, 1978

Somewhere in America there is a boy who picked up a newspaper at some point since last fall and read the name David
Wojnarowicz for the first time. Somewhere there is another

boy who was surfing the internet, and another who caught *Live at 5*, and another who was walking along F Street in Washington and saw a construction trailer with a droopy banner for a Museum of Censored Art and thought, Cool. And all of these boys—in the dark about art because why wouldn't they be? in the dark with their sexuality because it's still scary, in the dark about the social machinery of seduction and death because the political culture is so adept at sleight of hand—are now poised to discover wondrous and fiery things because Brent Bozell of the Media Research Center and Bill Donohue of the Catholic League and Congressmen John Boehner and Eric Cantor complained that the work of David Wojnarowicz is too hot to handle.

Sometimes the censor is the best friend knowledge has. He is often one of the best friends art has. In the latest case, the censor has retrieved Wojnarowicz's sensitive, sexy, fiercely rebellious legacy from the elite world that, since his death from AIDS in 1992, has hung him in hushed halls as if to say, *Yes, he did deserve to live, after all*.

In October the Smithsonian Institution's National Portrait Gallery opened a show called "Hide/Seek: Difference and Desire in American Portraiture." It assembled 106 works, by artists from Romaine Brooks to Jasper Johns to Andy Warhol, around the concept that sexual outlaws have responded to repression with "creative acts of resistance" by which they defined themselves and, in the process, redefined the lines of American culture. The first queer-themed exhibit in a national museum, it would have been as conspicuous as rain on a distant sea if it weren't for a few dank straight men who don't like gay people.

Those men huffed and puffed and blubbered that Christmas was insulted by eleven seconds of a Wojnarowicz video, and agreed with Donohue that its use of a crucifix was "hate speech." A nice touch, that, always a prelude to shutting someone up. Liberals, take note: it *will* be used against you. The Smithsonian's top man, G. Wayne Clough, yanked the video from the show on November 30. From then on, protest has rung through the blogs, the print press and the streets of DC.

It is almost as if Wojnarowicz had reached from the grave to orchestrate against his own domestication. As an artist, he wanted acknowledgement, but as a man alert to the ways that the system pulls the trapdoor on people, relegating most to the shadows while handing out a few rewards, he was at a remove from an art world convicted by faith in an elect set apart.

In his diaries, collected by Amy Scholder under the title *In the Shadow of the American Dream,* he is a lonely kid observing nature, a young man experiencing life on the road, a free man in Paris studying the senses, falling in love, worrying over his future and scorning "this self-searching in the face of a world that kills people with bombs."

He was eight in suburban New Jersey when his father started killing the family pets; sixteen when he dropped out of school and narrowly survived the violence of life on the streets; twenty-one when it struck him that his homosexuality was "a wedge that was slowly separating me from a sick society"; twenty-four and in Normandy when he wrote the passage quoted at the start, so ripe with erotic innocence; twenty-five when he first gained public notice, for a series of portraits of men behind a mask of Rimbaud; mid- to late twenties when he scavenged the midnight of Reagan's America and became the unintentional chronicler of a sexual Atlantis on the Hudson River piers; thirty when AIDS had killed 7,699 Americans but Reagan had yet to mention it, and the Catholic church opposed condoms; thirty-three when he made *A Fire in My Belly,* the unfinished film that has offended Reagan's heirs; thirty-six when he made his famous untitled self-portrait as a child set in the center of a nail-storm of words describing the cruelties that will befall this kid "in one or two years when he discovers he desires to place his naked body on the naked body of another boy"; thirty-seven when he died. His loved ones held a demonstration.

I had never seen *A Fire in My Belly* until I stepped into the frigid construction trailer that Mike Blasenstein and Michael Dax Iacovone opened in front of the National Portrait Gallery on January 13, the aforementioned Museum of Censored Art. Like me, like most people, the two Mikes had never seen the video until it was censored. Blasenstein had never even heard of Wojnarowicz. Nor had many of the young volunteers who sat for hours to keep the trailer open and free to the public; nor many of the 6,476 people who have stepped into this rough metal box to watch the film on a clunky TV powered by batteries.

Like that trailer, *A Fire in My Belly* is raw. Animals fight, humans fight, policemen preen, slums flash outside a car window, and a machine's wheels turn. Traffic veers around a legless beggar. A man hammers at the concrete bridge that holds him. Everything violent flourishes. Everything beautiful is consumed: a martyr in flames, a leopard pacing in its cage. St. Lucy holds her eyes in a dish, patron of the blind. Bread is not free; speech is not free. Only blood drips freely. Mummies stare out their skulls. A colony of ants goes about its business, crawling over money, over a crucifix, over a shrine to the dead. Jesus weeps. Wojnarowicz bleeds, mouth stitched closed. This is my body; this is my blood. Someone washes his hands, but you get the feeling there will never be enough water.

If someone hadn't been offended, I'd have been offended for the artist. A visitor to the trailer said the Smithsonian should have put up a sign in the gallery noting the piece had been censored, and then held a panel discussion. This is not a polite, go-to-panel kind of work. It is an incitement, a hoarse shout into the moral wilderness. The world you tolerate, it says, is one of force and suffering, liberal until the handcuffs come out, or the executioner's gurney, or the predator drone; liberal because you can step around the casualties of everyday horror on the way to work and believe *They brought it on themselves*, except the bodies keep piling up. The pious censors shouldn't have been insulted because of a plastic Jesus; they should have been insulted as accessories to a crime.

Before the two Mikes had the idea for the trailer, they stood outside the "Hide/Seek" exhibition with leaflets in hand and the video playing on an iPad hanging from Blasenstein's neck. "Every time someone took a leaflet, security swarmed around," Blasenstein told me. "This was maybe the most disappointing thing: everyone who took a leaflet gave it back." After ten minutes, security brought out the handcuffs and called the DC police, who made the Mikes sign a document, since rescinded, recognizing that they would be banned from any Smithsonian museum. They are not sure what to do next with their guerrilla museum concept, but Blasenstein, a website manager in daily life, says he is forever changed.

Jonathan David Katz, one of the curators of "Hide/Seek," said he chose *A Fire in My Belly* for the show because it offered the densest metaphor for life with AIDS under Reaganism. It offends some in the art world that he edited Wojnarowicz's thirteen- and seven-minute rough cuts down to four, the most the Portrait Gallery would allow. It offends some that he gave it a soundtrack, an audio recording of an ACT UP demonstration that Wojnarowicz made and that includes his voice. The Museum of Modern Art, which previously had been indifferent to *A Fire in My Belly*, grandly demonstrated its defiance of censorship by buying the artist's cuts and installing them in its exquisite mausoleum for art in the age of AIDS. I wonder how long it would take the two Mikes to be hustled away if they stood in that temple with a loudspeaker quoting Wojnarowicz: "I don't want to be polite and crawl into the media grave of AIDS and disappear quietly."

Beyond rage, Wojnarowicz was posing a choice between love and barbarism, between "life ... ah yeah" and a culture of killing. Sex, love, these were not incidentals of a private identity; AIDS was not some temporary trip-up in the forward sweep of human kindness.

As it happens, on the same day that his video was yanked, the Pentagon issued a review of its "Don't ask, don't tell" policy on homosexuality. President Obama was so tickled by one observation therein that he cited it when he signed the law repealing the policy. Speaking of our nation's values, the president declared: "As one Special Operations warfighter said during the Pentagon's review—this was one of my favorites—'We have a gay guy in the unit. He's big, he's mean, he kills lots of bad guys. No one cared that he was gay.' And I think that sums up perfectly the situation."

If that summation is true, the army of lovers really is tottering at the cliff of defeat. The censors may be thanked for the bracing slap in the face.

(2011)

10

Faith-Based Justice

Paul Shanley

When it was announced, late in the afternoon of February 7, 2005, that the jury had reached a verdict in the case of *Commonwealth of Massachusetts v. Paul Shanley*, probably the only one who expected acquittal was the defendant. He has always maintained his innocence, and from his indictment, in June of 2002, to the opening day of trial at the Middlesex County Courthouse in Cambridge, on January 19, 2005, it appeared, to him at least, that the state's case was crumbling. Born of the *Boston Globe*'s sensationalist reports of sex abuse and priests, the case always depended on context more than content, innuendo more than fact, what the public believed more than what it knew. Shanley became the scandal's most notorious figure, yet there was no evidence for the charges, and none emerged at trial. Where once there had been four accusers claiming to have recovered memories—of "unnatural sexual intercourse" endured repeatedly—now there was one. That accuser, twenty-seven-year-old Paul Busa, had the cleanest backstory but no stronger claim on memory. By his own account, his mind was vacant of experience of sex abuse until he heard of the rape memories recovered, as it's said, by his childhood friend Gregory Ford. For the finders of fact, the trial pivoted entirely on Busa's testimony. As Judge Stephen Neel instructed jurors prior to deliberations, nothing corroborated the accuser's central claims. They found Shanley guilty anyway.

In anticipating a happier outcome, Shanley was not entirely naive, assuming one proceeds on the basis of logic and law. The concept of repressed memory—which holds that the mind can submerge the most traumatic memories in some walled-off place, where they remain unaltered and retrievable in exact detail by a triggering event or by therapy—has been discredited in courts, psychiatric circles, even the popular press in the decades since children, prodded by therapists, and women, prodded by therapists, began reciting "memories" of horrific abuse and sending people to jail. Like the case against Shanley, the case for recovered memory depends on belief. In that sense the two were a match. Nevertheless, for those who still hold to the notion of courts as arenas for evidence, Busa's story was not the stuff of a strong legal claim. Late last year the state offered Shanley a deal: plead guilty to one minor charge and receive time served, plus two and a half years' house arrest. Shanley declined.

"I'm seventy-four years old," he told me during a recent visit to the Massachusetts Correctional Institution in Concord; "why would I take a deal?" Possessing a sharp sense of the absurd, Shanley projects nothing in person of the dour figure of media images. His eyes are given to tearing, but there's merriment in them, as if lighted by a crooked joke whose punch line he alone might deliver. "Can you imagine, here I am, the worst monster, a danger to children everywhere, and they offer me time served? Seven months [the time he'd spent in jail awaiting bail]. But for refusing to lie, I got twelve to fifteen years."

Shanley did not take the stand. Court TV, which broadcast the proceedings, stressed this, its commentators insinuating that silence equals guilt, and asserting that whether or not he did the things Busa claimed, Shanley had done "other things," vile things. By now the accepted narrative with respect to those other things is entrenched. It is, for instance, such common knowledge that Shanley was a founder of the North American Man/Boy Love Association that this falsehood was part of televised banter throughout the trial. In voir dire every prospective juror knew something about Shanley: most commonly, the NAMBLA connection.

The commentary demonstrated that what gets reported in the first twenty-four to forty-eight hours of any scandal is almost impossible to undercut later. After the verdict, Robin Washington of the *Duluth News Tribune* (formerly of the *Boston Herald*) wrote that Shanley's real trial had been the press conference in 2002 at which Busa's attorney, Roderick ("Eric") MacLeish, presented the priest as "the devil incarnate." With the "lawyer playing judge, jury and executioner," Washington wrote, journalists had merely to memorialize MacLeish's narrative as truth. The trial would put the seal of law to it.

Although irrelevant to the facts of Busa's case, Shanley is hardly the virgin priest. He admits to having had sex with men and teenagers; he has had a companion for more than twenty years. At least some of his encounters, most while he was a street priest in the 1970s, were bound to be exploitative, given that authority can further complicate the already complicated emotions around sex.[1] Many of Shanley's accusers came from violent homes, which may have made them more vulnerable, complicating things further still. Shanley has expressed remorse for the "wrongs of my life." He maintains that his sexual encounters were consensual. That hardly matters to the church, which defrocked him before trial, and is of interest to law only if the cases are within the statute of limitations (they are not). What should matter to society, the dense subject of human vulnerability—how people deceive themselves about sex, revising events to put their own actions in an acceptable light; how teenage sexuality is complex; how so much about sex can seem dirtier or lovelier in retrospect; how repetition, therapy, the lure of money and the evasions of memory may mean no one even knows the truth anymore—has not mattered. Scandal is a leveling wind.

Since 2002, the Boston archdiocese has settled a couple dozen new claims against Shanley for an undisclosed sum. He says he is never informed of the accusations, or given a chance to respond. There is effectively no way to determine the validity of any accusation independently, and the bar for what is considered credible is exceedingly low. The 2004 John Jay College study, commissioned by the US Conference of Catholic Bishops, defines an allegation as "any accusation that is not implausible." It need not have been the subject of legal challenge or any investigation; it need not have been substantiated or error free:

> An *implausible* allegation is one that could not possibly have happened under the given circumstances (e.g., an accusation is made to a bishop about a priest who never served at that diocese). Erroneous information does not necessarily make the allegation implausible (e.g., a priest arrived at the diocese a year after the alleged abuse, but all other facts of the case are credible and the alleged victim might have mistaken the date).

Although the DA ultimately refused to test Gregory Ford's accusations in court, Ford received more than $1.4 million from the church in a civil settlement and is counted as one of Shanley's victims, as are the other two dropped accusers, who were also paid. Busa got $500,000 even as criminal action was pending.

Paul Busa

On February 1, 2002, Busa was at Peterson Air Force Base in Colorado when his girlfriend, Theresa Mazzei, called from Boston to tell him about a *Globe* article the previous day that had reported on Shanley's alleged abuse of young men. Busa has stated under oath that his "first thought" about Father Shanley was "nice guy." Unlike Ford, Busa had not been in and out of mental institutions, had not accused others of rape or threatened to kill his family and burn down the house. He had attended community college, held jobs, got along reasonably well in the military, was considered cheerful despite a disturbed family life and problems with drink and drugs. He is now a Newton fireman, married to Mazzei.

Shanley did not come up again in Busa's daily conversations with Mazzei until February 11. A Newton newspaper had reported Ford's bombshell allegations. The setting for those, by now well known, was 1983, St. Jean L'Evangeliste, in Newton, Massachusetts, where Shanley was pastor and where Ford and Busa took religious instruction between the 9 and 10 o'clock Sunday Masses. Their class, with about twelve students, was said to be disorderly. Beginning when Ford was six, he claimed, either the teacher would send him to Father Shanley for discipline or the priest would come and pluck him out, take him elsewhere on church grounds and there commit a variety of atrocities. This went on for years, but Ford forgot each attack instantly. Mazzei told Busa the story, noting also that Ford had engaged Eric MacLeish for civil action against the archdiocese and would be pressing criminal charges.

Busa testified that when he heard Ford's story, his world collapsed. He felt panicked, nauseous. He called Ford, but said he can't remember the conversation. Like "a tidal wave," he said, memories virtually identical to Ford's hit him, and he cried for six hours. The next morning, he called MacLeish. He then went to the base psychologist. At trial, Busa said he couldn't remember what he told MacLeish or the Air Force counselor, John Drozd, but the latter's written notes indicate that Busa was seeking permission for a leave so that he could "consult with his attorney" about pursuing a lawsuit. On February 15, Busa flew to Boston, his ticket paid for by MacLeish. By April he'd been discharged from the Air Force and could devote himself to his civil suit against the archdiocese.

His first meeting with the base psychologist lasted all day, at least nine hours. Drozd suggested that Busa was suffering from post-traumatic stress disorder and recommended that he keep a journal. Drozd called it "an emotional barf bag," according to Busa in a sworn deposition. "He told me just to write down whatever I'm feeling that day, just to, you know, whatever is going to help me deal with it and get through it, just write, write whatever you want." Busa used the journal to reconstruct his memories. The first entry, written on February 12, was backdated to February 1. At the top of each page Busa notes: "Memo to Eric MacLeish, attorney confidential communication."

Journaling is a common technique among therapists who believe in repressed memory. The theory is that through free-association and quick writing, memories stored in the unconscious might break through the repressive filters of thought, screening, logic and control. In the annals of memory cases, such techniques tend to produce fantasies, which become false memories, as writing "whatever you want" morphs from game-like exercise into emotional release into documentary record. For Busa, the journal seems to have been both barf bag and serious business, which accounts for such anomalies as his references to Shanley as "that faggot" or "that fucking faggot" in entries for days when he admits he had no memories of sexual abuse but was making notes for himself and his lawyer that would later form the basis of his legal complaints.

So, in an entry dated at the start of February, Busa writes, "Still no memories." February 8: "Remembered Shanley used to pull me out of class to talk all the time." February 9: "Remembered Shanley leading me to the bathroom. Starting to get sketched out." As he said in his civil deposition, by the 9th he was "getting weirded out." This was all retrospective, as was his entry for the 11th: "Heard Greg was coming out, tidal wave." He gave that last entry an exact time, 1300. It was the wrong time; a simple misremembering, he said.

In the three years between Shanley's indictment and trial, errors of memory would alter the abuse story radically. Ford originally said Shanley began "brutally raping" him at age six, but the catechism teacher that year was his mother, Paula, and she swore in a civil deposition that she noticed nothing awry— no tears, flushed face, dishevelment—and had no memory of sending him to Shanley, or of Shanley pulling him out of class. Ford's earliest abuse was thus recalibrated to a year later. Busa's remained unchanged, although Paula Ford had no memory of him leaving class, either. None of the teachers over the six years in which ghastly crimes allegedly occurred at St. Jean's could support the accusers' claims. Testifying for the prosecution, two repeated this at trial.

Since initially Ford said he was raped weekly from ages six through twelve, and Busa said his own abuse was occurring every week or every other week from ages six through nine, and both of them said that often Shanley removed them from class with their friend Anthony Driscoll, this was a lot of rape for the church pastor to engineer and conceal on his busiest day of the week, and a lot of class disruption (regular removal of one-fourth of the students) for no one to notice. Such dereliction on the part of teachers would be especially remarkable since Massachusetts in the 1980s was gripped by lurid and well-publicized (though false) tales of child molestation at the Fells Acres Day School, and Shanley had been famously controversial for years before coming to St. Jean's. Simply shuffling children around to various unlocked rooms unnoticed, between Masses, when worshippers milled about along with ushers, lectors, Eucharistic ministers, practicing choir members and musicians, custodians, deacons—not to mention other priests and parishioners at the rectory—would have been a feat worthy of a magician.

Over time the story grew more reasonable. Ford revised his memories downward: seventy rapes, then a few, then not always involving penile penetration; then he and Anthony and the other man who was part of the original complaint didn't have to remember anymore. Dropping them was the prosecution's smartest move. Busa's memories of abuse also faded, so that at trial the jury would hear about only a few instances, thin on detail, vague as to time and less elaborate than first claimed. On the stand, Busa's memory continued to degenerate. He could not recall that he'd ever touched the priest. He could not recall being forced to perform fellatio. Judge Neel simply dropped the relevant counts from the charges.

Assistant DA Lynn Rooney ascribed such revisions of memory to a phenomenon whereby a person, having suffered total amnesia as a result of traumatic experience, "could remember something, find it too painful and then re-forget it." There is no evidence for such a phenomenon—or indeed for "massive repression"—in almost fifty years of research on memory and trauma, involving 120 studies and more than 14,000 persons with documented experiences of rape, sexual abuse, torture, death camps, war or other horrors.[2]

About the teachers' lack of memory, Rooney told the jury, "People remember what's important to them"; being taken off and raped was important only to Busa. That being the theory (despite Busa's own nineteen-year absence of memory), not only was every contradictory witness's memory irrelevant but a teacher's observational experience and responsibility for care were too. Four of Busa's classmates testified that the class was chaotic, that kids who misbehaved were sent from the room, and Busa misbehaved. Three said they didn't remember Father Shanley removing students. One, Brendan Moriarty, said the class got rowdy only as the kids got older (when, according to Busa, Shanley did not pull him from class, and the abuse amounted to a "caress," like a passing pat on the bum). Moriarty said that he recalled Busa leaving the class with Shanley once, and that he himself once misbehaved and went to the priest, who told him, "Shape up, be good, don't give the teacher a hard time."

What jurors were left with, then, was Busa himself, crying on the stand, begging to be released from cross-examination, surly and combative with Shanley's attorney, Frank Mondano. Busa had asked Judge Neel to bar the use of his name in court and the media, yet in 2002 he gave numerous interviews, posing for pictures and noting in his journal that he was miffed when *The New York Times* gave him only fleeting attention. The judge denied Busa's request, but the same newspapers that had freely used his name while building their case against Shanley, and that had just successfully challenged his request, turned demure in their trial coverage, referring to Busa as simply "the victim."

Mondano kicked up clouds of dust around Busa's memories and life story. His childhood acquaintance with violence had nothing to do with Shanley: "I was always punished," Busa had said in his deposition. His mother abandoned him emotionally, sometimes struck him; he rarely saw her after the divorce. His father beat him every time he got a report card, kicking him in the neck once, in the lower back, throwing him against a wall, slapping him. At sixteen he was tossed from the house, and spent part of high school sleeping outdoors. He started using steroids because he didn't like his body. He claimed to have played "semi-pro" baseball, but that was not true. He was unhappy in the Air Force, and had been looking for an exit. He did badly in military career development tests, Mondano said, and a superior officer wrote in one report, "If I was walking down a dark alley at night, I wouldn't be comfortable having him behind me."

Mondano argued that there wasn't reasonable doubt here; there was "massive doubt." He was operating under the assumption that the prosecution had to prove its case. From post-trial comments, jurors seem to have operated under the assumption that the defense had to prove that Busa's tears weren't real.

"It must have come back to him," juror Patrick Kierce told the *Globe*. "It was heartfelt." And the prosecution, having staked everything on Busa, turned the trip-ups of his life, oddities of character and contradictions in his testimony into further proof of abuse and sincerity. As Rooney said, if Busa had wanted to lie, "it would have been a better lie."

Busa didn't confront Shanley again at sentencing. Rooney read his statement. In it he wished for Shanley to die a slow, painful death in prison, "whether by natural causes or otherwise." Busa's wife, Theresa, who works for the Newton Police Department, and his father, who works for the Department of Corrections, had already intimated similar wishes. Signaling awareness of the criminal hierarchies governing prison justice, Paul Busa took care to add: "He is a pedophile, possibly the worst ever. He is a founding member of NAMBLA and openly advocated sex between men and little boys."

Dr. James Chu

In the trial's aftermath, *setback* was the word circulating among scientists, science-sensitive lawyers and citizens concerned about the repercussions of repressed memory claims. The setback occurred long before the verdict, actually, for if anyone but the defense had ever respected logic and law—meaning science and the admissibility of evidence grounded in verifiable research—the case against Shanley would never have proceeded. And if the defense had expended as much energy unmasking the junk science on which Busa's story depended as it did trying to discredit Busa himself, the outcome might have been different.

That is a mighty *might*. So many forces needed Shanley convicted, if only as payback for those "other things," or as symbolic sacrifice for all the priests who got away. The defense needed someone, preferably the judge, who would dispassionately evaluate the science relative to repressed memory and recognize that however fervently Busa may believe he lived in a state of amnesia for nineteen years and has now recovered his memory, there is no more support for that notion (absent a head injury, intoxication or other neurological impairment) than there is for the belief that space aliens abduct humans, insert anal probes and so on; and therefore no more support for legal claims dependent on those beliefs.

Judge Neel would not risk being labeled the judge who let the monster go by ruling recovered memory inadmissible. In a pretrial hearing he relied on a psychologist, Dr. Daniel Brown, whose testimony has been deemed unreliable in at least two states, and some of whose sources have been revealed as dangerous frauds in successful malpractice suits. Neel punted to the jury, thus to the narrative train of story, character, conflict and emotion. What disturbed defenders of science was the perception the trial may have left that in psychiatry not only is repressed memory accepted, if controversial, but its adherents have the edge in the controversy, with critics the marginal naysayers.

The opposite is true, yet Court TV advanced the lie relentlessly. The prosecution's expert witness, a confederate of Dr. Brown called Dr. James Chu, said repression and recovery of the type Busa claimed were "not at all rare." He said he's treated thousands of people for dissociative amnesia, or dissociated memory. The terms are less popularly linked with mass hysteria; Chu said he preferred them as more "neutral" than *repressed memory*. He spoke in reasoned tones about the mysterious mechanism that admittedly "doesn't make a lot of intuitive sense," but that nevertheless somehow causes people who have been seriously and repeatedly traumatized to erase all knowledge of the trauma until another mysterious mechanism unlocks the memory. Outlandish claims would raise questions, he said. He described his process of corroboration in terms of a clinician's alchemy, determining whether everything a patient says "make[s] sense in terms of trying to establish a reasonable and believable personal narrative." Because one believable narrative, now having attained the level of folk knowledge, begins with effects (a personal history of anger, instability, failure, addiction and the like) and from them deduces one cause (childhood sexual abuse), Busa's story naturally makes sense, the "common sense" the prosecution urged the jury to use as its guide in reaching a verdict.

Among Chu's qualifications as an expert is his former leadership of the International Society for the Study of Dissociation. At the time of trial he was editing its journal. An organization peppered with believers in satanic conspiracies, it was previously known as the International Society for the Study of Multiple Personality and Dissociation, co-founded in 1983 by Bennett Braun, one of Chu's mentors. Braun was a key figure in promulgating the theory of repressed memory (an idea Freud had pursued early on but ultimately rejected). He ran the country's first dissociative disorder clinical unit and promoted belief in satanic ritual abuse—also in a cult involving, among others, the Ku Klux Klan, the US military, the Mafia and FTD Florists. Braun's prominence as an expert ended in 1997 with a $10.6 million settlement of a lawsuit brought by a patient who went to see him for post-partum depression and came to believe, under hypnosis and memory therapy, that she was a flesh-eating satanic priestess.

The bizarre nonsense at the root of Chu's pedigree was not information available to the jury. On cross-examination, Mondano did not force Chu to acknowledge that the only "studies" supporting dissociative amnesia involve case reports from clinicians like Chu, or surveys of patients whose only evidence is their own claim. He did not confront Chu with the extensive research on documented trauma victims showing no evidence of such amnesia, or with surveys showing that dissociative amnesia is rejected by a majority of board-certified psychiatrists. He did not quiz Chu about the distorting effect of journaling and did not enter Busa's journal into evidence, the only document jurors requested during deliberations. Mondano did get Chu to admit that "there can be memories for events that did not occur." But he did not dissect the magical, hence untestable, thinking at the heart of repressed memory belief in another of Chu's statements: "There are patients who report no amnesia, and I don't know whether they in fact have no amnesia or that they just haven't yet remembered something that they forgot."

Forgetting was the prosecution's tool. Rooney repeatedly conflated the common human experiences of *not thinking* about something, or forgetting some extraneous details around a traumatic event, with *being unable* to remember that trauma at all—the "really pervasive amnesia" endorsed by Chu. The rational thus collapsed into the irrational, and seemed to ratify it. The defense failed to untangle the two, and then mishandled its only witness, Elizabeth Loftus, whose experiments on the processes of memory-making and the ease with which people can come to believe false memories have made her a formidable force in the memory wars in and out of court. On cross-examination Loftus mentioned a study by Richard McNally and colleagues at Harvard in which people with plainly false memories—abduction by aliens and spaceship experimentation—not only expressed total conviction (like Busa) but experienced surging heart rates, sweaty palms and facial grimaces when "remembering" their alien ordeals.[3] Busa testified that he had felt physically sick thinking about the abuse; so did abductees. He expressed intense emotion; so did abductees. Loftus had opened the door for the jury to think about how something unreal and untrue can come to seem excruciatingly real. Mondano shut the door by declining further questions on redirect.

Things are still too fresh to know whether the setback fears are founded, or whether, as R. Christopher Barden, a lawyer and psychiatrist who represented the suit against Bennett Braun, argues, the Shanley case was an anomaly. Trend lines are encouraging. From 1992 to 1994, 354 lawsuits based on recovered memory were filed in US civil and criminal courts. From 1995 to 1997, there were ninety-one; from 2000–04, twenty. One of the reasons for the decline—apart from a wave of successful malpractice suits against therapists whose memory treatments turned ordinarily unhappy women into quivering, pill-popping invalids—was a 1993 Supreme Court decision, in *Daubert v. Merrel Dow Pharmaceuticals*, stating that scientific expert testimony must be both relevant and reliable to be admissible.

Another decision, in 1999, extended the ruling to all expert testimony in federal courts, emphasizing the courts' gatekeeping responsibility toward evidence. Since the mid-1990s, states have adopted similar standards, and judges have been dismissing cases or overturning convictions based on recovered memories, often after pretrial hearings featuring legal-scientific teams. Such justice is not cheap. Barden, a proponent of the science-intensive approach, successfully led a team of five full-time defense lawyers and seven national experts in a monthlong landmark Daubert hearing in Rhode Island in 1999. A North Carolina ruling the previous year conveys the ascendant attitude in the courts: "There has been no general acceptance in the relevant scientific community of the theory of repressed memory"; hence, it is inadmissible, junk science.[4]

And yet even with the most science-savvy defense, Paul Shanley might have got no better than faith-based justice. Anticlericalists might say it serves him right. He'd had sex, and he lied about it. He railed openly against the Catholic hierarchy's sexual politics, but never disowned the institution. Caring little for human frailty, Shanley's deriders say simply that he is a hypocrite and predator.

In 1970, Shanley used to say Mass at midnight for freaks and street people in a Boston storefront under a banner proclaiming, "Go in peace, and may the peace of Christ disturb you profoundly." One night, police raided the place, drove out the longhairs and shut it down, in the middle of Mass. No one in polite society or the archdiocese complained. Wrong peace, wrong Christ, Shanley says now, thirty-five years later, in prison, where he thinks a lot about the religious revivalism that has elevated emotion over evidence in far weightier arenas than the Middlesex County Courthouse: WMDs, Saddam and 9/11, creationism, heterosexuality as nature's iron law. Far more information demolishing those myths has been far more widely circulated than has been mustered to unseat the myth of repressed memory; nevertheless, belief—that common sense—holds tight to itself. In this case, before there was a case, belief was heaped upon belief, pressed down, shaken together, running over. All those years as a priest Shanley was, one might say, life's contradictions incarnate, but somehow he had seen no contradiction between faith and justice. Prosecution, trial, finally conviction, have disabused him of some old certainties.

(2005)

11

Sexual Healing

In the beginning was sex. And sex begat skill, and skill (or its absence) begat judgement, and judgement begat insecurity, and insecurity begat doctors' visits, which begat treatments, which have flourished into a multibillion-dollar industry, so that sex between men and women is today almost inconceivable without the shadow of disorder, dysfunction, the "little blue pill" or myriad other medical interventions designed to bring sex back to some longed-for beginning again: a state of confirmed healthfulness, the illusion of normal.

Sex has been missing from the health care debate. A shame, because sexual health and disputes over its meaning reveal most nakedly the problem at the core of a medical system that requires profit, huge profit, hence sickness, or people who can come to believe they are sick or deformed or lacking and therefore in need of a pill, a procedure or device. Case in point: female sexual dysfunction (FSD), said now to afflict great numbers of women— 43 percent according to some, 70 percent according to others, an "epidemic" in the heterosexual bedroom according to Oprah. Ca-ching!

More on that in a moment, but first a bit about FSD's precursor, hysteria, and the rustic science of bringing women off.

In my room is an artifact of late nineteenth-century medicine, a heavy wooden captain's chair with a difference: from below the seat, a cast-iron lever extends up alongside each arm, within easy grasp of the sitter. Work the levers forward and back, and powerful springs activate a mechanism to rock or jolt the sitter (depending on the vigor of the thrust) in a manner meant to produce the healthful effects of horseback riding for ladies suffering from fatigue, insufficient exercise and "pelvic congestion."

This particular jolting chair was found in Chester, Vermont, by an antiques-dealer friend called Gilbert Ruff, but its provenance as an invention is said to reach back to a fabled arena of psychosexual medicine, the Salpêtrière hospital in Paris, and to Jean-Martin Charcot, teacher of Freud and father of modern neurology. Charcot was an enthusiast for the idea that women with a grab bag of complaints, from irritability to sleeplessness to sexual fantasies and ungratified desire, were diseased. Hysteroneurasthenic disorder was the name for their sickness then. For some, he prescribed long train trips over rough trackbeds. If they took another doctor's advice and leaned forward in the rail carriage, they might have got surprising relief. Such journeys were impractical, though, so a more homely vibration therapy emerged.

Various iterations of the jolting chair entered commercial self-help markets. Mine was manufactured in New York, and advertisements promoted it to strengthen "the parts that are usually most neglected by the fair beings." Now a woman might enjoy the chair's humpy bounce in a room of her own, varying the intensity, parting her legs, leaning forward and breathing deep, even calibrating her motions to the rhythms of a French dance tune, or gavotte, written for the purpose. The jolt never proved as efficient, though, at achieving the "hysterical paroxysm" or otherwise-named form of relief that doctors or midwives had been inducing since at least the time of Galen simply with their fingers. The jolting chair was soon consigned to the curio attic, outperformed by pulsing water cures and that ultimate women's aid, the vibrator, also invented by a doctor, who advised that, although his Manipulator could be beneficial in relieving pelvic congestion, those supervising its use ought to guard against women's "overindulgence."[1]

As Rachel Maines argues in her delightful book *The Technology of Orgasm*, making patients out of sexually unsatisfied women was good business. The afflicted would neither die nor be cured but required regular treatments, weekly, sometimes daily, for an hour or even three. By one 1863 estimate, she writes, massage therapies accounted for three-quarters of some physicians' business. Diddling women was work—"the job nobody wanted," she says—abstracted from sex (i.e., robust progression from male hard-on to vaginal penetration to male orgasm) and requiring time and skill. With the vibrator, Maines hypothesizes, doctors' productivity soared, as sixty-minute visits shrank to ten or five, raising more revenue from more patients, until the device became so technologically refined, popular and multipurpose (Sears marketed a home vibrator with attachments for beating eggs, churning butter, operating a fan) that the medical profession had worked itself out of a job. Miraculously the sick had been healed by the time the first vibrator popped up in porno in the 1920s.

Some sexologists and historians have blasted Maines for advancing an idea for which the evidence is patchy, debatable, unclear or nonexistent. Her footnotes have been challenged, along with her use of antique medical sources, her understanding of nineteenth-century medical attitudes toward female sexuality and her interpretation of evidence. Iwan Rhys Morus, author of *Shocking Bodies: Life, Death and Electricity in Victorian England*, tells me, "I can safely say that I have come across nothing in my researches on late nineteenth-century electricity and the body that lends any support at all to Maines' argument." Maines concedes that a lot of conjecture goes into creating a narrative from patent language, doctors' statements, manufacturers' marketing plans and fragments in medical texts where women's orgasm is de-eroticized, or "socially camouflaged," as she puts it.[2]

Something did happen on the way from the doctor's lab to the home. Leap across the decades, and that trajectory is positively progressive in that, willy-nilly, medicalization marched toward putting sexuality into women's hands, into their heads in terms of body knowledge, and into the mix of culture, personal relations and a polymorphous physicality beyond biological function alone. The white coats came out again with Masters and Johnson but bumped into a counterculture that pushed against their categorizations of normal or not. Every 1970s woman might not have attended one of Betty Dodson's masturbation workshops; every man was hardly reborn as an attentive, exploring lover. But nor was everyone straight, in all senses of the word, and the fluidity of sexuality as part of the great mishmash of human experience was out in the culture. It was sexual and also political. Today the cultural air is thick with sex, but the rhetoric of freedom largely serves a commodified notion of sexual performance. The liberationist politics has dropped out, and without politics we're all just patients, or potential patients.

How else to explain that a reality as old as God—that the vast majority of women do not climax simply through intercourse— has re-emerged as dysfunction? Or that another grab bag of indicators of dissatisfaction and low desire is renamed hypoactive sexual desire disorder, for which a female Viagra or a testosterone patch or cream or nasal spray must be developed? How to explain that middle-aged women go under the knife for vaginal rejuvenation (basically pussy tightening) and that young women go under the knife for laser labiaplasty (basically genital mutilation), saying that they want only to feel pretty, normal, and to raise their chances of orgasm through intercourse? How to explain that a doctor like Stuart Meloy of North Carolina has even one patient to test his Orgasmatron, an electrode threaded up a woman's spinal cord and controlled by a hand-held button that, Meloy promises, can make her clit throb with excitement during intercourse so as to reach the grail of mutually assured orgasm?[3]

A terrific documentary by Liz Canner, *Orgasm Inc.*, addresses those questions in terms of corporate medicine and the creation of need via pseudo-feminist incitements to full sexual mastery, as expressed by Dr. Laura Berman and other shills for the drug industry. Female sexual dysfunction, it turns out, was wholly created by drug companies hoping to make even bigger money off women than they have off men in the comparatively smaller market for erectile dysfunction drugs. That's capitalism; that's its nature. The more obstinate question is why so many people are willing to be its slaves, and whether a resistant politics can grow up to say not just "We want in" to health care but "We want out" of the profit system and, on the sex front, out of a medical model that elevates a doctor over "playing doctor" or a more sensual ease with oneself and others.

"So many times I don't think sex is a matter of health," Dr. Leonore Tiefer told me the other day. She is a sex therapist and founder of the New View Campaign to challenge the medicalization of sex. "I think it's more like dancing or cooking. Yes, you do it with your body. You dance with your body too. That doesn't mean there's a department of dance in the medical school. You don't go to the doctor to learn to dance. And in dancing school the waltz class is no more normal than the samba class." You might not be a good dancer by some scale of values. You might not get the steps right, or do steps at all. But even in wheelchairs people learn to move to the music.

(2009)

12

Through a Lens Starkly

"Taking nude pictures of yourself, nothing good can come of it."
—Police Captain George Seranko,
Greensburg, Pennsylvania

The police captain might be right, in one sense. Particularly for the unskilled or ill-equipped, getting the angle right, the focus and lighting just so, might be an effort—too much for the unsteady hand, the shy poser, the butterfingers, the compositionally challenged. Much better to take nude pictures with someone else, to make a game of it, an *amuse-bouche* before the banquet, or maybe in place of it. Safe sex unless you're a teenager, in which case someone might want to arrest you.

Captain Seranko made his observation after three girls and three boys at Greensburg Salem High School were charged with child pornography. The girls, ages fourteen and fifteen, are charged with taking pictures of themselves, nude or semi-nude; the boys, fifteen, sixteen and seventeen, with receiving them. The cell phone that lodged these dangerous images had been confiscated at school—not an outrageous exercise of authority had school officials merely stashed the phone in a drawer, unmolested, until the student could collect it. But the officials had to snoop. One can picture their fevered actions, fumbling with the student's phone, opening one screen, then another, maddened as they press the wrong buttons and must begin again, without the nimbleness of youth—curses!—their otherwise desiccated imaginations now fertile with anticipated indecency; scrolling through the teen's pictures and messages, expectant that their suspicions will be confirmed, certain that all they want is to protect the children ... And yet, there they are, instant oglers, prying into places not meant for them, gazing at images not made for them, drenching the relationship between school authority and student in sex.

The recent attention to teen sexting has focused quite a lot on the presumed self-exploitation of kids, not so much on the prurient reflex of grown-ups who spy on and punish them. It has dwelt quite a lot on the traps of technology, not so much on the desires that precede picking up a camera. Quite a lot on the question of whether the teens are sex offenders or merely stupid, sluttish or mean, not so much on the freedom to see and be. Quite a lot on the legal meaning of images, not so much on the ways that making them might delight, or on the cultural freak-out that colors law, images and how they are perceived.

No one knows how many kids are poised for long sentences, life sentences (a possibility under federal law), plea deals that cast them into the pariah-land of sex offenders. Prosecutors have gone after teens in at least Ohio, Wisconsin, Florida, Oklahoma and Pennsylvania. School and police investigators have searched students' phones, and now that the National Campaign to Prevent Teen and Unplanned Pregnancy has estimated that one in five teenagers is taking and sending nude or semi-nude selfies, and four in ten are sending sexed-up text messages, it can be assumed that kids generally are at risk of surveillance or worse.

Across the state from where Captain Seranko was discoursing on nude photographs, District Attorney George Skumanick, Jr., was threatening sixteen girls and four boys with felony charges. Officials at the Tunkhannock Area High School had confiscated phones, discovered about 100 photos and called the DA, who told reporters that the kids could face seven years in prison. Skumanick convened parents to say that their kids were involved in a child porn investigation but could avoid being nailed by submitting to a ten-hour re-education program, paying $100 and agreeing to an "informal adjustment" (in effect, a guilty plea before judgment in the juvie system), which would put them on probation for at least six months and subject them to random drug tests. If the kids get in trouble while on probation, they could end up with a juvenile record of a sex offense. And once Pennsylvania amends its laws to make sex offender registration apply to juveniles over fourteen, as required by the federal Adam Walsh Act, those laws will apply retroactively—meaning kids with records will have their names and pictures displayed on the state's sex offender website for at least ten years.

All but three families submitted to the DA's coercion. One father complained that his daughter was pictured simply wearing a bathing suit; Skumanick called the image "provocative," and she is being re-educated, writing a report on "Why it was wrong" to pose in her bathing suit, answering, "How did [it] affect the victim? the school? the community?" and learning "What it means to be a girl in today's society."

MaryJo Miller and Jami Day refused to inflict this madness on their daughters, who at thirteen were photographed lying side by side in their thick white training bras, while one, Marissa Miller, held a phone to her ear and the other, Grace Kelly, flashed a peace sign. Another mother, identified as Jane Doe, also refused on behalf of her seventeen-year-old daughter, Nancy, who was photographed coming out of the shower topless, with a towel wrapped around her. When Miller saw the picture of Marissa and Grace, taken during a slumber party at her house two years ago, she laughed and called the girls "goofballs"; to the DA they were "provocative," and he moved to prosecute. The Pennsylvania ACLU won a federal injunction barring Skumanick from filing charges against the three girls; Skumanick appealed, and the ACLU's Witold Walczak expects the case to be tied up for a year.[1]

"If this is criminal, you better go after Sears and J.C. Penney for their Sunday circulars," Walczak said of the photo of Marissa and Grace. A good line, but it leaves some questions floating in the spring air. What even defines what's criminal? Somewhere out in the wide world of sex there may be someone flushed and warm poring over those Sunday circulars, the torsos lined up in their mature brassieres or big lady briefs, just as somewhere a latter-day Humbert Humbert's pulse is quickening at the image of girls cavorting in school uniforms. Rationality invites us to say, So what? Fantasy has its place apart. Except the obsession with child porn and predators has ground fantasy into the dirt, and rationality flees like a hunted thing. The law invites us, instead, as the legal scholar Amy Adler brilliantly dissected in a 2001 *Columbia Law Review* article, to think like a pedophile, to read the lascivious, the sexually provocative, the potentially exploitative into almost any image.

"As everything becomes child pornography in the eyes of the law—clothed children, coy children, children in settings where children are found—perhaps everything really does become pornographic," Adler wrote in "The Perverse Law of Child Pornography." DA Skumanick only seems bizarre. In fact, he and school officials are doing what judges and juries in child porn cases have been doing for years, lingering over images, searching for signs of the erotic or proto-erotic, pondering *What if? Maybe so? One might think* ... and welding the child to sex.

But what of the teenagers—not Marissa or Grace or Nancy, but others, perhaps those kids in Greensburg—who mean to be sexy, for their boyfriend, their girlfriend, themselves? There is nothing new about teenagers being sexual and taking pictures, or indulging in fantasy; nothing new about the mixed thrill of having a secret and risking exposure, or sharing that secret, sometimes inelegantly. The new means of production carry pitfalls as surely as the fleeting passions of a teenager. The rude boy documenting a girl going down on him unawares, to share behind her back with his buddies, needs some schooling, but her problem, and his too, started before the shutter clicked. Privacy is not trifling, but sexual, or any, sensitivity is not achieved by threats. The girl who has mastered the nude self-portrait may later regret its mass circulation, but she may also have got comfortable in her skin while taking pictures. Maybe the Polaroid Land Camera should make a comeback. It is just possible, though, that the fifteen-year-olds are envisioning, however inchoately, a saner world than the one the grown-ups lecturing them have constructed, one where their life chances won't be ruined by a "compromising" photograph on the internet. If sexting really is as common as is claimed, it's more likely to proliferate than to abate, and then the issue won't be scandal or embarrassment but banality.

The truth is, a lot of good can come of taking nude pictures. Not so much the image as the act, the practice of seeing and being seen, the play of erotic imagination among friends. Remember play? Remember dalliance? Remember the captured glimpse of a lover stripped and weak with need? Grown-ups, don't get comfortable. A bill in the Massachusetts state legislature proposes to criminalize nude pictures of people over sixty and people who are disabled, for their own protection.

(2009)

13

Judgement Days

The photographers had worried all day about the fading of the light. It was already past 6, and four of them had deployed under a live oak in front of the Lawrence H. Williams Judicial Center at Fort Hood, waiting for a sentence in the court-martial of Pfc. Lynndie England. The grass crunched beneath them in a Central Texas landscape unrelieved by nature or human arts, parched in the 107-degree heat, uncommonly, achingly beige. Inside, the court was cool. MPs in battle dress uniform played cards to pass the time. In the jury room five men, officers in full dress greens festooned with insignia of merit and rank, major to full colonel, deliberated over fitting punishment for the twenty-two-year-old private first class, the "woman with the leash" in the Abu Ghraib prison abuse scandal who, the prosecution argued, had done more to disgrace their uniform than anyone within memory's reach. The two prosecuting attorneys, Army captains, strode out of their office from time to time as they waited; since winning conviction the day before on charges in this last of the torture trials that had commenced nine months earlier at Fort Hood, they exhibited a new ease. Reporters noted this, and had just begun talking among themselves about placing bets on the sentence when word came that the jury had a decision. It was 6:55 p.m.; day-for-night spotlights were readied outdoors.

England entered the courtroom as she had each day of trial, encased in her dress uniform, moving as if to remind herself to appear purposeful. Her school psychologist, a man who has known her since she was a twitchy, electively mute four-year-old, carried her infant son into the courtroom. "The best thing to come out of Iraq," England's mother had said of the blond, black-lashed boy, whose father was convicted here the previous January and whose mother now beamed back at him from the defense table, miming patty-cake and mouthing I-love-yous while spectators took their seats anticipating the final file-in and verdict of the jury. The baby squealed, whether with joy or agitation it was impossible to tell, and was removed just before the sentence was read. Within five minutes it was done. England, who'd been standing at attention, heaved for breath against the defense table, then cried in her mother's skinny arms. It was a sentence less harsh than it could have been but harsher than she had hoped: demotion to private, forfeiture of all pay, dishonorable discharge and three years in prison, three times—plus her baby's life. The child was brought in, as sparkling as his mother was numb, the only living being there unmindful of his own shipwrecked chances, and the courtroom was cleared. It was 7:35 by the time "the face of the scandal" finally stepped into the spectral light, puffy and blotched red now, the barest hint of the girl with the bowl cut and boyish frame whose snapshot smile the world had met less than two years before. In a case defined by pictures, one more would stand as the only record of this moment that mattered: Lynndie England flanked by MPs and inching down the long path from a law court, cuffed and in leg irons.

This is how the story ends, the simple story, about seven Army reservists in a Military Police unit who, in the fall of 2003 on the night shift at Abu Ghraib prison in Iraq, abused detainees and smiled for photographs, or took photographs, or watched and said nothing; and whose photographs, reproduced round the world in the spring of 2004, brought shame upon the US military, the Bush administration and its conduct of the war. Two besides England had been convicted in separate trials: Charles Graner, the father of her child and a former corporal, sentenced to ten years in Leavenworth; and Sabrina Harman, a former specialist depicted, like England, smiling and giving the thumbs-up with naked Iraqi men, sentenced to six months. Four others pled guilty as part of agreements with the prosecution: Ivan Frederick, former staff sergeant, sentenced to eight-and-a-half years in Leavenworth; Javal Davis, former sergeant, sentenced to six months; Jeremy Sivits, former specialist, sentenced to one year; and Megan Ambuhl, former specialist, discharged from the Army with no prison time. They were charged, variously, with conspiracy, maltreatment, dereliction of duty, assault, indecent acts, lying to Army investigators and taking pictures of detainees.

How the story begins is, as in every tragedy in which human weakness collides with historical force, a more tangled thing. At this late date it is unnecessary to reprise the volumes of government reports and journalists' accounts outlining the gestation of US torture policy, from September 11, 2001, to the president's February 7, 2002, directive suspending adherence to the Geneva Conventions in the Global War on Terror; from Afghanistan to Guantánamo to Iraq; from the Pentagon's "special-access program" of off-the-books abduction and assassination to the White House "torture memos" to the CIA's "extraordinary rendition" of terror suspects to the dungeons of foreign lands. The product of all this investigative industry is an uncomplicated fact, swiftly assimilated by the culture and entered in the column of what *everyone knows*.

In the Abu Ghraib trials the fact that, by official policy, America is a torture state and everyone knows was both critical background and inadmissible evidence. As to the ease with which the public arena has adjusted to this knowledge, two bracketing events beyond the Texas courtroom suffice as examples. On January 6, 2005, one day before jury selection in Charles

Graner's trial, the Senate Judiciary Committee was conducting televised hearings on the nomination of Alberto Gonzales—who as White House counsel authorized the legal struts for US torture policy—engaging him in debate over the application of pain before recommending him for the highest legal office in the land. On October 5, 2005, a week after Lynndie England's September 27 sentencing, the White House threatened a veto of any military spending bill that came to the president with a provision banning "cruel, inhuman or degrading treatment" of detainees. The Senate passed the ban, whereupon Vice President Dick Cheney and CIA director Porter Goss pressed for a cruelty exemption for CIA and other extra-military "clandestine counterterrorism operations conducted abroad."

The judge for the courts-martial, Col. James Pohl, would allow none of this larger picture into the trial phase of the proceedings at Fort Hood, a decision that, while prudent in a strict legal sense, consigned the Lawrence H. Williams Judicial Center to the world of make-believe. A narrative that makes sense only as part of a deeper story would be presented in fragments: a few minutes, a few hours of a few nights that were recorded in a few photographs. The bleeding specter of Iraq would hover over the proceedings, mostly as a mission that the photographs had grievously harmed.

Long before Judge Pohl's decision, it was clear that these would be trials by rank and photograph. As determined by the Army's internal review process and the convening authority—in this case, Lieut. Gen. Thomas F. Metz—only the lowest-ranked soldiers would be court-martialed, and only photographs they took that supported the government's limited narrative would be introduced. Anything that threatened to open more disturbing doors or lead down weedy paths was eliminated. Actions that were worse than or as bad as the charged activity, but were not photographed, did not make it onto the charge sheet. Confusion about the chain of command at Abu Ghraib, between Military Police and Military Intelligence, would become a leitmotif of the proceedings; confusion about allowable interrogation techniques would surface as an issue, then recede. "A red herring," the prosecution called defense efforts to explore the regimen of information-gathering at the prison.

So long as there were going to be trials, this duality—the contrasting demands of legal justice, rightly focused on direct evidence of an individual's deeds, and historical justice, considering such deeds as part of the collective enterprise that spawned them—was inevitable. The judge strove to finesse it by giving defense attorneys more leeway to fill in the story in the sentencing phase, during which mitigating or extenuating evidence was allowed. But the basic disjunction hobbled everyone. For the prosecuting attorneys, it meant their loftiest rhetoric of responsibility, honor and the rule of law had to be a lie. For defense attorneys, it meant they would concede that the pictures documented the deeds but would then try to raise doubt among the jury by slipping as much of that fuller story into the trial phase as their skill and the judge's temper would allow. For the members of the court—that is, the three jury panels—it meant there was effectively only one choice: conviction or nullification of the law. Since mustering the independence to exercise jury nullification in a military court, on a military base, was practically impossible for these career military officers, conviction was foreordained.

That everyone who wasn't thinking magically had to know it was foreordained added to the otherworldliness of the proceedings. For the decreasing number of reporters on the scene as the cases unfolded throughout the year, and especially for the two of us who witnessed all three full trials—Graner's in January, Harman's in May and England's in September, along with her aborted guilty plea in May—the proceedings became like a recurring opera whose familiar libretto is nevertheless compelling, whose players make their entrances and exits but here with a new detail, there with a different shading, and whose end, when it finally comes, leaves not the satisfied sigh of resolution but the shrill squeak of warped and homely beginnings.

Because the prosecution contended in each trial but explicitly in England's that "really, there are two sets of victims ... those men who've had their dignity stripped," meaning particular Iraqi prisoners, "and all those other men stationed in Iraq," meaning the Army men (and, no doubt, women) whose honor and safety were compromised by the resulting scandal, Fort Hood became both host to the trials and representative of that larger class of presumed victims. By implication, it was also the exemplary general model against which the behavior of the "morally corrupt" defendants might be contrasted.

Soldiers call Fort Hood the Army's "most deployable" post. It is its largest post. About an hour's drive northeast of the Bush ranch in Crawford, it houses two divisions, the 4th Infantry and the 1st Cavalry. Any of its 40,000 soldiers who have not already been to Iraq at least once can expect to be there soon. Access to its 340 square miles is controlled by armed guards at checkpoints, so I wasn't supposed to have just happened onto it one day in early January. While getting my bearings on the western outskirts of the post, I turned from one dismal road onto another and another until I found myself in what looked like an ordinary subdivision of two-story homes in the ordinary neutral tones, followed by similar subdivisions, with a school here, a playground there, a gas station with the usual SUVs and the usual busy moms filling up; except the streets where they lived were all named for conquered Indian tribes, and when the names became Battalion and Old Ironsides and Hell on Wheels, I knew I wasn't in civilian territory anymore. I drove on, hoping to be mistaken for one of those moms, waving at soldiers who passed, glad that my rental car had a yellow ribbon decal and wondering, as the road got muddier and the country more wild, as I came upon CATTLE CROSSING signs and rangeland studded with bunkers or targets, how long my determined air of casual confidence would carry me past the soldiers, now outfitted in what appeared to be full battle gear. I considered pressing on. I rehearsed excuses, then rejected them. More anxious than curious, I turned back, toward streets with names again: Warrior Way and Motor Pool and 761st Tank Battalion, where acres of bland block buildings were punctuated by banners urging SEEK, STRIKE, DESTROY or LIVE THE ARMY VALUES AND THE WARRIOR ETHOS. I came to Tank Destroyer Boulevard and recognized it as the military extension of a commercial strip I'd driven on earlier in Killeen, the post's largest supporting town. I hastened toward the East Gate and the vulgar rickrack of pawnshops and payday loan pits just beyond, on Rancier Avenue.

Like Fort Hood, Killeen sprawls because it can and exists because, by the calculus of national priorities, it must. Approached from the east on US 190, the town resembles any stretch of brand-name restaurants and hotels. Approached at night from the south on Highway 195, Killeen seems swallowed in darkness, with nothing to herald it but lighted orbs floating as if unmoored above the horizon, glowing PAWN, PAWN. By day, every business appears to advertise "Home of the Fort Hood Heroes" or "We Support Our Soldiers." Every public school declares its Army patron: "Fowler Elementary. Adopted by 1st Battalion, 67th Armor."

The post, which contributes as much as $7 billion to the Texas economy, is responsible for the vast majority of Killeen's. Locals debate which party reaps the greater benefit, and because so many landlords, business operators and political fixers are retired military, the lines blur; not so for the lower-ranked soldier, whose place in the scheme is quite clear. Pawnshops groan with "the shiny shit" that single young soldiers buy in the first flush of getting a paycheck, taking loans they can't afford, incurring car payments they can't sustain, then sinking themselves into a vortex of short-term loans with interest as high as 300 percent. Often the Army helps enforce repayment.

Killeen sacrificed itself to military necessity in 1942. Previously it had been an agricultural and ranching town. The government seized the property of 300 families to establish Camp Hood as a tank-destroyer training center during World War II. As the *Killeen Daily Herald* recounted it, "The complete economic foundation of the town, its very reason for existence, vanished in a matter of weeks, replaced by an economy dependent upon the federal government"; everything else was "relegated to the historical archive." Photographs of downtown Killeen in the early decades after the town's transformation present jolly scenes of bustling streets.¹ Today downtown is stripped, its low buildings like white bones against the sky. Killeen killed itself the way so many US cities did, with a highway project and a shopping mall, and then was resurrected as "The City Without Limits," strung along 190. Most of what's alive downtown is Korean, courtesy of the Korean brides of servicemen, and the extended families that followed those brides. Behind signs that the average Anglo cannot read and storefronts covered with white paper or white blinds, lies a brightly stocked grocery, a charming karaoke bar or the twinkling, fragrant dining room of Mama's Hen. Across the street from that restaurant, at the Armed Services YMCA, a mural featuring a combat soldier, the flag and a hand-lettered verse by a Marine Corps chaplain offers immigrants a civics lesson:

> *It is the Soldier, not the reporter,*
> *Who has given us freedom of the press.*
> *It is the Soldier, not the poet,*
> *Who has given us freedom of speech.*
> *It is the Soldier, not the campus organizer,*
> *Who has given us the freedom to demonstrate.*
> *It is the Soldier, not the lawyer,*
> *Who has given us the right to a fair trial.*

It is the Soldier who salutes the flag,
Who serves beneath the flag,
And whose coffin is draped by the flag,
Who allows the protester to burn the flag.

When the Abu Ghraib scandal broke, people wondered, *Why did they take pictures?* During jury selections, at least one battle-creased sergeant would always abandon euphemism and say, *If you're going to do something like that, why would you photograph it?* The simplest explanation is the best. They took pictures because they could. Soldiers in Iraq take pictures like crazy, especially, I was told, where signs instruct them not to. They take pictures because they're bored or want souvenirs. They take pictures of people they arrest (an abrogation of the Geneva Conventions), of fighters they kill (ditto), of bodies they desecrate (a war crime). They email them home, or send them with photos of their wives to a porno website, or string them together and add sound to make commemorative videos.

At trial the pictures of prison cruelty, now without the censoring blur that news media added in deference to the sexual delicacy of the viewing public, were reproduced in packets for each panel member. They were projected onto a screen that hung adjacent to the banked rows of the jury box. They were enlarged on 24"x36" foam core and propped on an easel. During England's trial they were displayed on individual computer monitors in the jury box. At some point in each trial, Judge Pohl advised the panel members that they would be given a CD-ROM containing all the photographs and a DVD of the video to replay privately during deliberations. The government's computer forensics expert had reviewed twelve CDs acquired from soldiers containing 16,000 photographs, and had identified 281 pictures pertinent to the Abu Ghraib investigation. Those used in court were, for the most part, the two dozen or so that made the news in 2004. With lights dimmed, the prosecution opened its case. For each trial, a slide show, lingering over the most sex-charged images: the leash, the human pyramid, the masturbation, the simulated fellatio. In each opening statement, a defining message to weld criminal action with moral degeneracy: "They were laughing, joking around"; "they thought it was funny."

The trials generally made a hash of chronology and the realities of Abu Ghraib, so it is best here to begin where the soldiers of the 372nd Military Police Company did, in October of 2003. By then they had been in Kuwait or Iraq for six months, and were expecting to return home when they got orders to report to Abu Ghraib.

A 280-acre area surrounded by twenty-foot walls, strung with four kilometers of razor wire and overseen by twenty-four guard towers, Abu Ghraib ("Father of the Raven") was designed in 1959 by a civil engineering firm from Mineola, New York. Shortly before the US invasion, it was emptied by Saddam Hussein. The Americans maintained its looted shell briefly as a monument to vanquished tyranny but soon rehabilitated it as the Baghdad Correctional Facility, leaving a good deal of rubble and filth but replacing Saddam's portrait with the slogan AMERICA IS A FRIEND OF ALL IRAQI PEOPLE. To aid the transition, they hired a private-prison executive, Lane McCotter, former director of the Utah Department of Corrections, who resigned in 1997 after a schizophrenic inmate died while shackled naked to a chair for sixteen hours. By the time England and the others arrived, mass arrests, which US troops had begun making a few months before, plus rampant crime amidst anarchy, had populated Abu Ghraib with thousands of inmates. England, twenty at the time, a former cashier at an IGA supermarket in Fort Ashby, West Virginia, later said, "I'd never been in a US prison." Abu Ghraib "was bigger than I thought, ... a lot more prisoners than I expected, not as many guards as I expected." At trial it was estimated that the prisoner-to-guard ratio climbed from 75:1 to 150:1. Soldiers were assigned minimum twelve-hour shifts with no days off. They slept in cells. Early on most got sick with vomiting or diarrhea.

Although an MP unit, the 372nd had no experience guarding prisoners. Its specialty was combat support, escorting convoys, providing security along supply routes. "We were never trained to be police officers," the company commander, Capt. Donald Reese, a home supplies salesman from Pittsburgh, testified. Before coming to Abu Ghraib, the reserve unit had some training in riot control, cell extraction and the use of nonlethal force, he said, but nothing on international law with respect to detainees. A generalized briefing in the States in early 2003 "rushed over everything." Once at the prison, he testified, the unit received no policy letters or written guidance from higher-ups on the treatment of detainees, and, with four missions to run simultaneously in and around Abu Ghraib, he never managed to hold training days.

This matter of training arose frequently throughout the trials, and frequently Capt. Chris Graveline, the lead trial counsel prosecuting England and Harman and the assistant trial counsel in Graner's case, barely contained his outrage as he asked, in one form or another, an obvious question: *What kind of training do soldiers need to know that you don't pile naked detainees into a pyramid, you don't force them to masturbate, you don't drag them by a leash like an animal?* During the trial of Sabrina Harman, a twenty-seven-year-old former assistant manager at Papa John's from Lorton, Virginia, Graveline pointed out that for five months prior to their assignment at Abu Ghraib the soldiers of the 372nd had effectively served as the police force in the town of Al Hillah without specific training and without incident. Indeed, photographs of Harman with the people of Al Hillah could be posters for the war the White House had promised, captured in the perfect smile of this comely blonde American soldier cheek to cheek with a beautiful dark Iraqi boy.

But Abu Ghraib, a city in lockdown, with all the appurtenances of violence but none of the resources, coherence or law associated with organized life, was not Al Hillah.[2] The clear lines and neat boxes of an aerial photograph offered as a prosecution exhibit occluded a fundamental disorder. Inside Abu Ghraib's walls the 372nd found a large tent city called Camp Ganci, meant to hold common criminals; another tent city called Camp Vigilant, meant to house classic prisoners of war; and the many-tiered cellblock compound, called the Hard Site. Technically, the Hard Site's Tier 1 Bravo was reserved for women and children, some arrested as criminals, most merely relatives of detainees swept up for information or because of local vendettas. Tier 1 Alpha was reserved for "high value detainees," those suspected of being insurgents or knowledgeable about the insurgency, who came under the control of Military Intelligence (MI). From defense and government witnesses, however, a picture emerged in which men were mixed with women and children (the youngest, eight); common criminals were mixed with POWs; lunatics were kept beside "MI holds" in isolation cells; targets for interrogation might have been anywhere. "We tried to keep the people with TB off by themselves," Reese testified. Otherwise, "we had no idea what category they were classified in."

Just providing for the prisoners proved overwhelming. The prison barely had water. The food was foul, and sometimes all that prisoners and soldiers had was a boiled egg, a piece of cheese or an Army-issue Meal Ready-to-Eat. Electrical generators would go out, and with them the lights. The Porta-John contractor often wouldn't show up, so toilets overflowed. Sgt. Hydrue Joyner, in charge of the day shift on Tier 1 Alpha, described the heat at times "like ten hairdryers blowing in your face all day long." Maj. David DiNenna, in charge of logistics at the battalion level, struggled for words to describe the stench. He testified that his requests for permanent generators and hand-held communication radios were denied. Prisoners detained in the summer were still there and without winter clothing in December. Medical care and blankets were in short supply. MPs were in short supply. Detainees staged uprisings, weapons were plentiful inside, and the prison was under constant insurgent attack. Joyner sent daily situation reports detailing needs to DiNenna, who sent daily reports to Brig. Gen. Janis Karpinski, head of the 800th MP Brigade, then in charge of prison operations in Iraq. The response, DiNenna said, was always "Got it, we'll work on it," but nothing changed. "We were abandoned," Joyner said.

Chaos and neglect served some purposes. Upon arrival, soldiers of the 372nd who were to work the tier got a tour by MPs from the unit they were replacing; at trial, typical defense inquiries went like this:

Q: "And what did you see?"
A: "Detainees in hoods, cuffed to the bars."
Q: "And your predecessor said that's how MI wanted it?"
A: "Yes."
Q: "You saw detainees wearing women's underwear?"
A: "Yes, sir."
Q: "He was naked, wasn't he?"
A: "Yes, sir."
Q: "And he was handcuffed to his cell?"
A: "Yes, sir."
Q: "Based on your experience, was that normal?"
A: "No, sir, that's illegal."
Q: "Did you raise the issue with your chain of command?"
A: "Yes, sir. Captain Reese told me, 'Follow MI.' Battalion Commander Phillabaum told me, 'Don't worry about it.' Lieutenant Colonel Jordan [MI and commandant of interrogation operations], I was asking him for guidance but never got any. I asked Major Thompson [MI] about rules and regulations, and he basically told me he'd check into it."
Q: "Who did you feel you were working for?"
A: "That's where it got confusing. I took orders from three different places. There was no clear sense of who was responsible ultimately in any given situation."[3]

All of the MPs charged in the scandal except England were assigned to work from 4 p.m. to 4 a.m. in the Hard Site. Reese made S.Sgt. Ivan Frederick the de facto night warden of the site because he was a corrections officer in Virginia. Frederick put Charles Graner, a mere corporal, in charge of Tier 1 Alpha because, though he had been fired from his last prison job in Pennsylvania, he did have experience. Sgt. Davis, from Roselle, New Jersey, worked in Tier 3. Spc. Sivitz, a factory worker and high school baseball coach from Hyndman, Pennsylvania, was a mechanic. Both Davis and Sivitz were on Tier 1 the night of the human pyramid because they had come to help with prisoners who had rioted. Spc. Ambuhl, a laboratory technician from Centreville, Virginia, was a guard on Tier 1 Bravo. Spc. Harman was a runner for Frederick on Tier 1. Pfc. England worked days as a clerk in another part of the prison but came most nights to the Hard Site to be with Graner, then her boyfriend.

It is necessary at this point to interrupt the sober historical narrative in order to dispense with a sub-story, the "soap opera" of Abu Ghraib, which attorneys on both sides occasionally exaggerated for their own purposes, and which, as time passed and the trials failed to produce political bombshells, overtook any larger themes in some of the press. In that story Charles Graner, a charismatic evil genius, then thirty-four, swept the easily led, socially awkward "little hillbilly" Lynndie England off her feet. He encouraged her to humiliate prisoners, to laugh and pose, not as her superior but as the dark god of her affections, and she responded as a girl, a rather dirty girl, who also posed for sex pictures with him and other soldiers at his urging. She became pregnant, the way bad girls do who aren't bad enough, but he, being a very bad boy, had already moved on, to her friend Megan Ambuhl, a fact that prosecutors brought out at his trial while Lynndie, miles away nursing the infant he refused to acknowledge, still pined for him. Megan and Charles had one last stormy night at a Killeen hotel, one last ardent kiss in a waiting room of the judicial center, before he was carted off in shackles. In May, *The New York Times* added to this daytime drama spin-off of the scandal, announcing that Megan and Charles were now Mrs. and Mr., wed by proxy.

This story never deserved as much attention as it got, not just because it was cast as melodrama or because the human dimension is irrelevant to that most stagy collision of private and public interests, the criminal trial. Charles Graner may indeed be a pathological narcissist and sadist. As a prison guard in Pennsylvania, he allegedly put a razor blade in one inmate's food and flooded the cell of another. His first wife got a protection order against him. Lynndie England may have the "overly compliant personality" that her defense described. Born a blue baby with a tongue defect, she refused to speak until kindergarten; and once she did speak, it was only to one person, a teacher's aide, and only when spoken to. On standardized tests, her school psychologist, Dr. Thomas Denne, testified, she registered at the top of the curve in visual comprehension and at the bottom in verbal comprehension, leading to lifelong confusion in apprehending the world. Her cognitive deficits, familiarity with abuse and tendency to model her actions to suit the demands of the person in charge, exhaustively detailed in court, may have made her a fool for love in the worst way.

But the perverse love story always sidled up too close to the Pentagon's theory that the humiliations at Abu Ghraib could be understood as the work of a few deviants. Just how close was illustrated by the Army's initial decision to heap more charges upon England than anyone, confronting this lowest-ranking of the accused soldiers with the possibility of the longest prison sentence, thirty-eight years, largely on the basis of photographic evidence intended to draw a straight line of moral decay from the girl who would blow her boyfriend on camera to a girl who would laugh at prisoners forced to simulate fellatio. Officials at Fort Hood dropped all but one of the consensual indecent act charges when her case was transferred there, and prosecutors ultimately would drop that one as well, but they reserved their most thunderous moral denunciations for England. In his closing argument Capt. Graveline shook a blow-up reproduction of her infamous portrait-with-masturbating-prisoners in the jury's faces, foisting upon them one last close-up of the weird-pixie pose of this small boyish girl, and crying in anguish, "These are men, gentlemen, ... men like us!" Plainly he was irritated that her attorneys had mounted a defense relying heavily on her enthrallment to Graner. But having raised the issue of the defendants' sex life when that was convenient, and advancing a theory of individual aberration, the government had dealt the cards that England's defense chose to play. It was not the most illuminating defense, only the most pathetic, which is soap opera's predictable dead end.

To the extent that biography can help at all in assessing what happened at Abu Ghraib, England's is worth pondering more for those aspects that make her typical rather than exceptional. Dr. Denne testified that from early childhood she had learned to take authority as her guide. For most of her life, obedience and deference worked. Then they didn't. In the purest moment of true feeling the trials would provide, Denne confessed that maybe it had been a mistake simply to teach Lynndie to do as she was told. "We didn't teach her to think!" he said in despair.

Had England been a subject in Stanley Milgram's famous experiments, she would doubtless have continued administering the "electric shock" to the unseen actor pleading for relief on the other side of the wall for as long as the doctor in the white coat told her to. But as Lieut. Col. Michael Russell, then the chief psychologist at Fort Hood, reminded me, "most people obey authority to the point that they will do very questionable things." At trial the judge would emphasize for the panel that distinguishing right from wrong was not England's problem. How it is, though, that people know better but do worse exceeded the jury's scope.

Not to underrate the vertiginous power of love, but England had reason to visit the Hard Site every night without it. Night was the most dangerous time at Abu Ghraib, and as a sergeant with the JAG corps told me, in Iraq "wherever your friends are, that's where you feel safe." It hardly mattered that night was also the freakiest time on Tier 1 Alpha, when prisoners had their clothes taken away, when they were being "stressed out" for interrogations, when Americans without name tags, "OGA"—Other Government Agencies, a euphemism for the CIA—came through the back door bringing prisoners who officially didn't exist ("ghost detainees"), leaving MPs the vaguest instructions. That England might have felt most secure amid the madness is, the sergeant explained, not unlike his feeling most secure at the wall of the Green Zone that was under the heaviest mortar fire: "Safety is extremely relative in Iraq." Also, within an alarmingly short time after taking up residence in the prison, the soldiers on the Tier 1 night shift, and England as well, had accommodated to barbarism.

"They say if you want to cook a frog, you don't just throw him in a pot of boiling water," Sabrina Harman's lead attorney, Frank Spinner, an easy-mannered former Air Force lieutenant colonel, told the jury at her trial. If you do that, he's liable to jump out. No, to cook a frog, "you put him in water and you turn up the heat slowly." By the time the frog figures out he's in trouble, it's too late to jump; he's already cooked.

Spinner was focusing the jury's attention on the time before the pictures, a tack that strained prosecutors' patience. There were documented actions, they countered. For the defense in each case, though most pointedly in Harman's, none of those actions made sense without the backstory. If the government could argue that the Army had suffered collective injury—and in the context of a court-martial the Army, rather than the violated Iraqis, emerged as the primary injured party—then the defense could try to put the Army on trial. "The prosecution says, Shame on you, Sabrina Harman," Spinner said in summation. "I say, Shame on the Army. Shame on the Army for putting an ill-equipped, ill-trained junior specialist in a position where she has to challenge her NCO leadership to do the right thing." He and his co-counsel, Capt. Patsy Takemura, never contended that their client had done right; they showed how disaster at Abu Ghraib was inevitable, and then asked the jury: "Do you have the integrity" to find her not guilty?[4]

For the observer, the moral dilemma at the heart of the matter was sharpened with each trial, as one defense (Graner's) argued that torture was part of the job, then another (Harman's) that the Army leadership had failed its soldiers, then a third (England's) that the soldier had only "partial mental responsibility," while the prosecution reran its picture show. Because the facts of the defense arguments were essentially true, the findings of individual guilt represented increasingly cynical abdications of command responsibility; yet the alternative flirted with the notion that everyone is guilty, which is to say no one is.

In the circumstance, Spinner's observations about cooking a frog were more meaningful sociologically than legally. For the larger society, the only reason these trials could matter, the only opportunity they offered the country for wrestling with the problem of justice that law itself is too limited to solve, lay in that backstory—the very thing that daily news reports of fractured narratives presented in court and summarized on deadline were incapable of providing with any coherence.

So let us cast back to that point when the heat in Abu Ghraib was rising. During a head count his first night on the job in October of 2003, Graner told the court, he opened the door of one bleak cell and found a man lying naked on the slab floor, then witnessed the same behind another door and another, until at the end of his rounds he discovered that a prisoner was missing. He finally found the man in an airless, dark 3'x10' isolation cell, naked, on the floor, in restraints. "That's when I learned about the sleep program," he said.

The program was known as "sleep management," a polite term for a form of sensory deprivation considered torture under the Geneva Conventions. Old soldiers argue that during the Korean War it was exactly this tactic used by the Chinese, causing American POWs to suffer psychotic breaks, that fed theories of the ruthless Oriental. Elements of the US military, intelligence and domestic prison establishments have studied and employed sensory deprivation ever since, and witnesses acknowledged it as a normal occurrence at Abu Ghraib. "Terrorizing prisoners" became part of Graner's job, he said in court.

Say, he explained, "you're in isolation for seventy-two hours and you have a restricted sleep regimen. You're allowed to have four hours of sleep within that period. ... Sometimes there are written plans: the prisoner eats at this time; he can sleep at this time." The plans, intended to scramble a person's sense of day and night, time and place, were drawn up by an interrogator and given each night to MPs to execute. The prisoner was kept alone without light or ventilation, without water or clothes, in a cell either very hot or very cold, with music or screaming all around at different times.

Sleep management worked tongue and groove with "food adjustment." Graner again: "I would go in the cell [screaming and yelling, often in Arabic]. ... Usually I'd like to have a second person with me. ... It's pitch-black in the cell, and the first thing I do is shine a Sure-fire light into your eyes. Now you're temporarily blind." You're brought out naked and set in front of an MRE that you can't see. The feeding plan says, "Give him five minutes, two minutes, thirty seconds to eat." And "the entire time you're eating," or trying to, "I'm screaming at you.

Someone else is screaming at you." If you don't eat, "a half-hour later we come back and do the same thing—'We gave you an opportunity to eat; you just didn't want to.' I lost my voice. Sergeant Joyner lost his voice. We yelled and screamed a lot. MI comes on with throat lozenges: 'Hey, great job; keep it up.'"

Because it was part of his job, not part of his criminal charges, Graner was able to talk about this. The account above comes from his statement to the jury prior to sentencing, and as such was unsworn testimony, not subject to cross-examination. In courts-martial these statements may not address activities for which a soldier has just been convicted. For more than three hours this pale, doughy soldier, big-eared and bespectacled, calmly laid out a scene of ceaseless screaming, hitting, darkness, forced nudity, shadowy drop-offs, threats, pain and "the anticipation of pain." He called it "the bizarro world" of Abu Ghraib, one in which the first "counseling statement" he received from his MP superior both scolded him for smashing a prisoner's face against a wall and acknowledged that, in other respects, MI "says you're doing a fine job."

"There's a lot of things we did that were so screwed up that if you didn't laugh, you couldn't deal with them," Graner told the court. "We got numb to a lot of things real fast." He had been convicted for acts of abuse in addition to those documented in the notorious photographs, but none involved interrogation and none involved ordinary cruelties, like shackling prisoners to bars or putting panties over their face (no one was charged for those). Graner, it has to be said, is not the most trustworthy witness, but the substance of his statement, outlining the tag-team relationship between physical and psychological brutality and interrogation, was never disputed in court.[5]

Sabrina Harman illustrated that relationship in a letter to her girlfriend, Kelly Bryant, describing a night on the job when it was time to "mess with" the MI prisoners. The letter was written on October 20, 2003, three days before the charged activity took place:

I cant get it out of my head. I walk down stairs after blowing the whistle and beating on the cells with an asp to find "The taxicab driver" handcuffed backwards to his window naked with his underwear over his head and face. he looked like Jesus Christ. At first I had to laugh so I went and grabed the camera and took a picture. One of the guys took my asp and started "poking" at his dick. Again I thought, okay thats funny then it hit me, Thats a form of Molestation. You can't do that. I took more pictures now to "Record" what is going on. They started talking to this man and at first he was talking "I'm just a taxicab driver, I did nothing." ... Then he stopped talking. They turned the lights out and slammed the door and left him there while they went down to cell #4. This man had been so fucked that when they grabbed his foot through the cell bars he began screaming and crying. After praying to Allah he moans a constant short Ah, Ah every few seconds for the rest of the night. I don't know what they did to this guy. The first one remained handcuffed for maybe 1 ½ – 2 hours until he started yelling for Allah, so they went back in and handcuffed him to the top bunk on either side of the bed while he stood on the side. he was there for a little over an hour when he started yelling again for Allah. Not many people know this shit goes on. The only reason I want to be there is to get the pictures to prove that the U.S. is not what they think. But I dont know if I can take it mentaly, what if that was me in their shoes. These people will be our future Terrorists. ... I thought I could handle anything. I was wrong.

Other female MPs testified to participating routinely in sleep management, to taking away blankets from naked detainees, accompanying men to the shower, pointing at their penises and laughing, all at the behest of Military Intelligence. The MPs on Tier 1 Alpha kept a logbook noting the prisoners who were brought in and the treatments MI had specified for them. Always the prosecution asked, Did the logbook say anything about stacking detainees in pyramids? Ordering them to masturbate? Did anyone tell MPs they could abuse detainees for fun? No and no again; no further questions.

During a break in the trial proceeding in May, I visited the 4th Infantry Division Museum at Fort Hood. A group of school-children was just exiting as I came upon a TV set replaying a video made by soldiers from the 44th Air Defense Artillery, documenting what they did in Iraq from April 2003 to February 2004—the same time period that the soldiers standing trial were in-country. Because Iraq had no aircraft to shoot down, the men of the 44th ADA did almost anything but the job for which they had been trained. That summer of 2003 they began rounding people up. The insurgency had erupted, and word had come down that insurgents or anyone with information about them had to be found, arrested and questioned. The soldiers' video, a composite of still photographs, had been approved by their commander, although exposing prisoners to "public curiosity" violates international law; he also inserted helpful quotations, including "It Is the Soldier" from the mural in Killeen. The soldiers added a soundtrack:

> (*Warden threw a party in the county jail ...*) Soldiers are detaining Iraqi men outdoors in daylight, leading them along in flexicuffs and white hoods.
>
> (*Prison band was there and they began to wail ...*) Handcuffed men sit beside a road; one appears to be pleading with a soldier.
>
> (*The band was jumpin' and the joint began to swing ...*) Soldiers lead blindfolded men along a road; others are being herded into a personnel carrier.
>
> (*You should've heard those knocked out jailbirds sing ...*) A soldier poses with a hooded detainee, then reveals the man's scared face for the camera. (*Let's rock, everybody, let's rock ...*)

Such detainees wound up at Abu Ghraib. In the historical as opposed to legal narrative of the scandal, this is how the story begins on the ground, with Iraqi resistance and US reaction, with house-to-house searches and mass arrests, with little cruelties, routine pranks and an occupier's insouciance toward formal conventions. The video thus supplies the pictures before "the pictures," those at the heart of court proceedings not a mile away, concerning events that unfolded on a few specific days.

October 23–24, 2003. Graner needed to free up an isolation cell for MI and asked Ambuhl and England for help in "extracting" a prisoner nicknamed Gus. Soldiers were profligate nicknamers, and even in court Shooter, Shitboy, Taxicab, Froggie, the Iraqi Houdini and Gilligan were often used in lieu of the victims' known names by everyone, including lawyers. Gus had been arrested for simple assault and was in isolation for throwing rocks at MPs in Camp Ganci. On this night he was smeared with excrement. Graner said he didn't want to touch him, so he made his rifle sling into what he and Ambuhl called a tether and others called a leash. According to Ambuhl and England, Graner put the leash around Gus's neck and handed the other end to England, who told Judge Pohl, "I assumed it was okay, because he was an MP, he had the background as a corrections officer, he was older than me. I didn't question it." The prisoner, she said, was not dragged but crawled out of the cell, and was then escorted away. Graner snapped three photographs, and England "realized it was for his own amusement." Graner's defense argued that subjecting a naked Arab man to the authority of a small American woman was a legitimate exploitation of culture, an approved element of US military psychological-operations doctrine, and that the pictures simply documented the use of force, a standard procedure in civilian US prisons.[6]

October 24–25, 2003. Three male detainees were accused of raping a boy in Tier 1 Bravo. This is the only incident depicted in the batch of publicized photographs for which MI soldiers were also charged: Spc. Armin Cruz pled guilty to conspiracy and maltreatment and was sentenced to eight months in prison;

Spc. Roman Krol admitted pouring water on the detainees, forcing them to crawl low to the ground and throwing a foam football at their penises, and got ten months. At Graner's and Harman's trials, MI soldiers said the MPs had been in charge, cuffing and uncuffing the prisoners in sexually evocative poses. MI Spc. Israel Rivera witnessed the action for up to thirty minutes but never reported it to superiors; he testified that he was afraid of Cruz and uncertain about his own chain of command, "it changed so often." He never tried to stop Graner or Frederick, who was also there: "If they were willing to do this to a detainee, why wouldn't they do it to me?" Rivera was not charged; Harman, who was present for a minute or two, was charged for failing to intervene or report. MP Sgt. Kenneth Davis testified that MI soldiers were giving the orders. The next day, Davis said, he told his platoon leader, 1st Lieut. Lewis Raedor, "MI was doing some pretty weird things with naked detainees." No action resulted.

November 4–5, 2003. Mr. Abdou Faleh, Detainee #18470, pictured wearing a cape and hood, standing on a box with arms outstretched, was, alone of all the detainees whose pictures figured in these trials, the subject of interrogation. He had been brought onto Tier 1 Alpha, suspected of having information about who killed four US soldiers. Frederick testified at Harman's trial that an Agent Romero of the Army's Criminal Investigative Division (CID) told him, "I don't give a fuck what you do, just don't kill him. I need him to talk tomorrow." Frederick then attached a wire to the detainee's left hand. Another guard attached another wire. The wires weren't live, but, per Frederick, "Sergeant [Javal] Davis told him he would be electrocuted if he fell off" the box. The guards were "laughing and joking." After a week CID decided Abdou Faleh, nicknamed Gilligan, knew nothing, but he remained at Abu Ghraib. After the pictures were discovered, Harman, like the other six MPs, waived her right to counsel and told CID investigators that she attached the wires as a joke. Abdou Faleh told CID agents that a male or two males attached them. The government entered Harman's statement into evidence and successfully suppressed Abdou Faleh's, which they called possibly untrustworthy. The man in the most iconic image of the scandal was never deposed under oath. Then he was released, and, prosecutors said, he was simply lost.

November 5, 2003. Manadel al-Jamadi was killed in the shower of Tier 1 Alpha. The event belongs in this chronology because it was so glaringly absent from the trials, Judge Pohl refusing to allow photographic documentation into evidence; because a picture of Sabrina Harman's smiling face beside the corpse on ice is profoundly unsettling; and because everyone in court knew that while these exercises in justice were underway, someone had got away with murder. The soldiers on Tier 1 knew it that day. Al-Jamadi was a ghost detainee, no name, no number. Arrested on suspicion that he had bombed a Red Cross facility, he had been beaten by Navy SEALS. He did, however, walk into the shower room under his own power, escorted by CIA interrogators, who did not wear nametags. Roughly an hour later he was dead. An autopsy report acquired by the Associated Press indicates that he died while strung up in a "Palestinian hold" (named for a practice widely used by Israeli torturers), suspended by his wrists, which were tied behind him. On the day shift, Sgt. Joyner asked his soldiers about the new smell and the water trickling from the shower room. "Oh, that's the dead guy," they said. Ice bags were melting. Later MI Lieut. Col. Steven Jordan rigged up a medical evacuation, with stretcher and ambulance and an IV line jabbed into al-Jamadi's cold dead arm so that it might appear to other detainees that nothing so awful had occurred.[7]

November 7–8, 2003. Seven detainees in Camp Ganci had rioted over food and were brought to the Hard Site for "cooling off." They were clothed but hooded, their hands cuffed behind their backs. Frederick, who was short on guards, asked Sivitz the mechanic to help out. The detainees were thrown to the floor in what was called in court a "dog pile." Some were also tossed from soldier to soldier or slammed against a wall. Sgt. 1st Class Shannon Snider, the ranking officer there, hurled a prisoner to the floor. Soldiers were yelling; Iraqis were screaming. England arrived, and Graner asked her to get his camera. As Snider looked on, she photographed Graner on top of the prisoners. Soon others were snapping pictures. There were signs prohibiting cameras, but most soldiers had one, Sgt. Snider had one; and they used them openly, according to much trial testimony. England and Harman began matching detainees' dossiers to the faces beneath the hoods and discovered that one man was being held for rape. Someone pulled the man's pants down, and Harman wrote RAPEIST on his bare buttock with a black marker. The detainees were still on the floor when Sgt. Davis flung himself on them from a running leap. Sgt. Snider, now watching from an upstairs balcony, said, "Enough," and made a cutting motion across his throat. It was the only order Snider gave that night. Then he left and spent the night, as was his custom, on Tier 1 Bravo, where, Frederick testified, he kept company with a female detainee. Snider was never charged. Davis left as well. Graner punched the alleged rapist in the temple, knocking him cold, and Frederick traced an x across the chest of another, striking him there so forcefully that Sivitz checked that he was still breathing. Frederick called for an inhaler, and Ambuhl, who spent most of the night in the office upstairs, ran for one. England gave the prisoner water.

Standing to the side, Spc. Matthew Wisdom, then twenty and ordinarily assigned to work the tower on Tier 4, had been watching with disquiet. He returned to his usual post to consult with his sergeant. While he was gone, Frederick, Graner and Sivitz stripped the men naked. They uncuffed them, and Graner began seating one on the floor facing the wall, another on the first man's shoulders facing out. Harman was taking pictures. England pointed trigger-finger style at the men against the wall and at the one marked RAPEIST. Harman also posed with him, but even at Harman's trial it was England's image that prosecutors repeatedly displayed. While the women snapped and posed, Graner positioned the prisoners into a pyramid, methodically adjusting the bottom row and thoughtfully placing the man who had just had the wind knocked out of him, Hussein Mutar, at the top.

At the tower on Tier 4, Sgt. Robert Jones, with nineteen years in the Army and Marines combined, told Spc. Wisdom that he had probably witnessed "a justified use of force." Jones did not imagine, when he sent Wisdom back to the tier, that the young soldier would find stripped, hooded detainees "jerking off," and Mutar and another man simulating fellatio. "He's getting hard!" Wisdom heard someone whom he identified as England cry out. Sivitz, Ambuhl and Harman were gone by this time. They had been there when Sgt. Frederick initiated the masturbation, and when Cpl. Graner photographed England, cocked at the hip, chewing a cigarette and pointing at one in a line of masturbating Iraqi men.

"Initially, I refused [to pose that way]. I said, 'No, gross,'" England told Judge Pohl.

"Why did you change your mind?" Pohl inquired.

"They were being very persistent, bugging me, so I thought, Well, okay ... I'm saying 'they' because I can't remember which one it was."

"So Graner or Frederick basically convinced you to do it?"

"Yes, sir."

"Did they order you to do it?"

"It was more or less peer pressure."

"Did they force you to do something you didn't want to do?"

"Yes, sir."

In court testimony Frederick said that although the detainees were under his control and he ordered them to stroke themselves, "quite frankly, I was surprised that they did." He also remembered Graner shouting something to England like, "This is your birthday, a present for your birthday." At some point in the hour and ten minutes during which these events occurred, Lynndie England had turned twenty-one.

Private England completed the long walk in chains down the path from the courthouse that September evening after her sentencing. A white van ferried her to jail, and the photographers killed the lights. The few reporters hastened to file their stories. The prosecuting attorneys had departed long before without comment. Judge Pohl, appearing diminutive off the high bench, walked smartly to his car, where a soldier engaged him in amusing banter. From the barracks just beyond, military wives or female soldiers in civilian clothes came pushing strollers. At a nearby playground other children were having the day's last go of it, their happy cries mingling with the mournful squeak of a merry-go-round.

Four months earlier, following Sabrina Harman's sentencing, Frank Spinner had said: "I guarantee that in ten years, this same kind of thing is going to happen again." We were talking in the entrance of the judicial center, within view of a photograph of its namesake, Maj. Gen. Lawrence H. Williams, who had directed one of the Army's investigations into the My Lai massacre. The crime at My Lai had shocked the conscience of the nation not because it was unique in the Vietnam War but because it was emblematic, an event in which the everyday regimen of body counts, racism, search-and-destroy missions, command deceit and free-fire zones converged in spectacular fashion. Scandal resulted in policy corrections. Army documents afterward emphasized the necessity of training soldiers in the laws of war and protocols for reporting war crimes. In the arena of war fighting, a host of theoretical and practical adjustments followed, from raising or supporting proxy armies rather than committing US troops in Central America in the 1980s, to mustering a worldwide mujahideen in Afghanistan and Pakistan, to relying on air power and the "overwhelming force" of a US-dominated coalition in the Gulf War, to the almost allergic rejection of body counts in Iraq. Those adjustments changed the form of atrocity—satisfying much of the populace, insulated from the moral sting of death squads in El Salvador, for instance—while leaving its roots undisturbed.

Like My Lai, Abu Ghraib has entered the vocabulary as a synonym for atrocity, and like the courts-martial in that earlier scandal, these latest trials were not convened to settle the great issue at their center—in this case, torture and accommodation. If only in a perverse way, Graner's lead attorney, Guy Womack, did force a consideration of atrocity at its roots. With nonchalance, he recognized violence as the unvarnished business of war and detention. He aimed to neutralize horror, to suggest that meaning and moral judgement were matters of situation and perspective, comparing the man at the end of a leash with "children in the shopping mall tethered by Mommy and Daddy." He mocked the prosecution's fixation on rules and procedures. Regarding every detainee as a potential terrorist, he defined every action by his client as an adjunct to information-gathering. Hand slaps, kicks, stripping, hooding, stacking, isolation, humiliation through cultural exploitation (though not sexual degradation, which he abhorred and attributed to Frederick): these were the tools with which the job got done. "When you make an omelet, you break some eggs," he said in closing. "It may be that in interrogations at Abu Ghraib you ... might have to use approaches that we wouldn't use with our own children." When a reporter asked him if he believed the American people would stand for his vision of discipline and punishment, Womack grinned, incredulous: "But we do stand for that. We strip and hood prisoners. We do it in American prisons."

That the jury chose not to reward Womack with an acquittal represents a rejection only of extremity. Womack was embarrassing; torture no longer is. In 2004, lawyers and policy intellectuals gathered at Harvard, invited by its Kennedy School, Law School and the US Department of Homeland Security to draw up rules for coercive interrogation—"torture lite," as *The New York Times Magazine* called it in a respectful essay. All but one of the discussants concluded that a little torture was sometimes necessary, provided it was accompanied by warrants, rules and strict oversight. The Bush administration rejected the Harvard team's regulatory proposals. Niceties for the use of torture are superfluous once everyone agrees it needs to be used. But euphemisms—*coercive interrogation, stress*—are appreciated. They allow the president to declare, "We don't torture."

If the Abu Ghraib trials are reducible to a single motto, it is this: we don't torture for fun, and certainly not for pornography; we torture for information and control. The Army sent that message with its choice of indictments, but it would be cheap to lay the burden only at the Army's door. Like the actions of the soldiers at Abu Ghraib, war, scandals of war and the institutions that must manage them develop within a context of human society. Those soldiers have taken to marking themselves with a tattoo of a bad apple, a stylized worm in the fruit, claiming their place in the story. Americans at large have yet to claim theirs. Because punishment of "bad apples" seems not to satisfy the full demand of justice, we look to bigger apples. We are moved by arguments to assign responsibility up the chain of command; to reaffirm the Geneva Conventions and the Law of Land Warfare; to establish clear rules in Congress limiting the CIA, foreclosing "black" operations, stipulating the rights and treatment of prisoners; to shut down Guantánamo and the global gulag; to drive Bush and Cheney and their cohort from office: in other words, to set America right again, on course as it was after the Vietnam War, a chastened empire, still wielding a fearsome arsenal but with liberal intentions. We cannot yet bring ourselves to pull up the orchard, to forsake the poisoned ground.

(2006)

14

Stripped

"Apparently without touching the detainees, an officer looked at their ears, nose, mouth, hair, scalp, fingers, hands, arms, armpits, and other body openings."

So writes Supreme Court Justice Anthony Kennedy in the majority decision in *Florence v. Board of Chosen Freeholders*, which affirmed a jailer's right to command just about anyone in police custody to submit to a strip search. How redolent of the slave auction. That was my first thought. Then, in a different key, how evocative of a scene in *Henry V*, in which Katherine of France recites some English words that the gentlewoman Alice has just taught her:

> d' hand, de fingres, de nails, d' arm, d' elbow, de nick, de sin, de foot, de coun.

The scene is comic—Shakespeare's audience would have heard *foot* and *coun* as puns on *fuck* and *cunt*—and it is dark. Katherine is the daughter of the besieged French king, upon whose armies Henry is gaining. Should Henry win the war, or her father make a deal, Katherine will be part of the trade: her hand, fingers, nails, arm, elbow, neck, shin, foot and gown the English king's possessions as surely as every other piece of France.

Sex is swept into the pageant of state violence, Shakespeare is saying, as potent a presence in the chitter-chat of a lady's bower as it is at the gates of Harfleur. (The townsfolk submit, thereby sparing themselves and their children from Henry's ghastly promises of rape and murder; Katherine weds.) In our own time, sexual menace is embedded in the prison complex, in its elaborations of control and projections for public entertainment—in what other context are rape jokes acceptable? Inevitably it must seep into the august language of the law. And so it has. *Pornographic* is too pleasant a word to describe the creepy fetishism that animates the court's decision and the Obama administration's supporting brief in the case.

The petitioner, Albert Florence, says he was stripped, humiliated, unmanned, held for six days, after police in New Jersey stopped his BMW for a traffic violation and arrested him, separating him from wife and family, in the belief that he had failed to pay a fine. He had not, and had a notarized receipt of payment, which he showed police to no avail.

Florence's lawyers did not challenge the state's right to strip-search some detainees, just not him or those like him: people arrested for minor offenses who give jailers no probable cause to suspect violence or weapons or contraband. It sounds reasonable. Like the four liberals on the court who agreed, however, the argument does not fully apprehend, and thus could not contest, just what it takes to be the world's biggest jailer. Justice Kennedy asks us to see things as they are. His opinion makes plain the amoeba-like nature of the violence system just below the surface of everyday life, always moving, always grasping, capable of engulfing anyone—especially if he's black, if she's poor, if s/he's on "the wrong side of sex"[1]—and absorbing so many persons as to suspend personhood, making distinctions moot. In the transit from freedom to handcuffs to lockup, the individual vanishes. What remains is a body, really a collection of parts, notable for what they may conceal.

As previously established by the court, police can arrest a body for any infraction, driving without a seat belt, for instance. In practical terms that means many millions of bodies are jailed across the country each year following an arrest. Consider, Kennedy says, the difficulties those bodies pose for the officials responsible. The jailer can be certain of nothing, not even their identities. Demeanor can be no guide. Past acts can be no guide. The alleged crime can be no guide. Each body is potentially a breeding ground for lice, contagion, dangers unseen; a palimpsest for tattoos inviting violence; a drug mule; a repository for weapons or proto-weapons, "something as simple as an overlooked pen"; a secreter of "cash, cigarettes, or a penknife" with which "to survive in jail" but prone to deadly purpose.

In the onrush of this ever-flowing stream, "correctional officials … must have substantial discretion to devise reasonable solutions to the problems they face." Reasonably, they rely on things seen. *Strip search* is an exaggeration, Kennedy writes. The body is not physically stripped. It is instructed to shed its clothes, lift or expose its genitals and spread its buttocks; ordered to squat, to cough, to shake its head, open its mouth, raise its arms, display its instep, expose its ears. The official may inspect from a distance of, say, five feet, or perhaps from "a closer, more uncomfortable distance." But the official does not touch. He does not intentionally humiliate. He does not single out. Petitioner Florence would have the jailer discriminate, but the jailer cannot.

He cannot, Kennedy doesn't quite say, because nothing about his workplace is reasonable. It is insane—overcrowded, unsanitary, ruled by a code of all against all. Kennedy acknowledges those conditions, but the violence system is beyond question, so he, the court, the jailer, can do no more than try to thwart human cunning.

Here, Kennedy gestures to US Solicitor General Donald Verrilli's brief, a phantasmagoria of rectums and double-edged daggers, jack-knives, eight-inch scissors, more rectums, more knives, seven inches, three to five inches, vaginas, razor blades. Not since Ken Starr's report on Bill Clinton's trysts in the Oval Office have the footnotes of a government document made for such salacious reading:

man arrested on drug charges found with golf-ball-sized bag of crack cocaine in his rectum ... woman booked into jail on a warrant "filled two condoms with methadone, tied them, hid them inside her vagina, and used electrical tape to keep them from falling out" ... man smuggled marijuana into jail in his rectum ... man placed 20 bags of heroin in his rectum ... inmate hospitalized after trying to smuggle a knife into jail inside his body ... "some inmates cut pockets inside their mouths" in order to smuggle razor blades ... inmate hid red-and-silver "flip-style" cellular phone in his rectum ... "and not only that, but with a charger" ... man arrested on probation violation found with methadone, Oxycodone, and Xanax in a bag in his rectum ... woman arrested for driving with a suspended license died shortly after her arrival at jail due to a drug overdose from pills she had concealed in a body cavity ... crack pipe found in body cavity of man pulled over for failure to wear a seatbelt ... man booked into a county jail on misdemeanor disorderly conduct charge was found with a cigarette lighter, rolling papers, a golf-ball-sized bag of tobacco, a bottle of tattoo ink, eight tattoo needles, an inch-long smoking pipe, and a bag of marijuana all concealed in his rectum ... man arrested for selling bootlegged CDs was found concealing a nine-millimeter handgun between rolls of fat.

And people say American ingenuity is dead.

Outraged by his majority colleagues' reliance on incidents ripped from the headlines, Justice Stephen Breyer wrote for the minority that "no one here has offered any reason, example, or empirical evidence" for intrusive searches in the absence of reasonable suspicion. Again, a good liberal argument, but it misses the point. Once a country accommodates itself to 13 million annual detentions following arrest—and 2.3 million incarcerations, and 46 million poor people—it is all just horror in, horror out.[2]

Meanwhile, in the years since Albert Florence was pulled over, arrested, strip-searched, locked up and moved by the experience to file suit, stripping for pleasure and an income has been increasingly constrained. States and municipalities throughout the country have decided that the live nude sex showplace is an evil so large it ought to be banned, restricted, run out of town, drowned in bright lights, deprived of alcohol, burdened with extra permits and taxes, extra clothes, "opaque" clothes, enforced distances between dancers and patrons (six feet generally, more than the five or less in lockup). This is for the dancers' own good, naturally, as the community's sense of values soars and the dancers' tips tumble.

Although joining the majority in the *Florence* decision, Chief Justice John Roberts felt compelled to write a concurring opinion, highlighting that the court "does not foreclose the possibility of an exception to the rule it announces," this being necessary "to ensure that we 'not embarrass the future.'" It is late for that.

(2012)

Make the Rules, Break the
Rules and Prosper

Brett Kavanaugh cannot prove a negative, his supporters say, and should not be judged on something he may or may not have done as a youth. On those two points, they are correct. I might think they were also sincere if the right-wing powers behind him had ever cared about poor people, asylum seekers, anyone who's been in prison, any kid held as an adult, anyone branded a sex offender, anyone convicted by the press before trial, or by police on the side of the road, or by the architects of Guantánamo—that is, the multitude in the crosshairs of suspicion, commonly denied equality, due process and the possibility of redemption.

Kavanaugh's sexual inquisitors are similarly flippant about justice. They ignore the problem of proving a negative and simply declare him a liar; they then focus on the story of Christine Blasey Ford, declare it true and steam ahead, affirming that accusation equals guilt and the bad acts of youth should forever color the life chances of an adult—scourges that those in the crosshairs mentioned above know intimately.

The sophomoric meanness of Kavanaugh's supporters, belching from the internet and in live threats, only bolsters their opposite number's argument that man is forever juvenile. The late-hour accusation by a former Yale classmate has the odor of pile-on and is flimsy, in *The New Yorker's* new panting approach to reporting.[1] I'm tempted to say that when it comes to sexual politics, a lot of grown-ups are acting like high-schoolers, but that would be a slur on youth.

Virtually everything about this spectacle except the tentative, then stoic intervention of Ford reeks of bad faith. Wisdom crouches in the corner, silent. Yet wisdom—have we forgot?—is the fundamental and ancient criterion for a judge. Kavanaugh has failed the test of wisdom, not by what he is accused of doing when he was seventeen and drunk but by his adult neglect of reflection and his indifference to suffering, something this moment puts in a sharper light.

That does not get his unwise antagonists off the hook, though.

For anyone who still cares about principle, the Kavanaugh case is not a matter of belief, nor will it come down to proving or disproving Ford's allegations. A confirmation process is not a trial. It is, however—in theory if not in fact—an arena for considering the problems and promise of justice, for taking the measure of a man, in this case, and his capacity to think deeply, to search bravely, to act humanely, beyond the limit of ambition. Ford's intervention puts the hard stuff of humanity at the center of that arena, something that has been absent, most strikingly in the Senate's approach to Kavanaugh's greatest ethical failure in government: his response to torture. For reasons probably of prejudice (and partly prurience), torture has never raised the temperature of politics to the same fever as sexual accusation. Ford's entrance and her story, which is so particularly human, call the profound questions on that subject. (Whether they will have that effect on the Senate is doubtful.)

We cannot know what happened one night in suburban Maryland in 1982. Pretending we can is dishonest. But what do we know?

We know that Ford has suffered. We know that she is brave; like Anita Hill, she can gain nothing that compensates for the slings and arrows, the scandal-mad press, the overwhelming din, whether of support or suspicion, that she is enduring. We know that as teenagers she and Kavanaugh occupied a social set where fun was fueled by getting blind drunk and being stupid. Maybe her story is completely true; maybe it became confused over time, in small or consequential ways. Her lawyer has said she had one beer on the night at the center of the story. Maybe it hit her hard; maybe there was so much drinking among so many of her friends so often that details of time and place blur or slip away, especially in a culture where forgetting is often played for laughs.

I spent most of high school going to drunken parties. Everyone was drunk, including the kids behind the wheel in the car home. Afterward—amazing that we lived—a standard line was *Oh my God, you were so wasted … I was so wasted … he was so wasted …* Everyone laughed, sometimes memorializing the events later in cryptic yearbook messages. One time a girl woke me in the morning to check if the car was in the yard; she couldn't remember driving home. Plenty of kids forgot making out, passing out, throwing up. In the time since, I have not heard of anyone from that crowd accusing another or being accused of assault, but an accuser's years of silence would not be surprising—sexual honesty was not our strength—nor would dumbfounded blankness on the part of the accused or anyone else. Why were we so insecure with one another? Longing for connection, attention, a kiss, why were all of us, girls and boys mustered in our single-sex schools, so afraid that we were willing to be foolish pretending not to be, pretending that we couldn't hurt or be hurt?

What do we know?

Wasted is the title of a lightly veiled memoir about being stupid drunk at Georgetown Prep and beyond by Mark Judge, Kavanaugh's high school friend, who Ford says was in the room and involved on the night of the assault she alleges. In a letter, Judge has told the Senate Judiciary Committee, "I have no memory of this alleged incident." Blacking out, remembering nothing, were regular experiences for Judge, going by his book, so it is entirely possible this statement is true. Others whom Ford named as being at the party have said they had no memory or knowledge of it, which proves nothing. A group of women, some of whom have known Kavanaugh since high school, have written that he was typically the sober boy on the side, eager for a chat about philosophy. Maybe. But it is hard to believe that the treasurer of the Keg City Club, accomplice in the blotto culture outside school and at Rehoboth Beach in summer, where kids tore up houses without a care, was not more like Bart O'Kavanaugh in *Wasted*—drunk and passed out in a car—at least some of the time. That's how high school works.

Kavanaugh claims he never got so drunk as to pass out or not remember. And the truth is, even if he had, none of this proves he attacked Ford. Granting the accused the full benefit of the doubt, we will probably have to live with uncertainty. We shouldn't have to live with Kavanaugh on the Supreme Court.

The past does impinge on the present: one should learn something from it. Kavanaugh has had thirty-five years to think about high school, specifically the formative culture of elite men. Thirty-five years to reflect on why so many felt the need to annihilate their personalities, why they were so careless and aggressive, how they thought about women and, especially, the privilege of breaking rules and getting away with it. This former member of the "Rehoboth Police Fan Club" seems not to have thought about it a bit.

If his first statements after Ford went public were typically bland denials vetted by lawyers, he had a chance, in a recent Fox interview, to offer some insight on the culture that fortified him and anguished Ford. Martha MacCallum prodded him for any thoughts on women's expressed experience, on memory, on competing versions of the past, on whether anyone (say, someone who might come before him in court) should forever be judged by youthful behavior. Kavanaugh was a robot. He ventured no ideas, no interest in the human condition, no sense of moral grappling, even in the abstract. He had his talking points.

Ambition says, *Stick to the script, even at the risk of being a depthless drone.* Wisdom would say otherwise. Intellectual curiosity and a feeling for justice would say otherwise.

When Kavanaugh was assistant White House counsel from 2001 to 2003, his office triggered one of the most momentous debates in this country's history. His boss, Alberto Gonzales, sought legal justifications for torture, for detention without trial, for ignoring the Geneva Conventions and pissing on habeas corpus, obstacle to tyranny since the twelfth century. The Bush administration, that is, was debating how to break the rules and get away with it. At issue was not the anodyne "power of the president" but the power to inflict pain.

There has been much attention to Kavanaugh's record over this period: the documents withheld or belatedly released, the rooms he was in, the secrets yet to know. So many in the Senate were so busy posturing that they forgot that the most important answers were not to be found in records, however illuminating, but in this nominee's ability to address the central questions: where is justice to be found in the contest between the mighty and the meanest, as Solomon put it; and how do the just respond in the face of suffering?

By simply entering the arena, a person in pain, Ford casts in shadow all of the procedural wrangle and makes plain what has been obfuscated on a host of issues, but on torture most acutely: the human person and the exercise of power. This figure of the person prompts a different consideration of the record, one grounded not in documents but in ethics, in human sympathy, where the issue of torture always belonged but got displaced by years of parsing the intricacies of cruelty. How much pain? To the point of organ failure? Who was in charge? Who authorized? Who was in the loop? Shifting the focus lights up Kavanaugh's deficits, though hardly his alone.

Kavanaugh has long repeated he "was not involved" in US torture policy, and technically he was not authorized even to know about it. "I don't recall having any conversations with Brett about torture," Gonzales has said. Of course Brett knew something about it; everyone knew something, if only by watching CNN in January of 2002 as masked US soldiers met prisoners from Afghanistan coming off a plane in Guantánamo—orange jumpsuits, manacles, turquoise hoods over their faces. Those men had been diapered and chained to the plane for 8,000 miles. We know Kavanaugh was involved in at least one heated discussion about denying detainees legal representation. He is not reported to be among those who got heated, and years later on the federal bench, he would deny a habeas corpus petition from a Guantánamo prisoner in *Bihani v. Obama* (arguing, contrary to the court on which he hopes to sit, that the US government has no obligations under international law that haven't been codified by domestic statute).

Job duties notwithstanding, everyone in the White House counsel's office was confronted with a moral choice: will you accommodate suffering? Will you be part of the machinery that seeks to exact and justify it?

Kavanaugh was willing to accommodate suffering. How many additional meetings he may have attended are incidental. More, his "not involved" involvement is either gutless evasion or further evidence of an incurious mind, a profound apathy toward knowing, questioning, reasoning independently. In 2004, as the president's staff secretary, he was copied on a White House email outlining a damage-control strategy to persuade the public that Bush had "never considered authorizing torture under any circumstances." It was a lie, put about after an infamous "torture memo" was revealed in the press. Kavanaugh told the Senate in 2006 that he hadn't known of the memo until it was leaked; maybe so, but once he did know he had a chance to intervene, to oppose the deception at least, and he did not. He accommodated deception.

Torture was officially discomfiting by 2006 (though still in use). Ambitious for a federal judgeship then, Kavanaugh was safe telling the Senate: "I do not agree with the legal analysis in the memorandum, including with respect to the definition of torture." Ambitious for a lifetime appointment to the Supreme Court now, he flattered Senator Dianne Feinstein for her staff's 2014 report on the CIA torture program. Then he declined to say what he thought about President Trump's enthusiasm for waterboarding, danced around a question on the Bush torture policy, and presented himself as a mere paper-pusher for a 2005 signing statement in which Bush declared that he could ignore the congressional prohibition of torture that he had just autographed. "It would've crossed my desk," Kavanaugh said about that statement, again playing the dimwit.

Except for a handful of low-level working-class soldiers, everyone who ordered, justified, implemented or looked the other way at the torture policy got away with it. Elite men and women got a step up. George Bush got to paint all day in retirement at his ranch. Gina Haspel got to be CIA director. Jay Bybee, who signed the memos authorizing torture, got to be a federal judge, just like Kavanaugh. Harvard used to tell its students, "You are the best and the brightest," the future ruling class. I don't know how Yale greeted Kavanaugh, but the vital lesson he seems to have taken from Georgetown Prep is a corollary to Harvard's: the ruling class makes the rules and breaks them and prospers in blameless irresponsibility.

One could joke that with Kavanaugh at least there's truth in advertising, but again the figure in pain enters to cut the laughter. Titan and CACI, multimillion-dollar private security contractors, had translators and interrogators who tortured prisoners at Abu Ghraib. They got away with it too. Kavanaugh gave them the pass. He joined the 2009 opinion of the DC Circuit Court of Appeals that not only prevented Iraqi victims from suing the corporations in civil court but established sweeping immunity from liability for private contractors in battle arenas into the future. The language of that opinion is obtuse, antiseptic; reading it, one may be forgiven for forgetting what the case is even about. It took Judge Merrick Garland, in dissent, to recognize the suffering subject—the human person beaten, blinded, humiliated, strung up, shocked, raped, forced to watch his father die, extinguished.

No one would be held to account. Kavanaugh washed his hands.

(2018)

James Baldwin:
Habits of Thought

These are times ripe for reading Baldwin. Not just the essays on racist policing; those are, in a way, too easy. "A Report from Occupied Territory" burns hot a half-century after it was published. That its depiction of black vulnerability and police volatility could describe the contemporary scene; that its central metaphor of occupation is not too hyperbolic to have been echoed by Attorney General Eric Holder; that even its particulars ("If one is carried back and forth from the precinct to the hospital long enough, one is likely to confess anything") feel gruesomely fresh from what we know of torture regimens—all of these examples confirm what we already tell ourselves in weaker words.

The police are brutal, the government is brutal, the populace is aroused (taking to the streets) or accommodating (switching from CNN to *Homeland* to football), brutalized or brutal too. America, cauldron of damaged life.

Baldwin wrote "Report" in 1966, about Harlem, not Staten Island, where Eric Garner died gasping for breath; during the war in Vietnam, not the War on Terror; amid dim promises of the Great Society and Top 40 radio playing "The Ballad of the Green Berets." We may study that past, track the news and shout the louder, but that is not why Baldwin is the most important US writer of the twentieth century, or why we should read him now.

A passage from a famous essay called "Everyone's Favorite Protest Novel," written in 1949, suggests a better reason:

> What constriction or failure of perception forced her to so depend on the description of brutality—unmotivated, senseless—and to leave unanswered and unnoticed the only important question: what it was, after all, that moved her people to such deeds?

The *her* refers to Harriet Beecher Stowe, the protest novel is *Uncle Tom's Cabin*, and Baldwin ventures the question that he would examine his whole life: who are we, as individuals and Americans, and what are our responsibilities? That *who* for Baldwin was no flimsy thing. It involved spirit and flesh, history and what we do with it, both in our intimate relations and in social, common life.

Uncle Tom's Cabin fails, in his reading, the way so much well-meaning protest does. It is so busy crying *This is horrible!* that it does not trouble to inquire into what makes those who have executed that horror, and who maintained, benefited from and accommodated it, do the things they do. A protest novel closer to him, *Native Son*, disappoints because Richard Wright has so constricted the frame of social life to fit white categories, has so reduced Bigger Thomas to his fears and hatreds—or white fears and hatreds of him—that Bigger "admits the possibility of being sub-human and feels constrained to battle for his humanity" in the only available arena, which is violence.

In either case, what the protest writer offers is a victim, maybe a saint (Tom) or a sinner (Bigger), plenty of villains but no demand on thought as to the roots of villainy or the effort required of us to live in defiance of it.

What any of this has to do with the present is superficially plain. Stowe's catalogue of cruelties evokes the Senate's partial catalogue of CIA tortures and any itemization of police killings. The latest fashion for martyrs and monsters is on display in bulletins from Paris since the *Charlie Hebdo* murders, absent the record of terror visited upon the Arab world by the United

States, its allies and creatures for decades. We might trace the roots of official violence to imperialism, capitalism, oligarchy, white supremacy. The words are not incorrect, but they are insufficient. And here is where Baldwin is hard.

Money, he writes elsewhere, is not sufficient to explain the deeds of white people in the time of slavery, or in the dehumanizing system that *Jim Crow* does not begin to express—just as, in our time, profit and empire were never sufficient to explain why multi-hued majorities backed the organized killing of strangers after September 11, 2001, and the designation of a worldwide class of people as subhuman. They do not explain why Americans adapted to the prison state or why, to take a banal example, Sony Pictures and everyone involved in *The Interview* figured it was a good bet that Americans would find assassination funny. White supremacy cannot fully explain the culture of police departments, or President Obama's penchant for murder-by-drone, or any routine instance of entitlement. Oligarchy cannot explain our apparent contentment with a pantomime of democracy: free expression as the freedom to insult.

Baldwin does not say that systems of power are unimportant. He insists that liberation is also a mandate on individuality: how one separates oneself from the "habits of thought [that] reinforce and sustain the habits of power"—in essence, how one comes into his or her humanity.

Baldwin came into his, profoundly, by leaving the country. But he began the process years before, as a black child given charge of successive black children. As a poor child introduced to the world of arts while mortally aware of the world of privation. As a man-child when a thirty-eight-year-old Spanish-Irish racketeer fell in love with him. It was a dangerous love in 1940; it would be today. It made him feel beautiful for the first time, and, though not without anguish—a word that appears frequently in Baldwin's explorations of human relations—this love shattered "all of the American categories of male and female, straight or not, black or white" that work to define the totality of a person and so thwart self-definition. "I will be grateful to that man," he wrote, "until the day I die."

The culture has not ceased trying to reinforce those categories, to which we may also add poor or not, citizen or not, Judeo-Christian or not. It was always bent on categorizing Baldwin: a black writer, a homosexual writer, a black writer who wrote a homosexual novel, a writer with a "juvenile" obsession with sex (as Langston Hughes put it), a melodramatic "Harriet Beecher Stowe in blackface," as Henry Louis Gates, Jr., said in a rather pitiful attempt to demolish the young Baldwin's essay on Stowe fifty-seven years after the fact.

Gates' flirtation with gay-baiting would not be worth mentioning (it is hardly famous) if his critique did not so precisely mirror mass culture's shallow conception of sex, as opposed to Baldwin's capacious view of sexuality's role in the creation of the self and of social attitudes. As a young man, Baldwin had written that in Stowe's treatment, Uncle Tom had been "robbed of his humanity and divested of his sex." He did not mean, as Gates damply inferred, that Tom was sexually impotent, not a shtupping man. Sex, as anyone who has seriously read Baldwin knows, meant far more to him than the act—though perhaps no one has written so sensitively about lovemaking and the body's effort to express what words cannot or dare not. Carnal knowledge in the old sense—knowing another, and so perhaps oneself, nakedly—gives a better sense of his concerns. Tom was deprived of such knowledge because he was a cardboard saint. Stowe could not but deprive him because she could not *see* him. Because she could not see him, as a figure of ethics and desires and history, the jumble of sometimes competing qualities that make up human personality—in other words, as a man—she could not really see his tormentors either, "her people," white people, or begin to fathom the sources of their inhumanity and complacence.

Baldwin's writing does not settle the question of why America developed its particular habits of power, or why those persist;

why it is so easy still for color to blind us, class to confuse us, sex and gender to trap us; why as a nation we are staggeringly cruel yet stubborn about our innocence; why love is so hard. His essays and novels do, however, prod us to assess our habits of thought.

It is not simple, this assessment. If so many of his fictional characters seem incomplete, alienated from one another, from their own deepest desires, uneasy in their skin or too easy until events disrupt their cozy assumptions, it is because they are ordinary people, prone like us to self-deception, scarred like us by history, and scratching toward something authentic. As the story ends, they may have failed to get there; they may be left in midstream. If they are left alive, chances are they have fought their way out of cliché, which, while not the same as succeeding, is a necessary start—cliché being another name for capitulation to what is.

We should read Baldwin because *what is*—the world of power in its many forms—is barbaric but inventively adept at enlisting our consent. No American writer since DuBois dissected the problem of the color line with such intimate and ferocious grace. No other so persistently explored the price of our history and the price of love. And no other so embodied the convergence of liberationist energies that once and briefly spared the culture from utter rot. The problem of the twentieth century continues into the twenty-first; the promise of liberation—full-fledged humanity—still calls to us; rot hurries near, and we are in the breach.

(2015)

Afterword

On February 25, 2020, under "The Lessons of #MeToo's Monster," a *New York Times* editorial featured a silhouette of Harvey Weinstein with a couch where his mouth would be, its legs evoking vampire fangs. While the *Times* hailed Weinstein's conviction for forcible oral sex and third-degree rape despite "a lack of physical or other corroborating evidence," and the DA praised women who "pulled our justice system into the twenty-first century," the demon graphic captured the premodern quality of the state's case at trial. From opening—"He was the Old Lady in the Gingerbread House, luring the kids in, missing the oven behind"—to summation, prosecutors created a theater of emotion that merged metaphorical and physical monstrosity. Weinstein was "deformed," "abnormal," "intersex," with no balls but a vagina, "disgusting," "scarred," "grunting," with bumpy skin, lumpy semen, "fat," "hairy," stinking of "shit, sorry poop," a beast, unmanned, subhuman. They showed jurors pictures of him naked, a drawing of his penis (which supported no key testimony). Never has body shaming and the "normal" trap been so wielded as a weapon of presumed progressive justice. Weinstein's shaming inevitably required that his accusers be ashamed too; that they be child-like, simple and will-less, beautiful but absent adult responsibility. Although jurors rejected the gravest charges, predatory sexual assault, a win is a win, as carceral feminists put it. Liberation reduced to making monsters, and caging them.

1. Nushawn Williams is confined, forcibly and indefinitely, to a psychiatric prison, having been declared a "sexually dangerous person" by New York State after taking a plea and serving his full twelve-year sentence for consensual, unprotected sex with two minors. He is among the 6,400 people in the US who have been civilly committed to mental institutions after serving their sentences for sex offenses. In ruling that no constitutional protection is violated by locking people up again this way, the Supreme Court has affirmed that fear alone is sufficient grounds in the US to deny a person freedom forever.

2. The #MeToo phenomenon has amplified or encouraged countless voices. It has also encouraged silence. Julian Assange was not accused of rape when two Swedish women went to police in 2010 to ask if they could compel him to take an STD test, but rape was the claim when Sweden put out an Interpol Red Notice for his arrest, an alert usually reserved for terrorists and fugitive dictators. Rape became at once the fulcrum for a series of international state actions and a muzzle on opposition. (See Andrew Fowler's 2012 investigation for Australian ABC's "Four Corners" program; also Tariq Ali and Margaret Kunstler, eds., *In Defense of Julian Assange*, O/R Books, 2019.) The muzzle has worked to astonishing effect. In May of 2019, the US Justice Department indicted Assange under the Espionage Act for publishing hundreds of thousands of US military documents about the wars in Iraq and Afghanistan. Earlier, the US pressured Ecuador into expelling Assange from its London embassy. A US judge ordered Chelsea Manning, the ex-Army intelligence analyst previously tortured and then convicted for releasing classified information, back to jail for

refusing to testify before a grand jury seeking charges against Assange. Manning, a transgender woman, told US authorities, "I would rather die of starvation than cooperate with you." No concerted left has risen to defend Assange or Manning or WikiLeaks or the First Amendment. No journalists' associations have taken the streets to protest this attack on press freedom. An obsession with sex and personality has trumped concern for state secrecy and the lengths governments will go to preserve their version of the facts. Assange sits in a British high-security prison, depleted, according to the UN special rapporteur on torture. Late in 2019, Sweden dropped its case, the phony rape investigation having served its purpose. The US began its argument for extradition in Britain on the same day that Harvey Weinstein was convicted, February 24, 2020. The next day's *New York Times* devoted almost four full pages to Weinstein; it gave a tenth of an inside page to the political persecution of Assange, with whom the paper profitably collaborated while the going was good.

3. Between 1999 and 2019, at least 1,011 persons were executed in the US. In 2009, President Obama expanded opportunities for imposing the death sentence or life without parole when he signed the Matthew Shepard and James Byrd Hate Crimes Prevention Act. #MeToo rhetoric about inherently violent "male sexuality" means that the root structure of violence and the gender traps for boys and men need be given little, if any, thought.

4. Sex education in America's 14,000 school districts is ad hoc, dominated by talk of danger, disease and dirtiness. Abstinence Only is the curriculum in thirty-seven states' public schools; talk of pleasure, of any positive or even substantive emotional aspect of sex, is rare or nonexistent. Marriage is to be the teacher of and solution to all sexual matters, though porno is the handier substitute.

5. *Sex* remains the largest-grossing illustrated book in the world. Until 2019, Oxford's Bodleian Libraries cloistered it in a restricted category of works considered too dangerous for young minds, giving it the shelfmark Φ (phi), along with about 3,000 risqué books, including *The Picture of Dorian Gray* and *The Love Books of Ovid*.

6. Woody Allen's estranged son, Ronan Farrow, became the #MeToo era's scribe of scandal from his perch at *The New Yorker*. Allen has been made a pariah in the movies and publishing—his last film iced in the US by Amazon in 2018, his memoir pulped in early 2020 after Hachette caved to staff demands for censorship, goaded by Farrow and company. Allen and Soon-Yi Previn are still together.

7. Mark Sanford retreated from politics but eventually returned. His short-lived challenge to Donald Trump for the 2020 Republican nomination was notable for his party's determination to squash internal dissent. Trump invoked the earlier sex scandal to mock him. Sanford (divorced) and Chapur are still together.

8. In 2018, reporters served as stenographers to another ambitious lawyer, Pennsylvania attorney general Josh Shapiro, whose inflamed twelve-page introduction to a grand jury report on sexual abuse in Catholic dioceses revived the priest scandal. The report is 1,356 pages. The only accounts based on a full reading that I know of were by David Pierre, Jr., in TheMediaReport.com, and Peter Steinfels in *Commonweal*. Overwhelmingly, the claimed criminal acts date back decades. Many of the accused are dead. Questionable and well-documented claims are treated alike. A prosecutorial undertaking, it includes no rebuttals or evidence from the accused. At least seventeen states have opened similar investigations and/or have dropped statutes of limitations for seeking

monetary damages, resulting in a rush of civil litigation and feverish media coverage, some of it retailing demonstrably fraudulent claims as true. Personal injury lawyers advertise for clients. Vatican factions have used allegations to strike politically at internal rivals, notably for a renewed crusade against homosexuality.

9. Museums increasingly have removed work because of the artist's biography or subject matter. In Britain, amidst a series of protests over the work of Eric Gill, Graham Ovenden (convicted of sex offenses and ordered by a judge to destroy his own art as well as his collection of nineteenth-century photographs) and others, Julia Farrington of Index on Censorship told *The Guardian* in 2017: "We don't yet live in a police state: they can't shut down a show unless it is breaking the law; they can only advise. But the police are very cautious, and if you ignore the advice that something is even potentially inflammatory, you could be arrested yourself." On book banning: in the US the practice is most common among state and federal prison authorities. Texas prisons alone ban 10,000 books, according to a 2019 Pen America report. The American Library Association compiles an annual list of Top 10 Most Challenged Books in school, university and public libraries. Typically, at least 50 percent of the titles deal with lgbtq subjects. In 2017, the list included *Sex Is a Funny Word*, a sex ed book, challenged because of fears it might lead children to "ask questions about sex."

10. Paul Shanley survived twelve years in prison and an effort by prosecutors to pack him off indefinitely to a mental institution as a sexually dangerous person. He was released, aged eight-six, in 2017. *The Boston Globe*, with a Pulitzer Prize for service to the public interest for its role in the scandal, has got a pass for its disservice to the public interest in re-legitimizing the baseless belief in repressed/recovered memory.

11. More on junk science: in June of 2019, the Food and Drug Administration approved Vyleesi, making the bet that, although it's a mystery how the drug acts to raise sexual desire and what its long-term effects might be, there's nothing like an injection forty-five minutes before lovemaking to satisfy a woman. Another firm, Sprout, has been pushing a woman's "right to desire" in the form of its FDA-approved pill Addyi, which may cause dizziness and low blood pressure if accompanied by alcohol. The work of the New View Campaign is archived at newviewcampaign.org.

12. In 2017, eighty years after Edwin Land's invention of instant photography, Polaroid announced its return with a new line of analogue and refurbished vintage cameras: "Polaroid is back with more ways to play."

13. As of 2020, every teenager and child in the United States has never known a time without war. Meaning that US bombings, troop deployments, killing of foreign civilians and soldiers, the burial or maiming of US soldiers, violence and grief on a global scale, are ordinary for an entire generation.

14. In 2018, police raided strip clubs in New Orleans, throwing exotic dancers out of work. The clubs reopened, but the crackdown—like a federal raid on *Rentboy* (2015), the shutdown of *Backpage*, the most popular internet ad site for sex work, and the subsequent nervous decision by *Craigslist* to discontinue its Personals section (both 2018)—was part of a putative safety campaign that has made sex workers less safe and less independent. The Justice Department's onslaught against *Backpage*, touted as a blow against sex trafficking, has had the opposite effect, because the site had closely monitored ads and alerted law enforcement to suspected exploitation. As so often, a protection campaign on behalf of women and children protects neither. Dulcinea Pitagora, a therapist and

former sex worker, described the impact on the trade thus: "Some people will ride it out, some people will be supported by their regulars, and some people will die."

15. Brett Kavanaugh gave a blubbering, bullying and maliciously partisan performance at his final Senate hearing, and was awarded lifetime tenure on the Supreme Court.

16. "One can be, indeed one must strive to become, tough and philosophical concerning destruction and death, for this is what most of mankind has been best at since we have heard of man. (But remember: *most* of mankind is not *all* of mankind.) But it is not permissible that the authors of devastation should also be innocent. It is the innocence which constitutes the crime." James Baldwin, "My Dungeon Shook."

Notes

1. The Secret Sharer

1. Of forty-nine bills concerning AIDS and HIV introduced in the New York State legislature in the heat of the scandal, only four promoted prevention or education.

2. When this essay was published, in 1998, there were no widespread effective retroviral drug treatments of the type there are today, which have dramatically reduced HIV transmission and arguably made the term AIDS obsolete—except among people who are living on the down low, disproportionately black and latin men, more likely to be poor, Southern, precarious or in denial, with inadequate transportation or access to health care; least likely to get treatment, to get it in a timely manner or follow it consistently. Although the rate of diagnoses has decreased overall, the number of diagnoses has remained stable, according to the CDC, with the highest rates among people aged twenty to twenty-nine. Risk of transmission increases with the number of partners but also depends on other factors: the presence of another sexually transmitted disease; the stage of infection; the strain of the virus; tearing or bleeding; anal sex. It is easier for men to pass the virus to women than vice versa, and repeated sexual interaction raises the risk—which is why women in relationships are so vulnerable if their regular partner is positive and untreated. In 2017, the latest year for which there is full data, 7,401 female adults and adolescents were newly diagnosed with HIV; 86 percent cited heterosexual contact; 59 percent were African American. The CDC reports: "At the end of 2016, an estimated 50,900 youth had HIV. Only 56 percent knew they had the virus." Of the 33,739 total new diagnoses in the US and territories in 2017, youth aged thirteen to twenty-four accounted for 21 percent.

3. In 2004, Thomas Shevory published *Notorious H.I.V.: The Media Spectacle of Nushawn Williams* (University of Minnesota Press), after extensive interviews with Williams. An illuminating study, it describes the teenage Williams finding in upstate New York an environment that was far safer and more lucrative than Brooklyn, and that, in its natural beauty, provided unique pleasures. The market for crack was large and diverse; with $2,000 worth of product a dealer could make $5,–$6,000 in an afternoon, an undercover cop told Shevory. Williams and his friends would " 'rent' cars from local crackheads and tool through" the countryside. "They would go snowmobiling through the forests and fields. ... Nushawn was even learning how to ski. He was, in fact, a classic example of the drug dealer who attempts to live his version of the American Dream." Shevory reports that Williams volunteered to be tested for HIV *after* some young women had listed him among their sex partners to health officials following their own testing— a sequence that reverses what officials told the press in 1997–98. When Williams, nineteen, was told of his HIV status, he received no counseling. In prison he was frequently harassed by guards and other inmates; he frequently spent long stretches in solitary. In his second letter to Shevory, Williams enclosed seventy-eight hand-written pages copied out of Lao Tzu's *Tao Te Ching*. "I hope these papers are as good to you as they are to me," Williams wrote.

4. As of 2018, according to the Center for HIV Law & Policy, thirty-four states have laws specifically criminalizing HIV exposure or allowing HIV status to be used to enhance sentences for other crimes. Some require proven intent; others still criminalize behavior that never could transmit HIV; all ignore the reduced risk of transmission. People have been convicted and imprisoned although their viral load is undetectable. Actual transmission (i.e., an infected sex partner) is not always required to charge or convict someone. Sentences related to HIV exposure can range from a few years to life in prison. Six states require people to register as sex offenders. Ignorance, then, remains the best way to avoid prosecution.

5. The CDC does DNA matching—an expensive, labor-intensive process—for epidemiological, not forensic purposes. The test cannot determine whether a particular virus was transmitted from person X to person Y. Still, popular belief that forensic magic can provide a simple solution to complex problems persists.

6. In 2019, the CDC called for "urgent action," as STDs in the US reached an all-time high. There were more than 115,000 cases of syphilis in 2018; cases of the most infectious stages of the disease rose to the highest number since 1991; syphilis in newborns, entirely preventable through testing and prenatal care, was up 40 percent from 2017. In

recent years more than 50 percent of local STD prevention programs across the country have experienced debilitating budget cuts.

2. What We Don't Talk About When We Talk About #MeToo

1. Portman credits this now-widespread idea to Rebecca Solnit, who argues that all women are "groomed to be prey" and live in "pervasive fear." Roxane Gay argues that women who escape violent or harassing male attention "escape because they are lucky." Stephen Marche condemns all men for "the grotesquerie of their sexuality," exhuming Andrea Dworkin to argue that the only nonviolent hetero sex is "sex with a flaccid penis." What's relevant here is language that requires no qualification. On terrorism, the most sweeping, insensate terms are acceptable; appeals to complexity must first assert that, of course, terrorism is awful.

2. Recent Democratic disavowals of the crime bill ought not erase the party's original enthusiasm for it. As the bill's legislative champion then-senator Joe Biden stated in 1994: "The liberal wing of the Democratic Party is now for 60 new death penalties. That is what is in this bill. The liberal wing of the Democratic Party has 70 enhanced penalties. ... The liberal wing of the Democratic Party is for 100,000 cops. The liberal wing of the Democratic Party is for 125,000 new State prison cells. ... I would like to see the conservative wing of the Democratic Party." Quoted by Naomi Murakawa in *The First Civil Right: How Liberals Built Prison America*, Oxford University Press, 2014.

3. See *The War on Sex*, Duke University Press, 2014. Also *Sex Panic and the Punitive State*, University of California Press, 2011; and, especially, Emily Horowitz, *Protecting Our Kids? How Sex Offender Laws Are Failing Us*, Praeger, 2015. Brock Turner, the former Stanford swimmer whose sentence of probation for sexual assault after a drunken party is regularly called a "slap on the wrist," is on the registry for life.

4. The Department of Education's Office of Civil Rights (OCR) does not require colleges and universities to document the race of accusers and accused in Title IX cases, but as Emily Yoffe, the most rigorously thoughtful journalist covering the campus sexual assault story, wrote in *The Atlantic* in 2017: "Black men make up only about 6 percent of college undergraduates. They are vastly overrepresented in the cases I've tracked." She notes instances where black males make up tiny percentages of the student body but account for 25 percent to 50 percent

of those accused in a given year. Asian and foreign students are also overrepresented. Harvard Law School professors have noted the over-representation of minority men in sexual misconduct complaints at Harvard. OCR agents are "aware of race as an issue in Title IX cases," Yoffe writes, "but [one investigator] was concerned that it's 'not more of a concern. No one's tracking it.'"

3. A Boy's Life

1. The order prohibited lawyers, witnesses, local, state and federal law-enforcement officers et al. from discussing the case. McKinney's friend who told me about the gun and the meth says he was visited by black-suited agents of the federal Bureau of Alcohol, Tobacco and Firearms shortly after McKinney and Henderson were arrested, and told them this story. Before it passed into his hands, says this friend, the gun had been stolen, which is consistent with court records. Henderson's grand-mother says she noticed nothing unusual about Russell when he visited her on October 5. McKinney's friend and other drug users, ex-users or dealers in Laramie spoke with me on condition of anonymity.

2. UW president Philip Dubois told me that the university had such a policy. But sexual orientation was not included as a protected category in the university's Equal Employment Opportunity/Affirmative Action Statement approved by the trustees, or in the anti-discrimination provisions for student admissions: the only formal statements of policy that have the force of law. This has changed in the years since.

3. Rerucha had brought capital murder charges against Henderson, but mounting two capital cases was never the plan; the county couldn't afford them. One of the defendants would have to plead. Henderson later argued that he was never properly informed about his options. His appeals have been rejected. For McKinney, Rerucha said he made no move without the Shepard family's permission. A jury convicted McKinney of felony murder (rejecting first degree murder), kidnapping and aggravated robbery. "I am going to grant you life," Matthew's father declared in court, the ultimate expression of privatized justice. McKinney received the same sentence as Henderson.

4. The judge who condemned Henderson to life in prison sentenced Menefee to four to seven years for killing Cindy Dixon. Menefee was out in four. In 2017, he was convicted of raping a nine-year-old girl in Ohio.

5. In 2013, having spent thirteen years following the drug connection, which this essay was the first to report, Stephen Jimenez published

The Book of Matt (Steerforth Press). Its details on McKinney and Henderson's partying differ somewhat from what's here, but it confirms the importance of drugs in the story. In Jimenez's account, Shepard and McKinney emerge as human commodities, working for rival drug circles to support their habits, and occasionally forced to pay their debts in sex. The two men knew each other, he reports. McKinney had hustled in a Denver gay club. Shepard had risked rough trade. Their police-scanner-carrying mutual acquaintance both facilitated the drug trade and ran male escorts. McKinney was his boy. Jimenez's evidentiary trail began with two bits of material from freshly unsealed court files: an anonymous letter to the prosecutor saying McKinney had worked as "straight trade" and felt guilty sexually; and a previously neglected portion of McKinney's confession in which he told police, "[Shepard] said he could turn us on to some cocaine or something, some methamphetamines, one of those two, for sex." The book has been attacked by the Shepard family for undermining the hate crime story; alternatively, it has been used to claim that the murder was nothing but a robbery gone bad. McKinney stopped talking to Jimenez once the latter reported that McKinney had had sex with men. It remains fatuous to believe that the murder conforms to any unalloyed explanation.

6. As of November 2019, more than 233,000 US kids had experienced a school shooting since Columbine. With so many schools targeted (243, according to *The Washington Post*'s count), it has become difficult to generalize about the shooters, other than that they are men or boys, sixteen being the median age.

4. The Wonder Years

1. All of the above was based on the most current research as of 2002. Contemporary research on any form of sexual interaction between adults and minors, for any population, is lacking because it has been made effectively impossible, with sexologists and other researchers fearing loss of funding, unemployment or prison. The internet has made all kinds of porn more widely available. The provenance of everything in cyberspace cannot, of course, be known, but sexual entrapment continues. Among men, the prevalence of pedophilia (defined as a primary or exclusive attraction to prepubescent children by an adult over sixteen) is estimated at 3 to 5 percent; among women a fraction of that. Levine tells me: "According to the Bureau of Justice Statistics, of the 20,000 cases of 'commercial sexual exploitation of children'

adjudicated from 2004 through 2013, fewer than 4 percent involved production—directly exploiting a child—and 96 percent were for possession. Independent scholar Marshall Burns' analysis of sex offender registries found that of the 2.8 percent of registrants convicted of child porn possession, less than 1 percent had also committed a contact crime."

2. Letourneau served seven and a half years in prison, and married Vili Fualaau in 2005. No one in this story was fine, but as Vili told Barbara Walters in a 2015 interview with the family, what hurt him most as a youth was the feeling that there was no one he could talk to about his emotions outside the context of crime and victimization. The couple are said to have divorced amicably in 2019.

3. As of September 2019, the US Census Bureau reported that 16.2 percent of US children (about 12 million souls) live in poverty. The National Center for Child Poverty reports that 43 percent of US children live in low-income families, a more telling measure of need. As Levine writes, "Poverty is the single greatest 'risk factor' for most every life-smashing condition a kid might be at risk for."

6. Grand Guignol, American-Style

1. In May of 2018, Moses Farrow wrote a lengthy blog post, "A Son Speaks Out." Now a family therapist, Moses supports Thompson's account, adding that he, too, witnessed videotaping, which extended over two or three days. He says he was in the room with Dylan and others on August 4 watching TV, watching his father. His mother had told him to stay alert, a command he took seriously. Moses says it is not true that Allen put his head in Dylan's lap or knelt in front of her. Ditto that Allen ever disappeared from his sight with Dylan. He describes the attic as a dirty, unfinished crawl space full of exposed nails and mouse droppings. He says there was no electric train set there, a haunting detail in Dylan's 2014 letter published by Kristof of the *Times*, though unmentioned in the 1992 investigations and custody proceedings. Moses discusses the events of 1992–93 as a microcosm of life in what he describes as a dark and punishing household: "coaching, influencing, and rehearsing are three words that sum up exactly how my mother tried to raise us." Moses' account made barely a ripple in media that otherwise had been hungry for the Farrow story; *The New York Times* emphasized repudiations from Dylan, Ronan and Mia.

8. Sin, a Story of Life

1. Because of structural differences, "it is effectively impossible to compare the incidence of abuse across [religious] denominations," Philip Jenkins notes in *Pedophiles and Priests: Anatomy of a Contemporary Crisis*, Oxford University Press, 2001. Scandals in the Baptist church, the second largest in the US after the Catholic, never extend beyond the congregation level; no hierarchical apparat exists to enable lawyers in one case to subpoena archives on other individuals, let alone track the accused throughout his life. Jenkins cites egregious molestation cases that arose in Baptist or Pentecostal congregations, registered a blip in the media and were forgotten, mentioned in none of the books or analytical articles on clergy abuse. The point is not to deflect attention from Catholic abuses, or to advocate spreading moral panic more widely, but to reflect on what any particular attention or inattention reveals about institutional structures and interests. In 2004, a report to the US Department of Education estimated that nearly one in ten schoolchildren, K through 12, is subject to sexual misconduct by teachers and other school personnel. In 2014, the Los Angeles Unified School District was discovered to have destroyed about 2,000 records of sexual abuse complaints from the late 1980s through 2008. Neither got much attention.

2. The victim and his mother testified to different circumstances. The victim said he suffered no lasting trauma. Geoffrey Packard, Geoghan's attorney, said: "If his name were Paul Smith and he did the same thing, he never would have been indicted; never would have been tried by a jury of twelve people; and there's no way the guy would max out on the sentence. He probably would have got probation." Geoghan was strangled, stomped on and beaten to death in his cell on August 23, 2003, by another inmate, Joseph Druce, already serving life without parole for murdering a man whom Druce believed to be homosexual.

3. By 2017, *BishopAccountability* estimated 3 to 6 percent since 1950. The extent of substantiation is not known. As of 2002, the most thorough study had been made by the Chicago archdiocese of all priests active there between 1951 and 1991; using a standard that erred on the side of accusers, it found justified complaints of sexual misconduct with minors or adults against 1.7 percent of the priests. The media regularly cited psychologist and former monk A. W. Richard Sipe to support a claim that 2 percent of Catholic priests are pedophiles and 4 percent ephebophiles (persons attracted to adolescents). Sipe's estimates refer not to behavior but attraction, that is, fantasy or desire—notoriously difficult to quantify.

4. That figure was approaching $4 billion by 2018, according to *BishopAccountability*.

5. *Baroque* does not describe this New Hampshire case. In 2005, its numerous affronts to justice were amply documented by Dorothy Rabinowitz in *The Wall Street Journal*. MacRae, as it turns out, was offered three plea deals. Others adding to the record are the National Center for Reason and Justice; Ryan MacDonald, summarizing legal papers and other developments on MacRae's website, thesestonewalls.com; and David F. Pierre, Jr., of *TheMediaReport*. In 2015, a federal court rejected MacRae's habeas corpus appeal, refusing to allow a hearing, or new witness testimony, or a statement from MacRae.

6. Daniel Lyons of *Forbes* was a notable exception. In June of 2003 his "Sex, God & Greed" explored the financial incentives for tort lawyers, quoting one of the most prominent, Roderick MacLeish, thus: "This is going to be a huge business." While acknowledging the legitimacy of many cases then being litigated, Lyons discussed the opportunities the scandal presented for extortion, lobbying legislatures to drop statutes of limitations to pursue civil claims, and exploiting insurance exposure. In September 2003, after the Boston archdiocese agreed to pay 552 claimants and their 57 lawyers $85 million, Lyons reported that MacLeish and Mitchell Garabedian expressed concern that some claims might not be legitimate. MacLeish was then pressing what Lyons called "one of the more dubious cases."

7. In 2002, the woman, Jacqueline Gavreau, added that the priest also grabbed the boy's crotch. That claim, absent from the file, was later asserted by the now-grown male in a civil deposition. Talkative and high-strung, Gavreau admitted having various, unrelated beefs with Shanley, and told me: "I told people, 'Don't go near him' ... [Law, everyone] they thought I was nuts. I was on the phone every minute."

8. Because initially the Boston archdiocese was going to fight the civil case (but settled, against the advice of its attorneys), a tremendous amount of material was generated in discovery, some of which I use here.

One extraordinary event at St. Jean's, which everyone remembers, occurred when the boys were eleven. Driscoll held a sharpened pencil on Ford's chair as a joke. Ford sat down and howled in pain. In the recollection of adults who were present, there was blood, Ford's mother was called, and she took her son to an emergency room. In Gregory's new memories, the pencil incident was prelude to a rape. According to medical records, Ford was treated for a puncture wound. MacLeish told me he considered the hospital report "physical evidence" that Ford had been sodomized.

9. Elaine Noble, a state representative in the 1970s and the first openly gay elected state official in the country, told the *Globe* that she had

relayed information about Shanley to police, a deputy mayor and several priests. The priests are dead, the deputy mayor cannot recall, the police and archdiocese have no record.

10. For a detailed, contextualized account see Mitzel, *The Boston Sex Scandal*, Good Day Books, 1980.

11. In our interview MacLeish expressed outrage because Shanley writes of being torn between leaving a teenager in the park all night with unsavory characters or dragging her to a shelter, which will force her to call her parents, something she refuses to do. Either way she is at risk of rape; he decides to leave her alone. Newspaper and magazine writers have told the story exactly as MacLeish did. At Harvard Square, where the Bridge mobile clinic was still offering confidential service in 2002, a fifteen-year-old hanging out with her younger sister and twentysomething boyfriend told me she appreciates the medicine but dismisses referrals to shelters. Those will force her to call home, she said, and home is a nightmare of violence.

12. The "troubled priest" quote was extracted in MacLeish's PowerPoint and has been used ever since to argue that "even the Vatican knew" Shanley was a sicko. Assiduously ignored is the context: an eight-page 1979 letter by Medeiros lamenting: the trend among homosexuals "to band together ... to secure their civil and human rights"; the existence of priests who "encourage the rising homosexual culture"; the difficulties attracting "healthier young men" because of homos in seminaries; and Shanley's chutzpah in publicly presenting "confusing and distorted teaching" on homosexuality.

13. Kathryn Ford had been firm in her recollection. After being contradicted in the press in 2003, she eventually recanted.

14. Pope John called Pio "a straw idol." Beyond suspicions and paranormal speculations, the Pio story reveals much about power, spectacle and the uses and abuses of belief, in the church and in society. As against countless hagiographies (some by the saint's Fascist and Neo-Fascist associates and admirers), I know of only one proper history: Sergio Luzzatto's extraordinary *Padre Pio: Miracles and Politics in a Secular Age* (translated by Frederika Randall), Picador, 2010.

15. In 2002 age and gender profiles were still up for discussion. Sipe said his research showed the majority of victims were female and most were adults. SNAP's website quoted a therapist saying he was seeing six times more female than male victims, adolescent and adult. Today, discussion is closed. The victim has been typed: he is a little white boy.

10. Faith-Based Justice

1. By about 2003, MacLeish had gathered nineteen affidavits from men who say Shanley used them sexually when they were younger. Together, they present an alarming picture of a man obsessed with sex, one who took advantage of his position. Individually, many lack credibility. All are untested. Some include particular detail while others are strikingly reminiscent of other well-publicized priest cases; some raise an issue studiously avoided since the scandal broke, teenage consent.

2. See Harrison G. Pope, Jr., Paul S. Oliva and James I. Hudson, "The Scientific Status of Research on Repressed Memory," in *Science in the Law: Social and Behavioral Science Issues*, American Casebook Series, West Group, 2002. One of Gregory Ford's therapists, Robert Azrak, testified in a deposition that "there is no scientific basis" for the traumatic amnesia described in this case. Commentators have hastened to argue that some combat soldiers and death camp survivors have reported no memory of particular battles or terrors. They never forgot the central traumatic experience of being in a war or a death camp.

3. R. J. McNally, N. B. Lasko, S. A. Clancy, M. L. Macklin, R. K. Pitman and S. P. Orr, "Psychophysiological Responding During Script-Driven Imagery in People Reporting Abduction by Space Aliens," *Psychological Science* 15/7, 2004.

4. On January 15, 2010, the Supreme Judicial Court of Massachusetts rejected science in favor of superstition, accepting, despite voluminous research and scientific opinion to the contrary, repressed memory as valid evidence in Shanley's case. This was the first time a Massachusetts court considered the evidentiary basis for what dozens of pre-eminent social science researchers in an amicus brief called "one of the most pernicious bits of folklore ever to infect psychology and psychiatry." The court's ruling begins dishonestly—"the victim was observed leaving the classroom with the defendant on several occasions"—and never deviates. It misrepresents or outright fabricates arguments made by the appellate attorney, Robert Shaw (who asked the court not to divine Busa's veracity or fault Judge Neel but merely to acknowledge that an unproven and unsupported hypothesis is not admissible, and that Shanley had ineffective counsel). The ruling ignores detailed affidavits from internationally recognized experts on research methodology and legal/psychiatric history. It offers no analysis of the impressive documentary material Shaw provided, none of which was available to Judge Neel. Finally, the court postures in a footnote that "there could be circumstances where testimony based on the repressed or recovered memory of a victim, standing alone, would not be sufficient" for conviction. *Just not for this perv*, it might have added.

11. Sexual Healing

1. The Manipulator was a large steam-powered table, invented in 1869 by US doctor George Taylor. The portable (though bulky) electric "percussor" was invented in the early 1880s by British doctor Joseph Mortimer Granville, who was at pains to declare that he did not use it on women. It's ironic that "Granville's hammer" should be the best-known technology of orgasm—an inspiration for Sarah Ruhl's 2009 comedy, *In the Next Room (or The Vibrator Play)*, and Hollywood's 2012 romcom *Hysteria*. There is no evidence that Granville used his hammer on women, though the force of his objection suggests somebody did.

2. On the matter of camouflage, Alabama law continues to forbid the sale of vibrators for erotic pleasure, though not for "a bona fide medical, scientific, educational, legislative, judicial or law enforcement purpose." The state Supreme Court affirmed this proscription in 2009. Alabama's adult shops still sell vibrating sex toys; customers must sign a receipt promising that their purpose is anything but sexual.

3. Beneath such questions is the fundamental one: why is something always wrong with the woman? Out of 2,000 erotic or obscene heterosexual jokes collected by Gershon Legman, "not one ... blames the man for the woman's not having an orgasm. It is *always* her inadequacy in the joke world. ... the only explanation is that the man's inadequacy is too threatening to treat even in a joke." So writes Susan Davis in her masterful *Dirty Jokes and Bawdy Songs: The Uncensored Life of Gershon Legman*, University of Illinois Press, 2019.

12. Through a Lens Starkly

1. It was, the girls and their families ultimately prevailing.

13. Judgement Days

1. Reality was never so breezy. The first African American employed here, helping to build Camp Hood, was locked in at night for his own protection. "You know what we used to say about Killeen?" a local businesswoman said to me. "Now, this is just black people talking among ourselves; we used to say it stood for Kill Each and Every Nigger." In 1944 Jackie Robinson, then an officer at Camp Hood, faced court-martial for refusing to board a bus at the back.

265

2. By 2005, Al Hillah was not Al Hillah as it had been when Harman and her comrades were embraced by locals. It had become a cauldron of violence, site of the single deadliest suicide attack of the war.

3. Juries heard such interrogatories only in shards, sometimes not until the sentencing hearings. Here, the first two questions were to Ivan Frederick under cross-examination in Graner's trial. The next three were to Sgt. Joseph Darby, the whistleblower in the scandal, who turned the pictures over to the Army, also under cross-examination in Graner's trial. The next question was to Graner in the course of his unsworn pre-sentencing statement (also regarding detainees shackled to cell bars), and the final two were to Frederick under cross-examination in Graner's and Harman's trials, respectively.

4. "Collective responsibility does not dilute personal responsibility," Graveline rebutted, and Harman was convicted. But collective irresponsibility does dilute personal responsibility, so Harman, facing five years in prison, was sentenced to six months.

5. While Graner was on Tier 1, Roger Brokaw, with the Army's Criminal Investigative Division, was questioning detainees in stairwells and showers, under pressure "to interrogate so many detainees per week ... to produce so many reports per week." At Graner's trial, Brokaw identified ten Pentagon-approved interrogation techniques. The list changed three times between mid-September and mid-November of 2003, he said, but he didn't have much use for deception, stress positions, military dogs, nudity or "fear-up, harsh," *aka* "put[ting] the fear of the Lord in them." No, Brokaw testified, "I would engage [prisoners] in conversation about their family. ... Many times they start crying, and then they start talking."

6. This disagreement was at the crux of England's mistrial in May. She had accepted a plea deal. In a Providence Inquiry to determine the soundness of that decision, the judge provisionally accepted her guilty plea, advising that if anything arose that offered a possible defense, he would be forced to enter a not-guilty plea on her behalf. Testifying before her sentencing, Graner gave his version of events, upon which the judge asked, "If this was a legitimate cell extraction, how can she be guilty?" Out went her deal. In September she was found not guilty of conspiracy in this incident. All exchanges here between England and Judge Pohl are from the Providence Inquiry.

7. Jordan was the only officer in the scandal to face court-martial, in 2008, the most cynical of all these legal performances. As earlier, al-Jamadi was invisible, so this detail from a Pentagon investigation went unmentioned. Also unmentioned by the handful of other reporters covering Jordan's trial was the government's rewrite of its story of prison command responsibility. At Fort Hood, prosecutors argued that

MPs controlled the prison; trying an MI officer, prosecutors argued that MI was in control. Jordan got off on all charges involving abuse and received a reprimand for one lesser charge, which the military convening authority then dismissed. On Jordan's record it is as if the court-martial never happened.

14. Stripped

1. The term is from Amber Hollibaugh, who uses it to describe herself growing up as part of a class considered deviant because of whom they love, how they love, where they come from, what they do with their bodies to make a living and make a life. See *My Dangerous Desires*, Duke University Press, 2000.

2. These were the latest statistics available in 2012. Numbers, too, are amoeba-like; annual variations, however, are less impressive than the aggregate picture they help describe. In 2018, according to the FBI, approximately 10,310,960 persons in the US were arrested. By the end of 2017, according to the Bureau of Justice Statistics, 2,234,563 adults were incarcerated in state and federal prisons and jails. At year-end 2016 (the latest available), adults under the supervision of the US corrections system (in confinement, under probation or parole in the community) totaled 6,613,500. The bureau notes that this represents the lowest rate since 1993. Progress thus means a return to the status quo before the enactment of Bill Clinton's law-and-order agenda. Those numbers do not include: juveniles, the 45,000 or so locked up, and the thousands on probation or parole; or the 860,000-plus adults and juveniles living under strictures of sex offender registration (not all of whom are still on probation or parole); or the thousands in indefinite detention in civil commitment. It does not include border-crossers in cages. The Census Bureau reported 38.1 million people in poverty in 2018 (earning less than $12,490 if single; $25,750 for a family of four). Albert Florence was not poor, but poverty increases the chances for arrest and incarceration.

15. Make the Rules, Break the Rules and Prosper

1. Authors Ronan Farrow and Jane Mayer approached Deborah Ramirez, who, they wrote, wasn't sure if the assault happened and was unwilling to make the accusation until after "six days of carefully assessing

her memories and consulting with her attorney." In September 2018, *The New York Times* reported that it could not corroborate Ramirez's claim. In September 2019 it printed an excerpt from a book by Robin Pogrebin and Kate Kelly saying that Ramirez's lawyers gave the FBI names of at least twenty-five people who may have had corroborating evidence; those were never contacted during the FBI's superficial review. Pogrebin and Kelly did not investigate further. They did raise a new allegation, which the *Times* had to qualify the next day, since the alleged victim "does not recall the incident," according to friends, and declined an interview.

Index